BIBB COUNTY GEORGIA

Inferior Court Minutes

- 1826-1831 -

(Volume #2)

Compiled by:
Michael A. Ports

Southern Historical Press, Inc.
Greenville, South Carolina

Copyright 2019
By: Michael A. Ports

All rights reserved. No part of this publication may be reproduced, stored in a retrieval system, transmitted in any form, posted on to the web in any form or by any means without the prior written permission of the publisher.

Please direct all correspondence and orders to:

www.southernhistoricalpress.com
or
SOUTHERN HISTORICAL PRESS, Inc.
PO BOX 1267
375 West Broad Street
Greenville, SC   29601
southernhistoricalpress@gmail.com

ISBN #0-89308-993-1

Printed in the United States of America

Introduction

The Georgia General Assembly created Bibb County on December 9, 1822, from parts of Jones, Monroe, and Twiggs counties, and established Macon the seat of the county government. No other county has been created out of land from Bibb County. The Inferior Court, made up of five elected justices of the peace for the county, tried any civil case, except those involving title to land. The Inferior Court had jurisdiction over all county business matters, such as care for the poor, building and maintaining the courthouse and jail, building and maintaining public roads, bridges, and ferries, issuing licenses to sell liquor, nominating justices of the peace, performing naturalizations, appointing guardians, authorizing apprenticeships and indentures, and administering county funds.

The following transcription of the court minutes is taken from the microfilm photographed on December 14, 1964 at the courthouse in Macon by the Genealogical Society of Salt Lake City, Utah, and available at the Georgia Archives in Morrow, Georgia. The heading on the microfilm reads

Bibb County
Georgia

Superior Court

Inferior Court Minutes

1826 – 1831

On the spine of the original record volume is printed the following

May	MINUTES	Bibb Inferior	Nov.
1826		Court	1831

The court minutes begin on May 22, 1826 and continue in chronological order through November 23, 1831. The original record volume contains no index; however, a complete full-name index follows the transcription. The reader should know that a lone surname in the index indicates that no first name appears in the minutes, for example Mr. Smith, Smith & Company, or said Smith. An index entry such as Smith, ___ indicates that a first name was entered into the minutes, but has been obscured by an ink blot, smear, tear, or other imperfection. Similarly, an index entry such as ___. Cynthia indicates that either no surname was entered or the surname is obliterated. The pages of the original record volume are not numbered. To assist the researcher in locating the original pages, the symbol ___ is placed at the bottom left-hand corner of each original page. By noting the date, or at least the court term, of an individual entry in the minutes, the researcher should not have too much difficulty in locating that entry in the original record or on the microfilm copy.

Martin Simmons served as clerk during the entire period covered by the transcription. However, based solely upon the handwriting, at least two other men served as deputy clerks, but their names were not recorded. The minutes contain numerous original signatures, mostly of the justices presiding, the clerk, attorneys filing various motions, petitions, and affidavits, as well as those parties filing bonds for appeals and stays of execution, as well as their securities.

For the most part, the handwriting is legible, and the quality of the microfilm is good, making the reading and transcription process straightforward and not too difficult, although several of the microfilm images are very faint, blurred, or very dark. The occasional ink blot, smear, or other imperfection is noted within brackets, for example [blot] or [faint]. The transcription follows Sperry's recommended guidelines for reading early American handwriting.[1] Generally, the transcription maintains the overall format of the minutes, but presents the case citations, jury panels, lists of witnesses, signatures, and other court proceedings in a standard and consistent format. No grammar or spelling errors are corrected in the transcription, although a few commas, semicolons, apostrophes, and periods are added for clarity. The clerks entered a vertical squiggly line to delineate case citations, affidavit and petition headings, and signature citations, replicated by the symbol } in the transcription.

Sometimes the clerk formed the letters "a" and "o" in a very similar manner, making abbreviations like Jas. and Jos. and surnames Bagg and Bogg or Shannan and Shannon difficult to distinguish. At other times, the letters "a" and "u" are too similar to differentiate such names as Burton and Barton or Barnett and Burnett, or Barns and Burns. At still other times, the clerk failed to dot the letter "i," making the name Silman

---

[1] Sperry, Kip, *Reading Early American Handwriting*. Genealogical Publishing Company, Baltimore, Maryland, Sixth Printing, 2008.

appear to be Selman. In a similar manner, the names Edmond and Edmund can be difficult to distinguish. The formation of the letters "n" and "r" at the end of surnames sometimes appear to be the same. Invariably, the formation of the capital letters "I" and "J" are identical. Determining which letter usually not difficult when the first letter of a name, but almost entirely a guess when a lone middle initial. The clerk often crossed the letter "t" by extending the horizontal line across the entire word, making it difficult to distinguish between such surnames as Watters and Walters. Compounding the problem, he sometimes neglected to cross any "t" in a word, making a "t" appear to be an "l," and making it difficult to distinguish Allison from Attison, Alloway from Attoway, or Motes from Moles. The letters "L" and "S" can be difficult to distinguish, confusing such names as Landers and Sanders or Liddle and Siddle. Careful researchers will consult the original record or the microfilm copy to either confirm the transcription or formulate an alternative interpretation of the clerk's handwriting.

To the right of many original signatures, the clerk entered a symbol consisting of a squiggly line in the form of a circle or oval with either the word "Seal" or the capital letters "L" and "S" in the center, as follows.

Those symbols are not included in the transcription.

The book is dedicated to the memory of the author's numerous Georgia ancestors, although none ever were residents of Bibb County. Many thanks are offered to the kind, patient, and generous staff of the Georgia Archives, for their assistance and suggestions, not only in locating the original records, but in understanding their historical context. Thanks also are offered LaBruce Lucas of the Southern Historical Press for his sage professional advice and counsel. Special thanks are offered to the author's late mother, Ouida J. Ports, who inspired and encouraged her son's interest in history and genealogy.

Inferior Court Minutes

May 22ⁿᵈ 1826

Georgia   } The Honorable the Inferior Court of the County of Bibb
Bibb County } Meet according To adjournment.

Present, their honors   Timothy Mathews }
                          Tarpley Holt   } Justices
                          Mathew Robertson }
                          Robert Birdsong }

The following Jury were impaneled to Serve at this Term.

Jury N° 1

1. John Bridges, Sen
2. Moses Pettis, Jun
3. ~~Reuben Williamson~~
   Solomon D. Chapman
4. William Scott
5. Lewis Hammock
6. Burrell McClendon
7. John Hall
8. James Busby
9. John McMurrian
10. Elijah Mathews
11. John F. Thompson
12. Hiram Man

Egan & McLaughlin }
        vs   } Case
James Thompson   }

I Confess Judgment to the plaintiff for fifty dollars, With interest and cost.

                                        James Thompson

Andrew McBryde }
      vs   } Debt
James Thompson }

I Confess judgment to the plaintiff for Eighty Nine Dollars and Seventy three and three fourth Cents, with Interest and cost.

                                        James Thompson

Alexander Lowery }
    vs   } Debt
Cyrus Cotton   }

I hereby Confess Judgment for the Sum of two hundred and twenty five dollars, besides Interest and Cost.

                        Cyrus Cotton

John W. Griffin }
    vs   } Case
Henry R. Foy   }

We, the Jury, find for the Plaintiff fifty Dollars, With All Cost.

                        S. D. Chapman, fm

Angus McLean   }
For the use of   }
Jonathan Peacock}
    vs   } Assumpsit
John Wilabee   }
Alias Willee   }

We, the Jury, find for The Plaintiff the Sum of Thirty Seven Dollars, with interest and Cost.

                        S. D. Chapman, forman

John S. Childers }
    vs   } Assumpsit for Rent
John Holzendorf }

We Confess Judgement To the Plaintiff for the Sum of One hundred And Seventy five Dollars, with interest And Cost.

                        Mandell & Campbell, Att[y] for Def[t]

Joel Rushin   }
    vs   } Assumpsit for Rent
Thomas Blancet }
& Mary Minor   }

We, the Jury, find for The Plaintiff the Sum of Thirty Seven Dollars, With interest and Cost of Suit.

S. D. Chapman, forman

Edward Bass having Returned a Pocket Book Belonging to Thomas Bass Containing Sundry papers, In obedience to the within Summons of Garnishment. Ordered that Said papers be Deposited in the

---

Clerk's office And that the Plaintiff, or his Consel, Have leave to inspect the Same in order to Assertain if the Sundry papers [faint] which will [smear] of the property of Said Thomas Subject to Levy, That all Note, if any, be Delivered up to be Collected Such persons as the Court May appoint in Order To Satisfy the Plaintiff Debt & Cost.

John Holzendorf }
     vs   } Summons of Garnishment
George Stovall }

Nine persons having been Summons in this Case, three Only of which it appear are indebted to the defendant. It is Ordered that The Defendant pay for Summoning the three Garnishment that Are So indebted. One Dollar Eighty Seven and a half Cents for the first & Sixty two and a half Cents for each of the two Others. And that the plaintiff pay at the rate of Sixty two and a half Cents for Summoning Each of the Other Six.

Ordered that William Cummings and Spencer Riley Be And they Are hereby appointed Constables for The 564th District, And that Nathan Carter be Appointed Constables for the 482nd District, And that Benjamin Allen be Appointed Constable for the [blank] District, And that James W. Howard be appointed Constable for the 483rd District.

Timothy Mathews, J. I. C.
Tarpley Holt, J. I. C.
R. Birdsong, J. I. C.
M. Robertson, J. I. C.

The Court then adjourned untill Court in Course.

May Term 1826

Abram Lowery }
    vs   } Debt & [smear]
Cyrus Cotton }

Came into Office Cyrus Cotton, the Defendant in the above Case, Who being Dissatisfied With the Verdict of the Jury, paid the Cost And Entered a Stay of Execution. Also at the Same time Came Daniel Cotton, his Security On the Stay of Execution, Whom Each of them Acknowledge themselves Jointly & Severally bound for the true payment of The eventual Condemnation Money According to The Statute in Such Cases Made & provided. Given under My hand and Seal this 26th Day of May 1826.

Test. Martin Simmons, Clk   Cyrus X Cotton, his mark
                                            Daniel Cotton

Georgia   }
Bibb County } In Chambers November 6th 1826

Present, their honors   Tarpley Holt   }
                                      Mathew Robertson} Judges
                                        Robt Birdsong   }
                                        William J. Danely }

The following Jury were Drawn to serve at November Term 1826.

1. Joseph Wiggins	25. David Patton
2. Edmund Gainey	26. Thomas Banks
3. James Curley	27. James Rowell, Sen
4. Barnett Wise	28. James Inglish
5. Josiah Carter	29. Reuben Williams
6. William Pickard	30. Murphey Champion
7. Benjamin Allen	31. George Wright
8. Maven Whalley	32. Aferd Johnson
9. Tird Parrot	33. William W. Stanford
10. Samuel Barry	34. Joseph H. Lee
11. Voluntine Rowell	35. William Williams
12. Benjamin Smith	36. Thomas Knight
13. Sampson Barefield	

14. Samuel Pace
15. Thomas Miles
16. Joseph Ducks
17. Allen Cosey
18. Joseph Mosely
19. Jonathan Wilder
20. Joseph Blanchard
21. William Russell
22. William Riley
23. Jacob Johnson
24. Richard Bullock   Martin Simmons, Clk

Georgia   } The Honorable the Inferior Court in & For Said
Bibb County   } County & State Meet agreeable to adjournment
November 27th 1826 }

Present, their honors   Mathew Robertson }
                               Tarpley Holt   } Justices
                               Robert Birdsong }
                               William J. Danely }

The following Jury Were empanneld to Serve at this Term.

Jury N° 1

1. Joseph Wiggins   7. Jonathan Wilder
2. Edmund Ganey   8. Sampson Bairfield
3. Josiah Carter   9. Jacob Jhonson
4. William Pickard   10. David Patton
5. Voluntine Rowell   11. James Rouell, Senr
6. Thomas Milles   12. Reuben Williams

Ordered that James Rea be and he is hereby appointed Notary Publick for the town of Macon & County of Bibb.

E. S. Stockton   }
for the use of   }
James B. Ransone }
       vs   } Debt
R. B. Shelman   }

8

We hereby Confess Judgement For the Plaintiff for two hundred Dollars, With Interest & Cost, this 27th November 1826.

Mandell & Campbell, Att^{ys} for Def^t

William H. Turpin }
     vs   } Debt
S. M. Ingersol   }

Judgement Confessed to the Plaintiff in the Sum of two hundred and Seven Dollars five & a half Cents, With interest and Cost.

John P. Booth, Defd^t Att^y

Edward Quinn & Co }
     vs   } Debt
Joseph Bennett   }
& Elisha Tarver   }

We Confess Judgement on the Within for four hundred and Eight Dollars, with interest and Cost of Suit, reserving right of appeal, this 27th November 1826.

Mandell & Campbell, Att^{ys} for Def^t

Eliza R. Bacon   }
administratrix of }
John Bacon, dec^d }
     vs   } assumpsit
Lewis H. Gregory }

I Confess Judgement to the Plaintiff The Sum of one hundred and Ten Dollars, With interest & Cost, Nov 27th 1826.

Lewis H. Gregory

John Murphey & }
Reuben Turner   }
     vs   } Assumpsit
John French   }

Jury Nº 1

We, the Jury, find For the plaintiff the Sum of Sixty two Dollars 56¼ Cents, with interest and Cost.

            Jacob Johnson, forman

John B. Gaudry }
  vs   } Case
John A. Sharp }

I Confess Judgement to plaintiff The Sum of one hundred & fifteen Dollars and forty three Cents, With interest & Cost.

            John A. Sharp

John D. Chapman }
& Abner Chapman }
  vs   } Assumpsit
James Holmes   }

We, the Jury, find for the plaintiff The Sum of forty Seven Dollars & fifty Cents, With interest and Cost.

            Jacob Johnson, forman

Robert Coleman }
  vs   } Debt
Seaborn Gray   }

We, the Jury, find for the Plaintiff Fifty five Dollars & forty three Cents, Besides interest & Cost, this 27th November 1826.

            Jacob Johnson, forman

R. & J. Habersham }
  vs   } Case
Charles Collins & }
Robert Collins   }

We, the Jury, find for the plaintiff the Sum of two hundred & Sixty Dollars and Ninety one & a quarter Cents, With interest & Cost.

            Jacob Johnson, forman

Archibald Darragh }
   vs   } Assumpsit for Rent
Sereno H. Dwight }
& Wade Harris }

We, the Jury, find for the Plaintiff the Sum of Seventy five Dollars, With interest & Cost, Nov 27th 1826.

            Jacob Johnson, forman

J. Freeman & Co }
   vs   } Assumpsit for Rent
Reason D., alias }
Rezen D. Bealle }
Hockey L. Towns}

We, the Jury, find for the Plaintiff the Sum of One hundred And twenty five Dollars, With interest & Cost.

            Jacob Johnson, forman

David Knox, bearer }
   vs   } assumpsit
M. L. Matherson }

Judgement Confessed to the Plaintiff in the Sum of Seventy Seven Dollars, With interest & Cost, 27th November 1827.

            Albert G. Clopton for
            Js S. Fryeron Def^t Att^y

Hugh McKay }
  vs   } Debt
Elezar McCall }

We, the Jury, find for the Plaintiff fifty Dollars, Will interest And Cost.

            Jacob Johnson, forman

B. & M. Ware }
    vs   } assumpsit
Nathan Carter }

I Confess Judgement to the plaintiff In Sum of Sixty four Dollars & Fifty three and a half Cents, with interest.

                                Nathan Carter

Wm H. Turpin }
    vs   } Debt
Ingersol & Ross }

We, the Jury, find for the plaintiff The Sum of Two hundred & ten Dollars And Sixty five Cents, with interest & cost.

                                Jacob Johnson, forman

Rufus K. Evans }
    vs   } assumpsit & Bail
Seaborn Gray }

I Confess Judgement to the plaintiff In the Sum of Sixty four Dollars, With interest and Cost of Suit.

                                Albert G. Clopton, for
                                Js S. Fryerson, Def^t att^y

It is ordered by the Court that Henry Smith be And he is hereby appointed Constable in and For Capt Rutland District.

Georgia   }
Bibb County }

Joel Rushin   }
    vs   } Casa
Thomas Blancet }
& Mary Minor } From the Inferior Court of Said County

Whereupon, it is Considered By the

Court that the Sheriff do pay over to Said Plaintiff the amount of Principal, interest, & Cost upon Said Execution.

Alexander Murray }
    vs   } Assumpsit
Rufus K. Evans }

We, the Jury, find for the Plaintiff two hundred and Fifty Dollars, With interest & Cost.

                        Jacob Johnson, forman

The Court then adjourned untill tomorrow Morning ten o'clock.

                        M. Robertson, J. I. C.
                        Wm J. Danelly, J. I. C.
                        Robt Birdsong, J. I. C.

            November 28th

The Honorable the Inferior Meet agreeable to adjournment.

Present, &c   Mathew Robertson }
                              Robert Birdsong   } Justices
                              William J. Danelly }

Rushin & Rodgers }
    vs   } Debt
William W. Leonard }

And Now Comes into Court the Said William W. Leonard, by his Attorney John P. Booth, and Confesses Judgement for The Sum of one hundred and Nine Dollars, for Value Received, With interest & Cost of Suit.

                        John P. Booth, Def^t att^y

Barton Helpburn }
    vs   } Assumpsit
David S. Booth }

And Now Comes into Court The Defendant, David S. Booth, By John P. Booth his Attorney, and Confesses Judgement for the Sum of Sixty Nine Dollars

And thirty Seven Cents principal, with interest & Cost of Suit, reserving right of appeal.

John P. Booth, Def^t Att^y

Rushin & Rodgers }
    vs   } Debt
Charles Ingram, Par }

And Now Comes Into Court the Said Charles Ingram, by John P. Booth his attorney, and confesses Judgement for the Sum of fifty Six Dollars and Ninety three and three Fourth Cents, With interest and Cost of Suit.

Jn° P. Booth, Def^t att^y

Rushin & Rodgers }
    vs   } Debt
Henry Terrell   }

And Now Comes Into Court the Said Henry Terrell, by John P. Booth his attorney, and confesses Judgement for the Sum of one hundred and ninety three Dollars, besides Interest & Cost of Suit.

John P. Booth, Def^t Att^y

William Perry }
    vs   } Debt
Joseph Dingley }

We, the Jury, find for the plaintiff Forty four Dollars & Eighty Seven Cents, besides interest & Cost.

Jacob Johnson, forman

R. Walton & Harris }
    vs   } Debt
George B. Wardlaw }

Personally appears in open Court George B. Wardlaw, defendant, who Confesses Judgement for the Sum of Seventy three Dollars and forty three Cents principal, With interest & Cost of Suit.

George B. Wardlaw

Robert Roffe }
    vs } assumpsit
Benjamin Grubb }

We, hereby Confess Judgement for the Plaintiff for one hundred & twenty Dollars, With interest & cost.

                 Mandell & Campbell, Att^{ys} for Def^t

John Murphey & }
Reuben Turner }
    vs } assumpsit
Caleb Smith }

We, the Jury, find for the Plaintiff the Sum of Forty one Dollars and fifty Six & one Quarter Cents, with Cost of Suit.

                 Jacob Johnson, forman

John Murphey & }
Reuben Turner } Indebtatus
    vs } assumpsit
Jordon Ivey }

We, the Jury, find for the Plaintiff the Sum of Sixty Six Dollars Seventy five Cents, With Cost of Suit.

                 Jacob Johnson, forman

A. McBryde & Brothers }
    vs } Debt
William F. Brown }

We, the Jury, find for The Plaintiff the Sum of Fifty Nine $^{6\frac{1}{4}}/_{100}$ Dollars, With interest and cost.

                 Jacob Johnson, forman

Charles W. Rockwell }
George Rolph }
Charles Kelsey & }
Charles McIntyer }
    vs } Debt
John W. Roberts }

We, the Jury, find for the Plaintiff the Sum of one thousand Eight hundred and Fifty Eight Dollars & Nine Cents, with interest & cost.

            Jacob Johnson, forman

William Moor }
  vs   } assumpsit
James Tobin }
John Philpot & }
John Scully }

We, the Jury, find for the plaintiff the Sum of fifty five Dollars Dollars Principal, With interest & Cost of Suit.

            Jacob Johnson, forman

Samuel Gillespie }
Robert Birdsong }
  vs   } assumpsit
James Holmes }

We, the Jury, find for the plaintiff The Sum of one hundred & three Dollars & thirty Eight Cents, with interest & cost.

            Jacob Johnson, forman

Samuel Gillespie }
Robert Birdsong }
  vs   } assumpsit
James Holmes }

We, the Jury, find for the plaintiff The Sum of Ninety Dollars, with interest & Cost.

            Jacob Johnson, forman

It is ordered by the Court that a Road be Cut out as Marked out by the reviewers to run from Dole's Meeting house to intersect the federal road about a Mile west of Bullock Mills on rocky Creek as Soon as Possible.

William H. Sayer }
     vs   } Debt
John M. Sanders }

We, the Jury, find for the Plaintiff The Sum of One hundred and Sixteen Dollars and twenty Seven Cents principal, with interest & Cost of Suit.

                                Jacob Johnson, forman

Benjamin G. Cray }
     vs   } Tresspass on the Case
Robert S. Patton }

We, the Jury, find for the Plaintiff the Sum of thirty Dollars For his Damages, with Cost of Suit.

                                Jacob Johnson, forman

Oliver Sage }
     vs   } Assumpsit
James R. Bennett }
& Ebenezer Keeney }

We, the Jury, find for the Plaintiff the Sum of forty Dollars and twenty one cents Principal, With interest & Cost of Suit.

                                Jacob Johnson, forman

Samuel Gillespie }
Robert Birdsong }
     vs   } Debt
Reddin Rutland }

I Acknowledge Judgment to the Plaintiff for the Sum of Eighty Six Dollars & fifty Cents, with interest & cost.

                                Henry Williams, Def[t] Att[y]

McComick Neal }
     vs   } Debt
Young Johnson }

I hereby Confess Judgment for the Sum of one hundred And twenty one Dollars Principal, With interest & Cost of Suit.

Young Johnson, By his
Att^y Mandell & Campbell

Alexander Murray }
    vs   } Assumpsit
Ebenezer Keeney }

We, the Jury, find for the Plaintiff the Sum of One hundred and thirty Eight Dollars & Six & one fourth Cents, with interest & Cost.

Jacob Johnson, forman

Rushin & Rodgers }
    vs   } assumpsit
Henry Williams }

I hereby Confess Judgment for thirty Seven Dollars & Sixty two & a half Cents, Besides interest & Cost.

Henry Williams

Hugh McNeil }
    vs   } assumpsit
Charles Collins }
& Robert Collins }

We, the Jury, find for the Plaintiff The Sum of one thousand four hundred And Eight Dollars, With interest & Cost.

Jacob Johnson, forman

John D. Chapman }
& Abner Chapman }
    vs   } Assumpsit
Thomas Pickard }

We, the Jury, find for the plaintiff the Sum of twenty four Dollars & Seventeen Cents, With Interest & Cost.

Jacob Johnson, forman

Alexander Murray }
     vs   } Assumpsit in
Rufus K. Evans   } Bibb Inferior Court

Mortimer R. Wallis, having been Garnished in the above Case on the part of the Plaintiff, Now Comes into open Court and deposes That he is unable to Say what he is indebted to deponent as their Accounts have not been liquidated, but That he believes that there is at least a balance due Defendant to the Amount of Two hundred Dollars.

Sworn in open Court   M. R. Wallis
This 28th November 1826
Martin Simmons, Clk

Alexander Murray }
     vs   } Assumpsit
Ebenezar Keeney }

John D. & Abner Chapman, Edward D. Tracy, Oliver H. Prince, William S. Norman, and Addison Mandell, having been Summoned as Garnishees at the last Court and Having then Duly answered the, the plaintiff having Established his Demand at this term, It is ordered That Executions for the Benefit of the plaintiff issue against the above Named Garnishees or So Many of Them as may Satisfy the debt & Costs for the Sums admitted by them respectively to be due to the defendant.

Hugh McNeal   }
     vs   } Assumpsit at May Term 1826
Robert Collins and }
Charles Collins   }

The Plaintiff having died Since the last term and Scire Facias having been issued by his administrator, Phillip H. Gibbs, Who brings his letters into Court, It is ordered That the Case proceed in the Name of the Said Gibb as plaintiff against the defendants.

Ordered that it be the Special duty of the Clerk of this Court to prosecute all persons who retail Spiritous liquors Without first obtaining licence.

Ordered that the Sheriff of this County proceed Forthwith to lay off ten acres of land around The Jail in Macon And Mark out the Same as Jail Bounds.

B. & M. Ware }
     vs   } Assumpsit & Judgment
Nathan Carter }

Came into Court Nathan Carter, the Defendant in the above Case, Who being Dissatisfied with the Verdict, paid the Cost and Entered a Stay of Execution. Also, at the Same time, Came Jacob A. Carter, his Security on the Stay of Execution, whom Each Acknowledge themselves jointly & Severally bound for the True payment of the eventual Condemnation Money according to the Statute in Such case made & provided.

Given under My hand & Seal	Nathan Carter
This 28th November 1826	J. A. Carter
Martin Simmons, Clk	

Ordered that Clerk of this Court pay to Spencer Riley, Jailor, the Sum of forty Seven Dollars and Sixty One Cents, it being the amount of his account For Keeping Hugh Gallagah in Jail to the present date and other things.

Ordered that the Clerk of this Court pay Benjamin Allen the Sum of five Dollars & forty four Cents, it being The amount of his account for apprehending and Bringing Alfred M. Elliott to Jail, including Justice's Cost.

Ordered that the Clerk of this Court pay Benjamin Allen the Sum of four Dollars for his Services as Bailiff During this term.

Hill & Caldwell }
     vs   } Casa
William M. Puryer }
& Chs J. McDonald }

The defendants, having entered into

Recognizance in the Sum of twenty Dollars for the Appearance of the Said Puryear at this term of Court and he Having failed to appear agreable therein, It is therefore Ordered that Execution issue against the Said Wm M. Puryear and the Said Charles J. McDonald, his Said Security, for the Amount of Said Debt & Cost.

The following Jury Were Drawn to Serve at May term 1827, Viz.

1. Henry Smith
2. Hezekiah McKiney
3. Henry Lamb
4. John Douglass
5. Zackariah Cowart
6. John Bridges, Sen
7. Thompson Powell
8. George Glover
9. Turner Smith
10. James Ashley
11. James Asburry
12. Thomas Scurly
13. Stephen Atkinson
14. Young Edwards
15. Eliah Neal
16. Isaac Metcalf
17. David Adams
18. William Ward
19. Joseph Shaw
20. Council Bryon
21. Charles McAlister
22. Edmund Wheless
23. Zackariah Jordon
24. Reuben Williamson
25. Willis Pitt
26. David Powell
27. John P. Ballard
28. Alexander Burnett
29. John H. Kimbro
30. Thomas G. Bates
31. Reddin Rutland
32. John L. Jones
33. Thompson Powell, Sen
34. William P. L. Brooks
35. William Harding
36. Glover Wright

The Court then adjourned untill Court in Course.

M. Robertson, J. I. C.
Wm J. Danelly, J. I. C.
Robt Birdsong, J. I. C.

November Term 1826

J. Freeman & Co }
        vs   } Debt & Judgement
Reason D., alias }
Rezen D. Bealle & }
Hockey L. Towns }

Came into office Reason D. Bealle, the defendant in this Case, Who being disatisfied With the Verdict of the Jury, paid the Cost and Entered a Stay of Execution. Also, at the Same time, Came Solomon D. Chapman, his Security on the Stay of Execution, Whoom Each acknowledge themselves jointly & Severally Bound for the true payment of the Eventual Condemnation Money According to the Statute in Such Case Made & provided. Given under our hands and Seals this 30th day of November 1826.

Test. Martin Simmons, Clk   Ren D. Bealle, by Herself
                                                  & Hockey Town
                                                  S. D. Chapman

John Murphey & }
Reuben Turner   }
     vs   } assumpsit & Judgment
John French   }

Came into office John French, the Defendant in this Case, Who being Disatisfied With the Verdict of the Jury, paid the Cost & Entered ~~a Stay of Execution~~ an appeal. Also, at the Same time, Came Joel Rushin, his Security on the ~~Stay of Execution~~ appeal, Whom Each acknowledge themselves jointly & Severally bound for The true payment of the Eventual Condemnation Money According to the Statute in Such Case Made And provided. Given under our hand and Seals This 30th day of November 1826.

Test. Martin Simmons, Clk   John French
                                                  J. Rushin

November Term 1826

Hugh McKay }
     vs   } Debt & Judgment
Elezar McCall }

Came into Office Elezar McCall, the defendant in This Case, who being disatisfied with the Verdict of the Jury, paid the Cost and Entered a Stay of Execution. Also, at the Same time, Came Thomas G. Bates, his Security on the Stay of Execution, Whom Each acknowledge themselves jointly & Severally bound For the true payment of the Eventual

Condemnation Money According to the Statute in Such Case Made & Provided. Given under our hands & Seals this Second day of December 1826.

Test. Martin Simmons, Clk   Elezar McCall
                                         Thomas G. Bates

Robert Roffe   }
     vs   } Assumpsit & Judgment
Benjamin Grubbs }

Came into Office Benjamin Grubbs, the defendant in the above Case, who being disatisfied with the Verdict of the Jury, paid the Cost and Entered a Stay of Execution. Also Came Benjamin Allen, his Security on the Stay of Execution, Whom each acknowledge themselves Jointly & Severally bound for the true payment of the Eventual Condemnation Money According to the Statute in Such Case Made & provided. Given under our hands & Seals this Second day of December 1826.

Test. Martin Simmons, Clk   Benjamin Grubbs
                                        Ben^j Allen

Georgia   } May 28th 1827. The Honorable the Inferior Court
Bibb County } Met agreeable to adjournment

Present, their Honors   Timothy Mathews }
                                  Tarpley Holt   } Justices
                                  Robert Birdsong }
                                  ~~David Ralston~~   }

The following Jury were empaneled to Serve at This Term.

Jury N° 1

1. Henry Smith   7. Willis Pitt
2. Hezekiah McKennie   8. Alexander Burnett
3. John Douglass   9. Thomas G. Bates
4. John Bridges, Sen   10. Redding Rutland
5. Isaac Metcalf   11. John Scully
6. David Adams   12. Ashburn D. Davis

Wm H. Turpin }
    vs   } Debt
Henry G. Ross }

I Confess Judgment to the plaintiff for Six three Dollars, with interest & Cost.

                                          H. G. Ross

C. Kelsey & Co }
    vs   } Case
Charles Ingram }

Judgment Confessed for the plaintiff Thirty five Dollars & ten Cents, With Interest & Cost.

                                John P. Booth, Deft Aty

Martin Simmons }
    vs   } Case
Henry G. Ross }

We, the Jury, find for the plaintiff The Sum of thirty three Dollars And fifty Cents, With interest & Cost.

                                Alexander Burnett, forman

John Oliver }
    vs   } Assumpsit
Arnold Johnston }

We, the Jury, find for the plaintiff One hundred Dollars, With interest & Cost.

                                Alexander Burnett, forman

Melins C. Leavenworth }
    vs   } Assumpsit
Clement Clements }

We, the Jury, find for the Plaintiff the Sum of thirty two Dollars, With Interest & Cost.

Alexander Burnett, forman

Charles P. Merriman }
     vs   } Assumpsit
Peter Leguiexx   }

We, the Jury, find for the Plaintiff the Sum of Three hundred Eighty one $^{45}/_{100}$ Dollars, with interest & Cost.

Alexander Burnett, forman

Josiah Freeman }
   vs   } Assumpsit
Elam Alexander }

We, the jury, find for the plaintiff The Sum of One hundred & Eighty one Dollars, With interest & Cost.

Alexander Burnett, form

Elliott W. Gregory }
    vs   } assumpsit
George B. Wardlaw}

I Confess Judgment to The plaintiff for the Sum of one hundred & One Dollars Ninety three Cents, with interest & Cost.

John P. Booth, Def^t Att^y

William H. Thompson & Co }
    vs   } Assumpsit
George B. Wardlaw   }

May Term 1827. I Confess Judgment To the plaintiff for the Sum of One hundred & Eighty two Dollars, With interest & Cost.

John P. Booth, Deftd Att^y

Thomas Napier }
    vs } Case
J. D. & A. Chapman }
Bullock & Wells }

We, the Jury, find for plaintiff Eight hundred & forty two Dollars & fifty Cents, with Interest & Cost of Suit.

Alexander Burnett, forman

Samuel Rockwell }
    vs } Debt
John C. Caldwell }

We, the Jury, find for the plaintiff The Sum of fifty two Dollars & Forty two Cents, besides interest & Cost of Suit.

Alexander Burnett, forman

Joel Rushin }
    vs } Assumpsit
Alexander D. Brown }

We, the Jury, find for the Plaintiff the Sum of thirty nine Dollars & seventy five Cents, With interest & Cost of Suit.

Alexander Burnett, forman

Crane & Legueux }
For the use of }
Thomas Napier }
    vs } Case
Elenor Davis }

We, the Jury find for the plaintiff one hundred Dollars, With interest And Cost.

Alexander Burnett, forman

Crane & Legueux }
For use of }
Thomas Napier }
    vs } Case
Thomas G. Bates }

Judgment Confessed to the Plaintiff for one hundred Dollars, With interest & Cost of Suit.

                          Thomas G. Bates

Joel Rushin & }
George A. Rodgers }
For the use of }
Seaborn Jones }
    vs } Assumpsit
John Loving }

We, the Jury, find for The plaintiff the Sum of Eighty two Dollars & twenty Seven cents, with interest & Cost of Suit.

                          Alexander Burnett, forman

Cadwell W. Rains }
    vs } Assumpsit
Seaborn Gray }

We, the Jury, find for the Plaintiff the Sum of fifty Dollars, With interest & Cost of Suit.

                          Alexander Burnett, forman

Peter J. Williams }
For the use of the }
Penitentiary }
    vs } Debt
Alexander Richards }

We, the Jury, find for the Plaintiff the Sum of forty Dollars principal, With interest And Cost of Suit.

                          Alexander Burnett, forman

Timothy Brewen }
     vs   } assumpsit & Bail
David Holt   }

We, the Jury, find for the Plaintiff one Hundred & fifteen Dollars & thirty Seven & a half Cents principal, with interest & Cost.

                                    Alexander Burnett, forman

---

Uriah Kinchen   }
     vs   } Debt
Samuel A. Plummer }

We, the Jury, find for plaintiff Sum of fifty Nine Dollars And forty two Cents principal, with interest & Cost of Suit.

                                    Alexander Burnett, forman

Peter J. Williams   }
for the use of the   }
Penitentiary   }
     vs   } Debt
Samuel A. Plummer }

We, the Jury, find for the Plaintiff the Sum of thirty Three Dollars, with interest & Cost of Suit.

                                    Alexander Burnett, forman

Timothy Brewen }
     vs   } Debt in Bibb Inferior Court
David Holt   }

Joel Rushin, having achieved To the Officer of this Court, The debt in the above Case for whom he was Bail. on Motion Ordered that the Said Joel Be hence discharged from any further liability on his Bail Bond in Said Case.

Georgia   }
Bibb County } Inferior Court May Term 1827

David Holt, having given due Notice To Wm G. Hansell & Timothy Brewer of his intention of Applying at this term of The Court to be admitted to take the benefit of the Act of the Legislature of this State for The relief of Honest debtors, & Said Holt Having Complyed with requisitions of the Statute, and having taken the oath required in Such Cases, On motion it is ordered that Said Holt be Allowed the Benefit of Said Act for the relief of Honest Debtors & that the Body of the Said

---

Holt be Henceforth free from Arrest on & on Account of any process issuing or Sued out In Consequence of any Demands, the Said Brewen & Hansell, or Either of them, May Now Hold or May have held at the time of the [blot]vier of Said Notice.

Shadrach F. Slatten, Ex^{or} }
of Solomon L. Slatten, Dec^d }
     vs   } Case
James Thompson }

We, the Jury, find For the defendant.

Alexander Burnett, forman

William Bivins }
     vs   } Assumpsit
Jonathan A. Hudron }

We, the Jury, find For the plaintiff Seventy One Dollars & Sixty Eight Cents, with interest & Cost.

Alexander Burnett, forman

Ordered that John S. Childers be paid the Sum of twelve Dollars for rent of Room For Grand Gury.

James B. Ransone }
     vs   } assumpsit
James T. Wofford }

We Confess Judgment To the plaintiff in the Sum of Seventy five Dollars for the principal Sum, [blank] for his interest, & the further Sum of [blank] for his Cost.

      Mandell & Campbell, Deft^d Att^{ys}

The Court then adjourned untill to Morrow Morning at ten O'clock.

Test. Martin Simmons, clk   R. Birdsong, J. I. C.
             Timothy Mathews, J. I. C.
             Tarpley Holt, J. I. C.

Georgia } The Honorable the Inferior Court Meet
Bibb County } agreeable to adjournment

Present, Their Honors   Timothy Mathews }
            Tarpley Holt   } Justices
            Robert Birdsong }

Francis Bacon   }
  vs   } Garnishee In Bibb Inferior Court
Ehud Harris &   } May Term 1827
Samuel Gillespie }

Samuel Gillespie, having answered as required By law in the above Case, & it appearing from Said answer that there is Nothing in the hands of The Garnishee as the property of the defendant, & No issue being joined Controverting Said Answer of The Garnishee, on Motion ordered that Samuel Gillespie pay over to the assigner of a order on Draft Drawn on him as County treasurer the Am^t due thereon, as the Same was transfered & the Legal interest passed from the Said Ehud prior To and Servis of garnishment & had Vested in W. P. Harris, the assignee of Said Draft.

Charles W. Rockwell }
George Relph   }
Charles Riley &   }
Charles McIntire }
  vs   } Assumpsit
David Ralston   }

We, the Jury, find for the plaintiff The Sum one thousand & Eighty Two Dollars & Forty Nine Cents, With interest & Cost of Suit.

Alexander Burnett, forman

Charles W. Rockwell }
& George Relph }
  vs   } Assumpit
David Ralston }

We, the Jury, find for the Plaintiff the Sum of Six Hundred And Sixteen Dollars, With interest & Cost.

Alexander Burnett, forman

Seaborn Jones }
  vs   } Assumpsit
Joel Rushin }

We, the Jury, find for the Plaintiff the Sum of three hundred And thirty four Dollars & Ninety Six Cents, With Cost of Suit.

Alexander Burnett, forman

Thompson Bird }
& John Loving }
  vs   } Assumpsit
J. J. Kaigler }

I Confess Judgment to the plaintiff In the Sum of thirty five dollars And Nine Cents, with Cost of Suit.

J. J. Kaigler

Thomas Napier   }
  vs   } Case
Edward W. Wright }

We, the Jury, find for the Plaintiff Ninety Seven Dollars & Fifty Nine Cents, with Cost of Suit.

Alexander Burnett, forman

Ordered that Samuel Powell be Appointed Constable for Capt Ross' Dist.

Ordered that Henry Smith be appointed Constable for Captain Rutland's Dist.

Ives & White }
  vs   } Assumpsit
Reuben Burroughs }

We, the Jury, find a Verdict for The plaintiff for four hundred & Nine Dollars & Eighty Seven Cents, with interest And Cost of Suit.

Alexander Burnett, forman

Henry B. Cone }
  vs   } Case
Henry G. Ross & }
Ge^o B. Wardlaw }

Judgment Confessed to the plaintiff For eighty Dollars, with interest & Cost of Suit.

Mandell & Campbell, Def^t At^y

George M. Troup, Gov &c }
  vs   } Assumpsit for Rent
David F. Wilson }
Benjamin Russell & }
George B. Wardlaw }

We, the Jury, find for the Plaintiff Forty Seven Dollars, With interest & Cost of Suit.

Alexander Burnett, forman

George M. Troup, Gov &c }
  vs   } Assumpsit for Rent
Perry & Coleman }

We, the Jury, find for the Plaintiff Seventy two Dollars, With interest & Cost of Suit.

Alexander Burnett, forman

George M. Troup, Gov &c }
   vs   } Assumpsit for Rent
Joel Rushin   }
George A. Rodgers & }
S. M. Ingersol   }

We, the Jury, find for the Plaintiff the Sum of Sixty Six Dollars, with interest & Cost of Suit.

              Alexander Burnett, forman

George M. Troup, Gov &c }
   vs   } Assumpsit for Rent
James S. Frierson   }
& Harrison Smith   }

We, the Jury, find for the Plaintiff Seventy two Dollars, with Interest & Cost of Suit.

              Alexander Burnett, forman

John Reddick &   }
Noah Reddick, Executors }
of Abraham Trice   }
   vs   } Debt &c
Luke Ross, administrator }
of James Bell   }

We, the Jury, find for The defendant, With Cost of Suit.

              Alexander Burnett, forman

Charles J. McDonald }
   vs   } Debt for Rent
A. D. Davis   }
William C. Crawford }
& E. Keeney   }

Judgment Confessed for The plaintiff the Sum of Ninety Dollars Sixty two & a half Cents, with interest & Cost.

              E. D. Tracy, deft[d] att[y]

William Cumming }
     vs   } Assumpsit
Mary Miner & }
John Chain }

We, the Jury, find for The plaintiff the Sum of Fifty Dollars, With interest & Cost.

                          Alexander Burnett, forman

The Court then adjourned untill Monday Next.

                          Robt Birdsong, J. I. C.
                          Tarpley Holt, J. I. C.
                          Timothy Mathews, J. I. C.

                    May Term 1827

Thomas Napier }
     vs   } [faint]
J. D. & A. Chapman }
& Bullock & Wells }

Came into office John D. Chapman, Abner Chapman, by his agent, Nicholas Wells, & Charles Bullock, the defendants in this Case, who being disatisfied with the Verdict of the Jury, paid The Cost and Entered a Stay of Execution. also, at the Same time, Came Solomon D. Chapman, their Security on The Stay of Execution, whom each acknowledge themselves Jointly & Severally bound for the true payment of the Eventual Condemnation Money according to the Statute In Such Case Made & provided. Given under our Hands & Seals this 30th day of May 1827.

Test. Martin Simmons, Clk   J. D. Chapman
                                           Abner Chapman
                                           By J. D. Chapman
                                           S. D. Chapman
                                           Bullock & Wells

May Term 1827

Georgia } June 4th 1827. The Honorable the Inferior Court in &
Bibb County } for Said County Meet agreeable to adjournment

Present,
        Timothy Mathews }
        Mathew Robertson } Justices
        Robert Birdsong }
        Tarpley Holt }

On or before the twenty fifth day of December Next, I promise to pay John S. Wallace, or bearer, one hundred Dollars for Value Received to bear interest from the date. Witness My hand & Seal February 4th 1827.

            Washington Ledbetter

Georgia } Bibb Inferior Court May Term 1827
Bibb County } Rule Nisi

It appearing to the Court that the original Note, of which the above is a Copy, is the property of John S. Wallace & that the Same is lost. on Motion, It is ordered that the Maker of Said promissory Note Appear at the Next Term of this Court & Shew Cause, if any he has, why the Copy filed in the Office of this Court Should Not be Established in Lieu of the Lost original & that a Copy of this Rule be Served by publication as prescribed by Law.

George M. Troup, Gov &c }
   vs   } Assumpsit
Jn° Perry   }
Robert Coleman   }
& Wm W. Brown   }

Wm W. Brown Not Served. On Motion of Plaintiff's Attorney, It is ordered that they have Leave To take from the file the Note on Which the Above Action is instituted to persue their Remedy against the Defendant, Wm W. Brown, who resides in another County And has not been Served, Leaving in place of the original Note a true Copy thereof.

Ordered that Albert G. Clopton be and he is hereby Appointed Notorry Publick for the town of Macon & County of Bibb.

Ordered that Samuel Thompkins, Hermon H. Howard, George Vigal, William Sanders, and Thomas Lundy Be & they are hereby appointed Commissioners of Roads for Capt Swearingin Dist.

Ordered that James Visage be and he is hereby Appointed Constable for Capt Swearingin Dist on his giving bond & Security in terms of The Law.

———

Matha B. Dawson, admint^{rx} } I^n Twiggs Inferior Court
& Charles Bullock, adm^r of }
William W. Dawson, Dec^d }
   vs   } fifa
James Holderness & }
Solomon Groce }

Same }
 vs } fifa from the Same Court
Same }

Bibb Inferior Court May Term 1827

On Motion, ordered that the Sheriff of this Court Produce the Above fifas, with his Actings & Doings thereon, & Shew Cause, if any he has, why He Should not pay over to John Carington, the Assignee of the above fifas, or his attorney, the Full amount of the principal & interest due thereon. May 29th 1827

          Strong & Lamar,
          Att^y for John Carington

Georgia }
Bibb County } Bibb Inferior Court May Term 1827

The Sheriff of this County, in Obediance To the Above rule Nisi, having produced the above fifas Therein Specified, With his actings & doings thereon, And No Sufficient Cause being Shewn Why he Should not pay over to the assignee the amount Thereof, And no Sufficient Cause being Shewn, on Motion it is ordered that the Sheriff aforesaid Pay to John Carington, assignee as aforesaid of Said Executions, the full amount of Money Due thereon. May 29th 1827

———

Georgia }
Bibb County } Bibb Inferior Court May Term 1827

Rule Nisi having been obtained against Edmund C. Beard, Sheriff of Bibb County, to Shew Cause, if any he has, why he Should not pay Over to John Carington, assignee of two Executions Issuing from Twiggs Inferior Court, returnable to January Term 1824, one for three hundred & thirty one Dollars & fifty Cents principal, With interest from The 2nd day of January 1823, the other for two Hundred & thirty Eight Dollars principal & interest Thereon from the 1st day of January 1823. Both of Said fifas are in favour of Matha B. Dawson, adm^x, & Charles Bullock, adm^r of Wm W. Dawson, Dece'd, against James Holderness & Solomon Groce, Defendants, and No Sufficient Cause being Shewn In Answer to Said Rule, and a rule absolute Being granted on Said Rule nisi against The Sheriff aforesaid, ordering him to pay To said John Carington the full Amount of The Money due thereon, And the Said Edmund C. Beard having failed to Comply And is Therefore in Contempt of the order & process of this Court, No we do Command You, Abner Cherry, the Corroner of Said County, After the first Tuesday in August Next to take the Body of the Said Edmund C. Beard, Sheriff as aforesaid, into Your Custody & him Confine & Keep in the Common Jail of this County Without Bail or Mainprize untill he Shall Have purged the Contempt by paying over To John Carington, or his attorney, or to you, the Full amount of principal & interest & Cost Due on Said fifas.

May Term 1827

It appears to the Court that Hardy, a Coloured Man, has been at Considerable Expense & trouble in Sheltering, Nursing, & Maintaining Sharp, a person wholly destitute of Sources, Since Dead, it is ordered that the Clk of this Court Pay to the Said Hardy fifteen Dollars of the County funds Not otherwise appropriated as a Remuneration.

The Application of Henry Clem & Jonathan Neal, on the part of themselves & others for Rebuilding of a bridge across the Tobasofka, Where Wadsworth's bridge formerly Stood, Was Read & on consideration it is ordered that the Petition be granted And that the Said Henry Clem, Jonathan Neal, & Joshua Jordon be appointed Commissioners to let at Public outcry the building of Said Bridge at a price not Exceding Two hundred Dollars, the undertaker to Give Bond for keeping the bridge in repairs for five Years and agreeing to take the Subscription of the Said Clem, Neal, & others, persons of the neighborhood, For one half the Cost of the Bridge.

~~Ordered that James Fitzjerold, James Thompson, and Quinton Hoy be and they are hereby appointed Commissioners To let out the erecting of a Bridge across Tobias So[blot] Creek at the Federal Road.~~

Ordered that James Flewellen have leave to Build a bridge at his own expence across the Tobasofka Creek at or near his own House, provided That the Said James Build a Substitute Bridge and Keep the Same in good repairs ten Years and at his own Expense open & Keep up a

---

Public road to intersect the present Knoxville at or Near Bullock's Mills. And ordered that Josiah Dixson and Lewis Lauchea have leave to open & Keep up a public road from Dixson's Mills on the Ichecona to Flewellen Mills at the Expence of the Said Josiah & Lewis, provided they will Keep up the present bridge in good repairs at Dixson Mills for ten Years at their own Expense, And provided that the Said James, Josiah, & Lewis ~~Mannify~~ indemnify the County against any damage of the road, or either of them, Should run through Cleared land.

May Term 1827

James Tobin }
    vs   } Casa from Justices Court
John Scully }

William Cumming & John T. Lamar, Who were Securities for the appearance of John Scully at this term, on the law for the Relief of Honest debtors, having brought the defendant into open Court & delivered him to the Sheriff. It is ordered that the Said Lamar & Cumming be Discharged from their bonds & that an Exoneration Be entered on the Said Bonds.

The Court then adjourning untill tomorrow Morning at ten o'clock.

Robt Birdsong, J. I. C.
Tarpley Holt, J. I. C.
Timothy Mathews, J. I. C.

The Honorable the Inferior Court Meet agreeable To adjournment June 5th 1827.

Present   Timothy Mathews }
                  Tarpley Holt   } Justices
                  Robert Birdsong }

Ordered that James Fitzjarrel, James Thompson, and Quinton Hoy be and they are hereby appointed Commissioners to let out and Contract for the Erecting of a Bridge across Tobias Sofca Creek at the Federal Road and that the Said Commissioners require and bind the undertaker in a Bond in double the amount of the Cost of the Bridge to insure it for five years.

Rushin & Rodgers }
    vs   } Casa and application for Relief
Charles Ingram   } under the Honest Debtors act

An arrangement having been Made in this Case Between the plaintiff & Defendant. It is ordered that Rice Durrett, Security for Said Ingram, be released From any further Responsibility upon the Bond for The appearance of Said Ingram & that Said Bond Be Considered as Satisfied & rendered inoperative.

Ordered that Spencer Riley be paid the Sum of fifteen Dollars ninety two Cents, it being for his Fees for Keeping Lewis in Jail.

Ordered that Martin Simmons be paid the Sum of Eight Dollars & twenty five Cents for Laying of & advertising Lots on Court House Square.

~~The Court then adjourned untill Court in Course.~~

~~Test. Martin Simmons, Clk~~

May Term 1827

Crane & Legueux }
for the use of }
Thomas Napier }
    vs   } Case & Judgment
Eleanor Davis }

Came into office Eleanor Davis, The defendant in this Case, Who Being disatisfied with the Verdict of the Jury, paid the Cost & Entered a Stay of Execution. Also, at the Same time, Came Thomas Howard, her Security on the Stay, Whom Each Acknowledge themselves jointly & Severally Bond For the true payment of the Eventual Condemnation Money According to the Statutes in Such Case Made & provided. Given under our hands & Seal This 5th day of June 1827.

Test. Martin Simmons, Clk   Eleanor Davis
                                           Tho[s] Howard

List of Jury Drawn to Serve at November Term 1827.

1. Thomas Patterson
2. Blunt Bazmore
3. Benjamin Philips
4. Henry B. Hill
5. Joshua Worrin
6. William Castlebery
7. John Patterson
8. Whiton Keith
9. William Taylor
10. William Manereth
11. Ambrose Killingworth
12. Henry Carter
13. John Jordon
14. Edmund Woods
15. David Carter
16. Enoch Green
17. Ebenezer Keeney
18. Abslom Jordon
19. John Potts
20. John Morgan
21. Joseph Wiggins
22. Andrew Voluntine
23. Nathan Jones
24. Samuel Pickard
25. James Smith
26. John McMarrian
27. Harrison Hammock
28. Moses Jones
29. James Fergerson
30. Charles C. Carter
31. Wiley Dorman
32. William Scott
33. Washington Durdon
34. Randal Stewart
35. James Jones
36. Elijah Garrett

The Court then adjourned untill Court in Course.

Test. Martin Simmons, Clk   Robt Birdsong, J. I. C.
                                Tarpley Holt, J. I. C.
                                Timothy Mathews, J. I. C.

Seaborn Jones }
     vs   } Assumpsit & Judgment
Joel Rushin   }

Came into office Joel Rushin, the Defendant in this Case, who being Disatisfied with the Verdict of the Jury, paid the Cost and entered an appeal, also, at the Same time, Came James H. Rodgers, his Security on the appeal, Who both acknowledge themselves Jointly & Severally bond For the true payment of the Eventual Condemnation Money according to the Statute in Such Case Made And provided. Given under our hand & Seal this 7th day of June 1827.

Test.   J. Rushin
                                Ja^s H. Rodgers

Thomas Napier   }
     vs   } Case & Judgment
Edward W. Wright }

Came into office Thomas Napier, by agent Nathan C. Munroe, the defendant In this Case, who being disatisfied with the Verdict of the Jury, paid the Cost & entered an appeal. Also, at the Same time, Came Robert Collins, His Security on the appeal, Who both acknowledge Themselves jointly & Severally bound for the true Payment of Eventual Condemnation Money according to the Statute in Such Case Made & provided. Given under our hands & Seals This 7th day of June 1827.

Test. Martin Simmons, Clk   Nathan C. Munroe, ag^t
                                for Thomas Napier
                                Robt Collins

John Reddick }
Noah Reddick }
Executor of }
Abraham Tice }
    vs } } Debt & Judgment
Luke Ross, adm^r }
of James Bell }

Came into office John Reddick, Noah Reddick, by their att[y], Mandell & Campbell, who being Disatisfied with the Verdict of The Jury, paid the Cost & Entered an appeal, also, at the Same time, Came Henry G. Ross, their Security on the appeal, who acknowledge themselves Jointly & Severally bond for the true payment of the Eventual Condemnation Money according to the Statute in Such Case Made and provided. Given under our hands & Seals this 9th ~~1827~~ day of June 1827.

Test. Martin Simmons, Clk   Mandell & Campbell
                                                  Att[os] for Plaintiffs
                                                  Henry G. Ross

---

Georgia } The Honorable the Inferior Court In and for Said
Bibb County } County Meet this day November 26th 1827 Agreeable to adjournment.

Present, their Honors   Timothy Mathews }
                                   Tarpley Holt   } Justices
                                   Mathew Robertson }

The following Jury were Sworn to Serve at This Term.

Jury N° 1

1. Henry B. Hill   7. Ebenezer Keeney
2. Joshua Warren   8. Absolum Jordon
3. Whiten Keith   9. Joseph Wiggins
4. Ambrose Killingworth   10. Mathew Jones
5. Henry Carter   11. James Smith
6. Enoch Green   12. John McMarrian

Jury N° 2

1. James Jones
2. James Fergerson
3. Harrison Hammock
4. Wiley Dorman
5. Jehu W. Hutcherson
6. Lewis Hammond
7. Howell Wooten
8. Benjamin Smith
9. ~~Stephen Carver~~
   Benjamin Philips
10. Abner Hammond
11. Benjamin Allen
12. George Collins

Thomas Thweatt, bearer }
    vs   } Case
John M. Shelman }

I Confess Judgment for Two hundred & Sixteen Dollars, With interest from the first day of January 1827, With Cost.

                John M. Shelman
                By his attorney
                Polhill & Cole

Roger McCarthey, Indorsee }
    vs   } Assumpsit
James Thompson, Indorser }

I Confess Judgment to the

Plaintiff for Two hundred and Twenty Dollars, With interest & Cost.

                James Thompson

John W. Gordon }
    vs   } Debt
John Hall }

We, the attorneys for Defendant, Do Confess Judgment for two Hundred & twenty five Dollars, With interest & Cost.

                Prince & Poe, def^t att^y

J. D. Weathers }
    vs   } Debt
James S. Frierson }

We find for the plaintiff Two hundred & twenty Seven Dollars & Sixty two & a half Cents, With interest & Cost of Suit.

                                              Benjamin Allen, forman

Daniel Gunn, bearer }
    vs   } Case
Temperane Rodgers }
& John C. Rodgers }

We find for the plaintiff Thirty Seven Dollars & Sixteen Cents, with interest & cost.

                                              Benjamin Allen, forman

Peter Clower }
    vs   } Assumpsit
John D. Chapman }
Abner Chapman }
John S. Childers }
& Samuel Thomkins }

We find for the plaintiff Thirteen Hundred & twenty one Dollars & forty two Cents, With Interest & Cost.

                                              Benjamin Allen, forman

———

J. H. Branscombe }
    vs   } Debt
Joel Sherrard }

                                    N° 2

We, the Jury, find for the Plaintiff One hundred & fourteen Dollars, With interest & cost.

                                              Benjamin Allen, forman

Anson Kimberly }
    vs   } Debt
John Philpot   }

Judgment Confessed in the Within Notes amounting in all to five hundred and three Dollars and forty Three Cents, with interest & Cost.

                Mandell & Campbell, Def^d Att^{ys}

Kimberly & Chisholm }
    vs   } Ind assumpsit
John Philpot   }

Judgment Confessed in favour of Plaintiff for thirty Seven Dollars and twelve Cents, With interest & Cost.

                Mandell & Campbell, Att^{ys} pro Def^d

M. R. Wallis   }
    vs   } Assumpsit
Wilder & Lewis }

                Jury N° 1

We, the Jury, find for the Plaintiff One hundred & Eight Dollars, With Interest & Cost.

                Absolam Jordon, forman

Benjamin Russell }
    vs   } Assumpsit
David F. Wilson }

                Jury N° 1

We, the Jury, find for The plaintiff the Sum of Forty Dollars & fifty four Cents for his principal Debt, besides interest & cost.

                Absolam Jordon, forman

Josiah Newton }
    vs   } Assumpsit
Zackariah Sims }

I hereby ~~Acknowledge~~ Confess Judgment to the Plaintiff in the Sum of three hundred & nine dollars and Sixty two Cents, With interest & Cost.

           Z. Sims

Thomas F. Cowles }
  vs   } Case
Elijah Wells   }

I hereby Confess Judgment for the Defendant for Sixty Eight Dollars Principal, with interest and Cost.

           Elijah Wells
           by his Brother
           Nicholas W. Wells

Ralph King }
  vs   } Assumpsit
John Loving }

       Jury N° 1

We, the Jury, find for the Plaintiff the Sum of fifty Six Dollars And Sixty Seven Cents for his principal debt, besides interest & Cost.

          Absolam Jordon, forman

Robert D. Ware   }
& William Harris   }
  vs   } Assumpsit
James S. Week, Principal   }
Jephtha V. George, Security }

       Jury N° 1

We, the Jury, find for the Plaintiff the Sum of one hundred & Nine Dollars & fifty Eight Cents for Their principal debt, besides interest & Cost.

          Absolam Jordon, forman

David T. Baldwin }
  vs   } Assumpsit
Alexander Richards }

I Confess Judgment to the Plaintiff the Sum of Seventy three Dollars and Eighteen Cents for his principal debt, besides interest & Cost.

         Alexander Richards

Hannah Harris   }
 vs   } Case
David S. Booth   }
adm^r of Thos Bagby }

      Jury N° 1

We, the Jury, find for the Plaintiff the Sum of forty One $^{25}/_{100}$ Dollars and Cost.

         Absolam Jordan, forman

Anson Kimberly }
 vs   } Assumpsit
Alexander Richards }

I hereby ~~Acknowledge~~ Confess Judgment to the plaintiff For the Sum of one hundred and eight dollars And Seventy four Cents, With interest & Cost.

         Alexander Richards

Samuel Cook   }
 vs   } Assumpsit
John D. Chapman }
Abner Chapman & }
Ambrose Chapman }

      Jury N° 2

We find for the plaintiff four hundred & Thirty five Dollars Twelve & a half Cents, With Interest & Cost.

         Benjamin Allen, forman

Anson Kimberly }
 vs   } Assumpsit
Elijah Cotton   }

Jury Nº 2

We, the Jury, find for the Plaintiff the Sum of fifty four dollars and fifty Cents for his principal Debt, besides Interest & Cost.

Absolam Jordon, forman

Anson Kimberly }
    vs   } Assumpsit
John M. Sanders }

Jury Nº 1

We, the Jury, find for the plaintiff The Sum of thirty Seven dollars for his principal Debt, besides interest & Cost.

Absolam Jordan, forman

Samuel Gillespie }
& Robert Birdsong }
    vs   } Assumpsit
Davis B. Braswell }

I Confess Judgment to the Plaintiff the Sum of thirty Eight dollars & Eighty Seven Cents for his principal Debt, Besides Interest & cost.

Davis B. Braswell

Anson Kimberly }
    vs   } Assumpsit
Young Johnston }

Jury Nº 2

We, the Jury, find for the Plaintiff thirty Nine dollars for his principal, besides interest & Cost.

Absolam Jordan, forman

Anson Kimberly }
    vs   } Assumpsit
David F. Wilson }
& John J. Kaigler }

Jury Nº 1

We, the Jury, find for the Plaintiff the Sum of forty Dollars & Eighty one Cents for his principal debt, besides interest & Cost.

Absolam Jordan, forman

Anson Kimberly }
    vs   } Assumpsit
John J. Kaigler }

Jury Nº 1

We, the Jury, find for the Plaintiff the Sum of Seventy Two Dollars & Sixty Seven Cents for his principal debt, besides interest & Cost.

Absolam Jordan, forman

Bibb Inferior Court November Term 1827

It having been recommended to this Court by the Judges of the Superior Court to Allow Mitchell Coxwell one dollar a day for Eight Days & Henry Smith one Dollar a day for Nine Days Attention as Bailiff on Said Court, it is therefore ordered that this Amount be Paid out of the Money Arising from fines & forfeitures.

John Bozman }
    vs   } Case
Elenor Davis & }
Marther Davis }

Jury Nº 1

We, the Jury, find for The plaintiff the Sum of Sixty Dollars, With interest and Cost.

Absolam Jordan, forman

Wallis & Bond }
    vs   } Case
Moore & Johnston }
& William Cumming }

Jury Nº 1

We, the Jury, find for Plaintiff One hundred And twenty five dollars & two Cents, With Interest & Cost.

        Absolam Jordan, forman

Henry Cosnard }
  vs   } Assumpsit
Evans & Moore }

We, the Attorneys for Defendants, do confess Judgment for one hundred & Eight Dollars And fifty Cents, with interest & Cost.

        Tracy & Butler, Att^y for Defd^t

Smith & Childers }
  vs   } Case
Zackariah Sims & }
Samuel A. Plummer }

Jury Nº 2

We find for the plaintiff One hundred & twenty dollars, With interest & Cost.

        Benjamin Allen, forman

Samuel Gillespie & }
Robert Birdsong }
  vs   } Assumpsit
John D. Alston }

Jury Nº 1

We, the Jury, find for the Plaintiff the Sum of one Hundred dollars for their principal debt, besides Interest & Cost.

        Absolam Jordan, forman

Luke J. Morgan }
  vs   } Assumpsit
Martin H. Brown }

Jury Nº 1

We, the Jury, find for The plaintiff the Sum of three hundred & Eighty five Dollars & Six Cents for his principal Debt, besides interest & Cost.

Absolam Jordan, forman

Anson Kimberly }
    vs } Assumpsit
Daniel Wardsworth }

Jury Nº 1

We, the Jury, find for the Plaintiff the Sum of Two hundred & Seventy Six Dollars & thirty Seven Cents for his principal Debt, besides interest & Cost.

Absolam Jordan, forman

The Court then adjourned untill Tomorrow Morning at Nine O'clock.

M. Robertson, J. I. C.
Timothy Mathews, J. I. C.
T. Holt, J. I. C.

November Term 1827

Georgia } The Honorable the Inferior Court in for Said County
Bibb County } Meet agreeable to adjournment

Present, their honors   Timothy Mathews }
                                    Tarpley Holt   } Justices
                                    Mathew Robertson}
                                    David Ralston   }

George M. Troup }   George M. Troup   }
Gov &c }   Gov &c   }
    vs } fifa   vs } fifa
James Frierson & }   Joel Rushin   }
Harrison Smith }   George A. Rodgers & }
                              Stephen M. Ingersol }

The State on the Motion of }
Solicitor General Harris }
      vs }
Edmund C. Beard }

          Rule to pay over Money

On Motion, ordered that the Clerk issue up to the Next Superior Court the proceedings In Said rule and that the Sheriff, in the Mean time, hold Said Moneys Subject to the Order of the Superior Court.

William Moore }
    vs   } Case
James Thompson }

          Jury N° 1

We, the Jury, find for The plaintiff Nineteen Dollars and Sixty five cents, with interest & Cost.

                        Absolam Jordan, forman

John Murphey & }
Reuben Turner }
    vs   } Indebitatus Assumpsit
Benjamin Smith }

          Jury N° 1

We, the Jury, find for plaintiff The Sum of forty four Dollars and forty four Cents, With Cost of Suit.

                        Absolam Jordon, forman

The Court then adjourned untill Tomorrow Morning at 10 O'clock A. M.

                        Timothy Mathews, J. I. C.
                        David Ralston, J. I. C.
                        T. Holt, J. I. C.

The honorable the Inferior Court in and And for Bibb County Meet agreeable to adjournment November 28th 1827.

Present, their honors   Timothy Mathews }
                            Robert Birdsong } Justices
                            David Ralston   }

The State   }
    vs   } habes Corpus to Edmund C. Beard, Sheriff
Benjamin E. Garry   }

I have the body of Benjamin E. Garry, With the Warrant Mittiamus & Bond upon which the Said Garry detained.

Edmund C. Beard, Sheriff

Whereupon, it is ordered and adjudged That the Said Benjamin E. Garry be liberated And discharged from further detention on the Warrant & Mittimus for the offence of assault and Battery on the body of Robert Minzins this 28th November 1827 on payment of Cost.

John Scully   }
    vs   } Case
Lemuel Merrell   }

Jury N° 1

We, the Jury, find for the Defendant, With Cost. November 28th 1827

Absolam Jordon, forman

William Mackie   }
    vs   } Assumpsit
John G. Polhill }

I Confess Judgment to the Plaintiff for the Sum of Sixty Six Dollars Ninety three and a half Cents, with interest & cost.

John G. Polhill, deft

Charles W. Rockwell &c }
     vs   } Debt
John W. Roberts   }
David S. Booth &   }
John Philpot   }

We, the Jury, find For the defendant.

                              Absolam Jordon, forman

J. D. Weathers, Indorsee }
     vs   } Case
Henry Mims   }

We Confess Judgment for the plaintiff fifty five Dollars, with interest & cost.

                              Mandell & Campbell, Defd^{ts} At^y

The Court then adjourned untill Tomorrow Morning at ten o'clock A. M.

                              David Ralston, J. I. C.
                              R. Birdsong, J. I. C.
                              Timothy Mathews, J. I. C.

                     November Term 1827

Georgia   } November 29th 1827. The honorable The Inferior Court
Bibb County } in & for Said County Meet agreeable to adjournment

Present, their honors   Timothy Mathews }
                                    David Ralston   } Justices
                                    Robert Birdsong }

John T. Rowland }
     vs   } Garnishment
John Bruce   }

It appearing to the Court from the Answer of the Garnishee, Ralph King, that he is indebted in the Sum of Nine Dollars, it is therefore ordered that Judgment pass for the Same.

James Venters }
    vs } Assumpsit
Rufus K. Evans }

Jury N° 1

Ramsone B. Campbell was Substituted on the Jury in the place of Henry B. Hill in the above Cas.

We, the Jury, find for the Plaintiff in the Sum of Eight Dollars and Thirty five cents, with interest and Cost of Suit.

Absolam Jordon, forman

Nathaniel Barker }
    vs } assum
John Scully }

We, the Jury, find for The plaintiff fifty three Dollars & Sixty Eight Cents, with Cost of Suit.

Absolam Jordon, forman

Peter P. Rockwell}
    vs } Garnishment
Charles Cotton & }
John Harrison }

Whereupon, it is ordered By the Court that the plaintiff Enter up Judgment against Said Cotton And Harrison, garnishees, forty Sixty Eight Dollars And thirty one Cents principal, with interest & Cost.

John Nesbit }
    vs } Assumpsit for Rent
Rachael R. Sweet }

Jury N° 1

We, the Jury, find for the Plaintiff the Sum of four hundred and thirty Seven dollars and fifty Cents for his principal debt, besides interest & Cost.

A. Jordan, forman

John Scully }
    vs   } Assumpsit
Charles Bullock}

                Jury Nº 1

We, the Jury, find for the Plaintiff thirty five Dollars, With Cost of Suit.

                                A. Jordan, forman

John Scully }
    vs   } Assumpsit & Bail
Alvanus W. Harris }

Exception to Bail Having been taken for Cause that a Copy of the original affidavit has Not been Filed in the Clerk's office & has Not been Indorsed upon the original declaration and Allowed, it is ordered that the bail bond Be Cancelled & John W. Jones be Discharged from the obligation.

John M. Fuller }
    vs   } Debt & Rent
John Ellis and }
William F. Brown }

                Jury Nº 1

We, the Jury, find for the Plaintiff the Sum of fifty dollars for his principal debt, besides interest & Cost.

                                A. Jordon, forman

David F. Wilson }
    vs   } Debt
Benjamin E. Garry }

We Confess Judgment for Sixty dollars principal, With interest & Cost.

                          Polhill & Cole, Att[ys] for Defd[t]

Peter P. Rockwell }
    vs   } Debt
Samuel A. Plummer }

I Confess Judgment for Sixty Eight Dollars $^{31}/_{100}$ Principal, with interest & Cost.

Prince & Poe, def^{ts} att^{ys}

Rushin & Rodgers }
    vs   } Debt
David F. Wilson }

Jury N° 1

We, the Jury, find for the plaintiff four hundred and twenty Three dollars Eighty Seven & a half Cents principal, With interest & cost.

A. Jordan, forman

Findley Holmes }
    vs   } Debt
John M. Shelman }

Judgment Confessed for Plaintiff fifty dollars, With interest & Cost.

Polhill & Cole, Att^{ys} for def^t

———

John Brownell }
for the use of }
Beverly Rew }
    vs   } Assumpsit
Samuel A. Plummer }

I Confess Judgment To the plaintiff for the Sum of thirty three dollars & fifty Cents, With With interest & Cost.

Prince & Poe, def^{ts} att^{ys}

Ordered, that the Clerk of this Court Pay to Henry Smith four Dollars for four Days attendance as Bailiff at this term.

William Moore }
    vs   } Case
John J. Kaigler & }
David F. Wilson }

Jury Nº 2

We, the Jury, find for plaintiff Eighty five Dollars principal, with interest & Cost.

Benjamin Allen, forman

Thomas Kenon }
    vs } Case
William B. Akridge }
& William B. Akridge }

Jury Nº 2

We, the Jury, find for Plaintiff Sixty Dollars, With interest & Cost.

Benjamin Allen, forman

Robert Burton }
    vs } Debt
Nathaniel Raines }

Jury Nº 2

We, the Jury, find for Plaintiff two hundred and Thirty five Dollars, With interest & Cost.

Benjamin Allen, forman

Jeremiah Smith }
    vs } Case
Robert B. Shelman }

Judgment Confessed for Plaintiff Sixty Dollars, With interest & Cost.

Polhill & Cole, pro Defendants

Berry Rodgers }
    vs } Case & Bail
Alexander Richards }

Judgment Confessed for plaintiff Ninety one Dollars and fifty Six Cents princ.[l], With interest & Cost.

Alexander Richards

Josiah Freeman & C° }
    vs   } Debt
James T. Wafford   }

Jury N° 2

We, the Jury, find for The plaintiff forty Dollars Sixty two and a half Cents principal, With interest & Cost.

Benjamin Allen, forman

Starr & Cleland   }
    vs   } Case
Eleanor Davis   }

Jury N° 2

We, the Jury, find for the Plaintiff Sixty Six dollars & Seventy five Cents Principal, with interest & Cost.

Benjamin Allen, forman

Rushin & Rodgers }
    vs   } Case
David S. Booth   }

Jury N° 2

We, the Jury, find for Plaintiff thirty four dollars, With interest and Cost.

Benjamin Allen, forman

Starr & Cleland   }
    vs   } Case
Swearingin & Hammond }

I hereby Confess Judgment for plaintiff Seventy three Dollars principal, With interest & Cost.

        Abner Hammond
        for Self &
        E. Swearingin

Starr & Cleland }
  vs   } Case
John M. Shelman }

      Jury N° 1

We, the Jury, find for Plaintiff the Sum of fifty Dollars principal, With interest & Cost.

        Absolam Jordan, forman

Starr & Cleland }
  vs } Case
Nathan Carter }

      Jury N° 1

We, the Jury, find for plaintiff one hundred and thirteen Dollars & Seventy two Cents principal, With interest & Cost.

        Absolam Jordan, forman

Starr & Cleland }
  vs   } Case
Benjamin Allen }

I hereby Acknowledge Judgment for plaintiff Thirty two Dollars And Seventy five Cents principal, With interest & Cost.

        Benjamin Allen

Andrew Low }
Robert Isaacs }
Surviving Copartners }
of Andrew Low & C° }
    vs } Debt
Ingersol & Coolidge }

                   Jury N° 1

We, the Jury, find for plaintiff two hundred & Eighty four Dollars & Seventy three Cents, With interest & Cost.

                            Absolam Jordan, forman

John R. Wooten }
    vs } Debt
James Butler }

                   Jury N° 1

We, the Jury, find for the Plaintiff Eight hundred & Thirty three Dollars & Eighty Six Cents principal debt, With interest & Cost.

                            Absolam Jordan, forman

———

Beverly Rew }
    vs } Assumpsit
Samuel A. Plummer }

Judgment Confessed for Plaintiff for one hundred And Seventy two Dollars $^{78}/_{100}$ principal, with Cost of Suit.

                            Prince & Poe, def[ts] att[ys]

William C. Daughtry }
    vs } Assumpsit
Samuel A. Plummer }

                   Jury N° 1

We, the Jury, find for Plaintiff fifty Seven Dollars, With Cost.

                            Absolam Jordan, forman

Archibald Colquhaun }
      vs   } Assumpsit
Samuel A. Plummer }

Jury N° 1

We, the Jury, find for The plaintiff the Sum of Forty Seven Dollars & thirty Cents, With Cost.

A. Jordan, forman

Howell Wooten   }
      vs   } Assumpsit
Samuel A. Plummer }

Judgment Confessed for Sixty Dollars & twenty Cents, With Cost of Suit.

Prince & Poe, def[ts] att[ys]

J. D. & A. Chapman   }
      vs   } Debt
Swearingin & Hammond }

I hereby Confess Judgment for plaintiff forty Eight Dollars and forty Eight Cents principal, With interest & Cost.

Abner Hammond, for Self
and E. Swearingin

Rushin & Rodgers }
      vs   } Debt
John Philpot   }

Jury N° 1

We, the Jury, find for Plaintiff the Sum of two Thousand and forty Six Dollars principal, with interest & Cost.

Absolam Jordan, forman

Smith & Dean }
    vs   } Assumpsit
John C. Rodgers }

I hereby Confess Judgment for Sixty Dollars and ten Cents principal, With interest & Cost.

                                    John C. Rodgers

The Court then adjourned untill Tuesday the 4th December.

                                    Timothy Mathews, J. I. C.
                                    Robt Birdsong, J. I. C.
                                    D. Ralston, J. I. C.

Georgia   } November Term 1827. December 4th 1827. The Bibb County } honorable the Inferior Court In And for Said County Meet agreeable to adjournment.

Present, their Honors   Timothy Mathews }
                                    Tarpley Holt   } Justices
                                    Robert Birdsong }

Ordered that Martin Simmons, Clk of this Court, Be paid out of the County funds Nine Dollars & Six Cents for his Cost in the Case.

The State   }
    vs   } Burglary
Negro Man Tom }

Ordered that Joseph Washburne be appointed Notory Public for the County of Bibb by his Taking the usual oath.

Ordered that Thomas Campbell be appointed Notory Public for the County of Bibb by his Taking the usual oath.

                            November Term 1827

Thomas Thweatt, bearer }
        vs   } Case & Judgment
John M. Shelman   }

Came into office John M. Shelman, The defendant in the above Case, Who being dissatisfied with the Verdict of the Jury, Paid the Cost and Entered an appeal. Also, at the Same time, Came Robert B. Shelman, his Security on the appeal, Whom each of them Acknowledge them Selves jointly & Severally bound for the true payment of the Eventual Condemnation Money according to the Statutes in Such Cases Made and provided. Given under our hands & Seals this 4th day of December 1827

           John M. Shelman
           R. B. Shelman

Findley Holmes }
  vs   } Debt & Judgement
John M. Shelman }

Came into office John M. Shelman, The Defendant in the Above Case, Who being disatisfied with the Verdict of the Jury, paid the Cost and Entered a Stay of Execution. Also, at the Same time, Came Robert B. Shelman, his Security on the Stay, Whom each of them acknowledge themselves jointly and Severally Bound for the true payment of the Eventual Condemnation Money According to the Statutes in Such Cases Made and provided. Given under our hands & Seals this 4th day of December 1827

           John M. Shelman
           R. B. Shelman

       November Term 1827

Starr & Cleland }
  vs   } Case & Judgment
John M. Shelman }

Came into office John M. Shelman, the [blot] Defendant in the Above Case, Who being disatisfied with the Verdict of the Jury, paid the Cost And entered a Stay of Execution. Also, at the Same time, Came Robert B. Shelman, the Security on the Stay, Whom boath acknowledge Themselves jointly and Severally bound for the True payment of the Eventual Condemnation Money According to the Statute in Such Cases

Made and provided. Given under our hands & Seals this 4th day of December 1827

         John M. Shelman
         R. B. Shelman

Charles W. Rockwell }
George Relph and }
Charles McIntyre }
  vs   } Debt & Judgment
John W. Roberts }
David S. Booth }
and John Philpot }

Came into office Prince & Tracy ~~and Butler~~, the The attorneys for the Plaintiffs in the above Case, who being disatisfied With the Verdict of the Jury, paid the Cost And Entered an Appeal. Also, at the Same time, Came Murdock Chisholm, their Security on the appeal, Whom Each of them Acknowledge themselves Jointly & Severally Bound for the true Eventual Condemnation Money according to the Statutes Made & provided in Such Cases. Given under our hands & Seal this 4th day of December 1827.

         Edward D. Tracy
         M. Chisholm

On or before the twenty fifth day of December Next, I promise to pay John S. Wallace, or bearer, one hundred Dollars for Value Re^d, to bear interest from the date. Witness My hand & Seal.

February 4th 1827   Washington Ledbetter

The above Copy of a Note being Lost & a rule taken last Court to Establish the Same by advertising the Same according to Law. It having been advertised according to Law, it is ordered that the above Copy be established in Lieu of the Lost orriginal.

Bibb Inferior Court May Term 1827

Ives & White }
    vs }
Reuben Barrough }

It appearing to the Court from the Records thereof that a Verdict Was rendered by the Jury at the last term of this Court & the Attorneys having Ommitted to Sign up Judgment. On Motion, it is ordered That Judgment be Signed Nunc pro tunc for the Amount found by the Jury.

To the Honorable Inferior Court of Bibb County.

The Petition of Solomon Humphries respectfully Sheweth that he is a free person of Colour residing in Said County & Your petitioner prays that Charles J. McDonald of Said County May be Appointed his Guardian according to Law.

4th December 1827   Solomon Humphries

I, Charles J. McDonald, do hereby Signify to the Honorable the Inferior Court of Bibb County My Willingness to accept the appointment of Guardian of Solomon, a person of Colour Resident in Said County.

4th December 1827   Charles J. McDonald

It is ordered that Charles J. McDonald be & he is hereby appointed Guardian of Solomon Humphries, a free person of Colour, & that he give Bond & Security in the Sum of Six Thousand Dollars. Security Accepted. Harrison Smith

Burrell Rabon }
    vs   } Casa from Justice Court
Charles Ingram, Jun }

The defendant and his Security, Zackariah Jordon, having been Called & Not Appearing, it is Ordered That the plaintiff in Said Casa enter up Judgment Against Said Security Upon his bond agreeable to Said Bond & the Statute in Such Case Made And provided.

The following Jury Were Drawn to Serve at May Term 1828.

1. Samuel Auston	19. Johnson Hammock
2. John Perkins	20. Kinchen C. Dudly
3. John Jones	21. James Douglass
4. William B. Cone	22. James Tobin
5. Nathan Jones	23. James Thompson, Senr
6. William L. McCree	24. Lewis Foy
7. Thomas Grimes	25. Thomas Watson
8. Stephen Williams	26. Jesse Palmer
9. Charles S. Lewis	27. Jonathan Jones
10. Hugh Morrison	28. James Williams
11. Samuel Wade	29. Lewis Collins
12. Iseral Keith	30. Thompson Field
13. Elijah B. Etherage	31. James Summerlin
14. Rufus K. Evans	32. John Evans
15. Angus McCallum	33. Zackariah Williamson, Jun
16. Micheal Mixson	34. Robert C. Hunt
17. John J. Kaigler	35. Littleton Williamson
18. Charles Biddle	36. John Gadist

The Court then adjourned untill Court in Course.

Robt Birdsong, J. I. C.
Timothy Mathews, J. I. C.
Tarpley Holt, J. I. C.

Henry Cosnard }
    vs   } Assumpsit & Judgment
Evans & Moore }

Came into office Rufus K. Evans, one of the defendants in the Above Case, Who being disatisfied with the Verdict of the Jury, paid the Cost & Entered a Stay of Execution. Also, at the Same time, Came Benjamin Russell, the Security on the Stay, Whom both of Them acknowledge themselves Jointly & Severally bound for the true payment of the Eventual Condemnation Money according to the Statute in Such Cases

Made and provided. Given under our hands & Seal this 8th day of December 1827.

> R. K. Evans
> Benjamin Russell
> By R. K. Evans

John Scully }
    vs   } Assumpsit & Judgment
Charles Bullock }

Came into office Charles Bullock, The defendant in the above Case, Who being disatisfied with the Verdict of the Jury, paid The Cost & Entered an appeal. Also, at the Same time, Came John S. Childers, his Security on the appeal, Whom both of them acknowledge themselves jointly and Severally bound for the true payment of the Eventual Condemnation Money according to the Statute in Such Cases made and provided. Given under our hands & Seal this 8th day of December 1827.

> Chas Bullock
> J. S. Childers

November Term 1827

Samuel Cook }
    vs   } Assumpsit & Judgment
John D. Chapman }
Abner Chapman & }
Ambrose Chapman }

Came into office John D. Chapman, one of the defendants & Atty in fact in the above Case, Who being disatisfied With the Verdict of the Jury, paid the Cost and Entered a Stay of Execution. Also, at the Same time, Came Solomon D. Chapman, their Security in the Stay, Who Acknowledge themselves jointly & Severally bound for The true payment of the eventual Condemnation Money According to the Statute in Such Cases Made and Provided. Given under our hands and Seals this 8th Day of December 1827.

            J. D. Chapman
            For Self &
            Abner Chapman
            Ambrose Chapman
            S. D. Chapman

Peter Clower   }
  vs   } Assumpsit & Judgment
John D. Chapman }
Abner Chapman }
John S. Childers & }
Samuel Tompkins }

Came in to office John D. Chapman, one of the defendants in the above Case & Attorney in fact, Who being disatisfied With the Verdict of the Jury, paid the Cost and Entered a Stay of Execution. Also, at the Same time, Came Solomon D. Chapman, their Security on the Stay, Who Acknowledge Themselves jointly & Severally bound for The true payment of the eventual Condemnation Money According to the Statutes in Such Cases Made & provided. Given under our hands and Seals this 8th Day of December 1827.

            J. D. Chapman
            For Self
            Abner Chapman
            John S. Childers
            Samuel Tompkins
            S. D. Chapman

Anson Kimberly }
  vs   } Assumpsit & Judgment
Elijah Cotton   }

Came into office Elijah Cotton, The defendant in the Above Case, Who being disatisfied With the Verdict of the Jury, Paid the Cost and entered a Stay of Execution. Also, at the Same time, Came Samuel Gillespie, his Security on the Stay, Who both of them acknowledge themselves

Jointly & Severally bound for the true payment of the Eventual Condemnation Money According to the Statute In Such Cases Made and Provided. Given under our Hands and Seals this 8th Day of December 1827.

                                               E. Cotton
                                               S. Gillespie

John Scully   }
      vs   } Judgment
Lemuel Merrell }

Came into office John Scully, The Plaintiff in the Above Case, Who being disatisfied with the Verdict of the Jury, Paid the Cost and entered an appeal. Also, at ~~That~~ the Same time, Came John Philpot & Thomas Moore, his Securitys on the appeal, Who acknowledge themselves Jointly & Severally bound for the true payment of the Eventual Condemnation Money according to the Statutes in Such Cases made and provided. Given under our hands and Seal this 8th Day of December 1827.

Test. Martin Simmons, Clk   John + Scully
                                           John Philpot
                                           Thomas Moore

                        November Term 1827

William Moore }
      vs   } Case & Judgment
James Thompson }

Came into office William Moore, The plaintiff in the Above Case, By his attorney Thomas Campbell, Who being disatisfied With the Verdict of the Jury, paid the Cost And Entered an appeal. Also, at the Same time, Came Solomon D. Chapman, his Security on the appeal, Who Acknowledge themselves jointly and Severally bound for the true payment of the Eventual Condemnation Money According to the

Statutes in Such Case Made and provided. Given Under our hands & Seal this 8th Day of December 1827.

        William Moore, By his
        attorney Thos Campbell
        S. D. Chapman

May Term 1828

Georgia   } The Honorable the Inferior Court in & for Said County
Bibb County } Meet this day May 26th agreeable to adjournment

Present, their honors   Timothy Mathews }
            Mathew Robertson}
            Tarpley Holt } J. I. C.
            Robert Birdsong }
            David Ralston }

The following Jury was Impanield to Serve at this Term.

Jury No 1

1. Samuel Austin	7. Stephen Williams
2. John Perkins	8. Hugh Morrison
3. John James	9. Rufus K. Evans
4. William B. Cone	10. Johnson Hammock
5. William L. McRee	11. Kinchen C. Dudly
6. Thomas Grimes	12. Charles S. Lewis

John Hardin, Guardian &c }
for the use of Thos Napier }
    vs   } Assumpsit
Ambrose Baber &   }
Albert G. Clopton, admrs }
of Joseph Morgan   }

Judgment Confessed to the Plaintiff for the Sum of one Hundred & forty Dollars and Twenty four Cents principal & Sixty two dollars & Sixty One Cents interest & Cost.

            Albert G. Clopton, Deft Aty

Francis Bacon }
    vs   } Assumpsit
Ehud Harris }

Judgment Confessed to the plaintiff for fifty Dollars, With interest & Cost, reserving the right of Appeal.

                        Strong & Lamar, Def[ts] Att[y]

John F. Thompson having been recommended by the Justices of the peace for the 483 or Cap[t] Brown's Dist, it is Ordered that he be appointed Constable for that District, on his Giving bond to the Justices of The peace payable to the Governor in terms of the Law With good Security.

William Cumming and Martin Riley having been Recommended by the Justices of the peace for the 564 Dist for the Appointment of Constables and they having Each Tendered bonds With good Security, it is ordered that They are hereby appointed Constables for Said District.

L. Q. C. Lamar }
    vs   } assumpsit
Samuel Gillespie }

I Confess Judgment to the plaintiff for four hundred & fifty Dollars, With interest & Cost.

                        Samuel Gillespie

Ordered that George W. Jackson be appointed Constable for the 481 Dist.

L. Q. C. Lamar }
    vs   } Assumpsit & Judgment
Samuel Gillespie }

On Motion, ordered that the Plaintiff in the above Case have leave to take from the office of the Clerk the Note on Which Said Action is founded in order to pursue other Parties thereto if it Should be Necessary, the Clerk retaining in Office a Copy thereof.

James Herring }
    vs   } Assumpsit
Isaac M. Tate }

We, the Jury, find for the plaintiff The Sum of four hundred and Twelve Dollars, With interest & Cost.

                        Charles S. Lewis, forman

The following Jury Were empanield to Serve at this Term.

1. James Thompson   7. Thompson Fields
2. James Douglass   8. Daniel Smith
3. James Tobin   9. Clement Clemmons
4. Lewis Foy   10. Aaron Robertson
5. James Williams   11. Alvanus W. Harris
6. Lewis Collins   12. Joseph Wainwright

George Relph & }
John H. Reid }
Surviving assignees }
of William Turner }
    vs   } Case
Absolom Jordon }

We, the Jury, find for the Plaintiff Sixty Nine Dollars Eighty Seven and a half Cents, With interest from the 3rd April 1827, With Cost of Suit.

                        Charles S. Lewis, forman

George Relph and }
John H. Reid }
Surviving assignees }
of William Turner }
    vs   } Case & Judgment
Absolam Jordon }

Came into office Absolom Jordon, the plaintiff in the above Case, Who being disatisfied with the Verdict of the Jury, paid the Cost and Entered An appeal. Also, at the Same time, Came James Thompson, his Security on the Appeal, Who Acknowledge Themselves both jointly and

Severally bonded for the true payment of the true Eventual Condemnation Money According to the Statutes in Such Case Made and provided. Given under our hands & Seals this 26th Day of May 1828.

Absalom Jordon
James Thompson

N. B. & H. Weed }
     vs   } Debt
Nathaniel Barker }

Judgment Confessed to the plaintiff for the Sum of one hundred and Sixteen Dollars & thirty one Cents, With interest & cost.

Albert G. Clopton, Def^{ts} Att^y

John B. Gaudry }
     vs   } Assumpsit
Zachariah Jordon }

Judgment Confessed to the Plaintiff for Eighty Eight Dollars and Eighty three Cents, With Cost.

E. D. Tracy, Att^y for Def^t

Alexander Y. Robertson }
     vs   } assumpsit for Rent
John Perry   }

We, the Jury, find for the Plaintiff the Sum of Thirty Seven Dollars Nine and a half Cents, With Cost of Suit.

James Thompson, forman

John Robertson }
     vs   } Assumpsit
John Crain   }

Judgment Confessed to the Plaintiff for the Sum of two Hundred Dollars, With interest & Cost.

Albert G. Clopton, Def^{ts} Att^y

John Scully }
    vs } Assumpsit
Alvanus W. Harris }

We find for the plaintiff One hundred & twenty Dollars, With interest & Cost of Suit.

                              James Thompson, forman

Leonard Bowman }
    vs } assumpsit
Ambrose Baber and }
Albert G. Clopton, adm^{rs} }
of Joseph Morgan }

We, the Jury, find for the Plaintiff forty Nine Dollars and Seventy five Cents, With Cost of Suit.

                              James Thompson, forman

The Court adjourned untill the Morning at half past 8 O'clock.

                              M. Robertson, J. I. C.
                              R. Birdsong, J. I. C.
                              Timothy Mathews, J. I. C.
                              Tarpley Holt, J. I. C.

Georgia } May 27th 1828. The honorable the Inferior Court of
Bibb County } Said County Meet agreeable to adjournment

Present   Timothy Mathews }
                                  Tarpley Holt   } J. I. C.
                                  Mathew Robertson}
                                  Robert Birdsong }

Leonard Bowman }
    vs } Assumpsit & Judgment
Ambrose Baber and }
Albert G. Clopton, adm^{rs} }
of Joseph Morgan }

75

Came into office Albert G. Clopton, the Attorney in the Case, Who being Disatisfied With the Verdict of the Jury, paid the Cost and Entered an Appeal, ~~also, at the Same time~~, Came Acknowledge them Selves both jointly Bond as administrators for the true Eventual Condemnation Money according to the Statute in Such Case Made and provided. Given under My hand & Seal this 2tth Day of May 1828.

Albert G. Clopton, Attorney
At Law for the administrators
of Joseph Morgan, Deaced
~~Tarpley Holt~~, J. I. C.
~~Timothy Mathews~~

John Scully }
    vs   } assumpsit
James Tobin }

We, the Jury, find for the plaintiff Seventy Dollars & Cost.

Charles S. Lewis, forman

John Scully }
Survivor &c }
    vs   } assumpsit
James Cowly }

We, the Jury, find for the plaintiff fifty Eight Dollars & Cost.

Charles S. Lewis, forman

Smith & Childers   }
    vs   } Debt for Rent
Moreland & Townsend }

We find for the plaintiffs two Hundred & fifty three Dollars & eighteen Cents, with Cost of Suit.

Charles S. Lewis, forman

———

John Scully } Case or assumpsit in Bibb
    vs   } Inferior Court Inferior Court
David Ralston }

on Motion, ordered that the Said Case be Withdrawn from This Court and refered to John Philpot, Thomas G. Bates for their arbitrament and award and Their award, When Made, be Sent up to this Court and remain the Judgment of this Court.

John B. Gaudry }
    vs   } Assumpsit
Bertrand Tessrau }
& Andrew Bie   }

We, the Jury, find for The plaintiff two hundred and fifteen Dollars & Sixty Eight Cents, with Cost of Suit.

                                Charles S. Lewis, forman

Bibb Inferior Court May Term 1828

Georgia   }
Bibb County } Rule Nisi

It appearing to the Court That Henry S. Cutler has Made oath of the Loss of an acceptance by J. & A. Bennett of his Draft for two hundred and Ninety three Dollars Dollars and fifty one Cents in favour of Charles Roe Payable Ninety days after date, Which Said affidavit Is Now on file in the Inferior Court of Said County, Describing Said Acceptance. It is therefore ordered That Said J. & A. Bennett Shew Cause by the Next Sitting of this Court Why a Copy of Said Acceptance Draft Should Not be established in lieu of the original and that Said Cutler publish this Rule in Some Public Gazett for three Months before the Next Sitting of this Court.

John Murphey   }
& Reuben Turner }
    vs   } assumpsit
Britain Braswell }

We, the Jury, find for the plaintiff forty Six Dollars & twenty five Cents principal, with Interest & Cost.

                                Charles S. Lewis, forman

George Rodgers }
Survivor &c }
for the use &c }
    vs } Debt
A. D. Brown }

I Confess Judgment to the plaintiff for Sixty four Dollars & Sixty Eight Cents, With interest & Cost.

                                Alexander D. Brown
                                By Polhill & Cole, his att^{ys}

Mortimer R. Wallis }
    vs } assumpsit for Rent
John B. Cumming }

We, the Jury, find for the Plaintiff the Sum of thirty four Dollars & thirty Eight Cents, with Interest & cost.

                                Charles S. Lewis, forman

Cadwell W. Raines }
    vs } Case &c
Clemant Clements }

We, the Jury, find for the Plaintiff thirty nine Dollars And Sixty Cents principal, with interest & cost.

                                Charles S. Lewis, forman

Henry G. Orick }
administrator of }
James Green }
    vs } Debt
Robert Roffe & }
Robert Burton }

We, the Jury, find for plaintiff forty Seven Dollars Six Cents Principal, With interest & cost.

                                Charles S. Lewis, forman

Samuel B. Skaggs }
    vs   } Debt
Daniel Wordsworth }

We, the Jury, find for plaintiff Eighty Dollars, With interest and Cost.

                        Charles S. Lewis, forman

Philip Powledge }
    vs   } Debt
Davis B. Braswell }

Judgment Confessed for plaintiff forty Seven Dollars twenty two & a half cents, With interest & Cost.

                        Edward D. Tracy, Def^{ts} att^y

Shadrick R. Felton }
    vs   } Case
Young Johnston }

I Confess Judgment for plaintiff for one hundred and twenty five Dollars, with interest & Cost.

                        Young Johnston

Theodore Nims }
    vs   }
Edward Varner & }
Henry W. Tripp }

It appearing to the Court That Servis in Said Case Has Not been perfected against Henry W. Tripp of Monroe County. On Motion, ordered that Said plaintiff have untill Next Sitting of this Court to perfect Said Servis.

Peter P. Rockwell } Case & bond given to take
    vs   } Benefit of the Insolvent Act
Robert S. Patton }

Robert S. Patton, the defendant, Having been arrested under Said Casa and having given bond & Security to Appear at the present Sitting of this Court to take the Benefit of the Insolvent Act and Said Patton having

Been Called & Not answering & Not having filed his Schedule or Cited his Creditors, it is therefore ordered That Said plaintiff enter up Judgment for the amount of Said Casa, interest, & Cost against the Said Robert S. Patton and Robert Collins, Security on Said bond, instanter Conformity with the Law in Such Case Made and Provided.

Reuben Turner } Casa from the Justices Court
     vs } And Bond given to take the
Lewis Collins and } Benefit of the Act for the
Martin H. Brown } Relief of Honest Debtors

Harmon H. Howard, Security on the bond, Lewis Collins, the defendant, having Been arrested under Said Casa And having given Bond & Security to appear & Comply With the requisition

---

of the Act by Virtue of which Said bond was received. And Said Collins having been Called & failing to Appear or to file his Schedule or to Cite his Creditors. It is therefore ordered that Judgment be entered Instanter against the Said Lewis Collins & also against The Said Harmon H. Howard in Conformity with The Statute in Such Case Made & provided.

David Ralston }
     vs } Casa & application for benefit
David F. Wilson } of Honest Debtors act

It appearing to the Court that David F. Wilson has filed his Bond for his appearance at this Term of the Inferior Court of Bibb County & has failed to appear & render in a Schedule & Notify his Creditors in terms of the Law, on Motion it is ordered that judgment be Entered up against the Said Wilson & Alexander McGregor, his Security on their Bond, for the Principal money, interest, & Cost.

Ordered, that the Clerk of this Court pay William F. Brown the Sum of Twenty Seven Dollars, it being The Amount of his account for Making Six Coffins for poor persons Whose estate are unable To pay therefor.

Ordered that Alexander McGregor be Released as Security on the bond With David F. Wilson To take the Benefit of the insolvent act.

Ordered that the Clerk of this Court pay Samuel Slate one Dollar and twenty five Cents for Guarding Prisoners one day & part of Knight at the Superior Court February Term 1828.

Wallis & Bond }
     vs   } fifa Bibb Inferior Court
William Moore } May Term 1828
Young Johnston }
& Wm Cumming }

The Cause of illegality in the above Case Having been heard and the Grounds being overuled by the Court. It is ordered that the illegality be Discharged And the Execution ordered to proceed.

The Court then adjourned untill Morning at ½ past 8 o'clock.

                                Robt Birdsong, J. I. C.
                                Timothy Mathews, J. I. C.
                                M. Robertson, J. I. C.

Georgia   } May 28th 1828. The Honorable the Inferior in and for
Bibb County } Said County Meet agreeable to adjournment

Present   Timothy Mathews }
                                 Mathew Robertson } J. I. C.
                                 Robert Birdsong   }

Ordered that the Clk of this Court pay Benjamin Russell the Sum of two hundred & Ninety Dollars & fifty Cents, it being one half the amount for Which Said Benjamin Russell undertook to build a Bridge across Walnut Creek on the Milledgeville Road.

John Scully   }
     vs   } Assumpsit & Judgment
Alvanus W. Harris }

Came into open Court Alvanus W. Harris, the Defendant in the above Case, Who being disatisfied with the Verdict, Paid the Cost and Entered an appeal. Also, at The Same time, Came William Sanders & David G. Worsham, his Securitys on the appeal, Who Each acknowledge themselves jointly & Severally bound for the true Eventual

Condemnation Money according to the Statute In Such Case made & provided. Given under our hands & Seals this 28th day of May 1828.

          A. W. Harris

          W[m] Sanders
          D. G. Worsham

Thomas A. Ranalds }
  vs   } Case & Bail
Clark & Coffin }

The Court having heard the Exceptions to the bail affidavit, Ordered that the Exceptions be Sustained and that the Bail in Said Case be & is hereby discharged.

William J. Danelly & C° }
  vs   } Assumpsit & Bail
Addison Mandell   }

The plaintiff, by their attornies Prince & Poe, Came into Court Wednesday the third day of this the Appearance term of the Said Case and Except to the Suffering of the Bail taken by the Sheriff in the above Case and That the Sheriff Stand as Special bail. The bail Having testified to the Satisfaction of the Court, it is Ordered that the Motion against the Sheriff be Discharged.

Andrew Low & C° } Fifa Prin[l] 284.73
  vs   } Affidavit of Illegality upon an
Ingersol & Cooledge } Execution from this Court

The Motion Set forth in this Affidavit having been duly Weighed and Considered by the Court and they being deemed insufficient to Effect the Validity of Said Execution. It is therefore ordered that Said Affidavit of Illegality be dismissed and that Said Execution forth With proceed.

Commissioners of }
Town of Macon }
  vs   } Case for Rent
James Tobin & }
Young Johnston }

Judgment Confessed for Eighty three Dollars principal, with interest and Cost.

James Tobin
Young Johnston

Ordered that the Clerk of this Court pay James Hughs the Sum of Six Dollars for Making a Coffin for a pauper by the Name of Youngblood.

John Bozman }
     vs   } Judgment in the Inferior Court
Eleanor Davis & }
Marther Davis }

It appearing to the Court that Plaintiff's att^y in Signing Judgment made an Error in the Calculation of interest. ordered That he have leave to Correct Said error by Signing Judgment for the Correct amount, Calculating interest from the first January 1826 & that the Clerk issue Execution for Said Balance at Plff^s Cost.

Ellis, Shotwell & C° }
     vs   } Rule in Case of Garnishment
Thomas Campbell & }
George Walker }

The above Named Garnishees having failed to appear and answer at this term of our Court in Conformity With Said Summons of Garnishment. It is on Motion Ordered That Said Garnishees do appear at our Next Inferior Court & depose in Manner as required by Said Summons or Shew Cause Why an Attachment Should Not issue against them.

Charles S. Lewis & C° }
     vs   } Rule in Case of Garnishment
Archibald Woodson }
Thomas Campbell }
Isaac Seymour & }
William Ward }

The Above Named Garnishees Having failed to appear & Answer at this term of our Court in Conformity With Said Summons of Garnishment. It is on Motion ordered that Said Garnishees do appear at our Next

Inferior Court & Depose in Manner as Required by Said Summons or Shew Cause Why an attachment Should Not issue against them.

William Moore }
    vs } Fifa from Bibb Inferior Court
John J. Kaigler & } Returnable to May Term 1828
David F. Wilson }

It appearing to the Court from the Sheriff's Returns upon Said fifa that There is No property of the defendants in Bibb County from Which the Cost in Said Execution can be Satisfied. It is ordered that the Clerk, Sheriff, and Attorneys in Said fifa be permitted to Enter up Judgment Instanter against Said plaintiff for the Cost of Said fifa.

Henry B. Cone }
    vs } Fifa from Bibb Inferior Court
Henry G. Ross & } Returnable November Term 1827
George B. Wardlaw }

It appearing to the Court from the Sheriff Return upon Said fifa that There is no property of the defendants in Bibb County from Which the Cost in Said Execution Can be Satisfied. It is ordered that the Clerk, Sheriff, and Attorneys in Said fifa be permitted to Enter up Judgment instanter against Said plaintiff for the of Said fifa.

The Court then adjourned untill Court in Course.

Test. Martin Simmons, Clk   Timothy Mathews, J. I. C.
                                                    M. Robertson, J. I. C.
                                                    David Ralston, J. I. C.
                                                    Robt Birdsong, J. I. C.

May Term 1828

John Scully }
    vs } assumpsit & Judgment
James Tobin }

Come into office James Tobin, the Defendant in this Case, Who being Disatisfied With the Verdict of the Jury, paid The Cost and Entered an

Appeal. also, at the Same time, Came John M. Shelman, his Security on the appeal, Who Each acknowledge them Selves Jointly & Severally bound for the true payment of the Eventual Condemnation Money according to the Statute in Such Case Made & provided. Given under our Hands & seals this 31st day of May 1828.

Test. Martin Simmons, Clk   James Tobin
                                 Jn° M. Shelman

L. Q. C. Lamar   }
       vs   } assumpsit & Judgment
Samuel Gillespie }

Came into office Samuel Gillespie, the Defendant in The Above Case, Who being disatisfied With the Verdict, paid The Cost and Stayed the Execution. Also, at the Same time, Came Solomon Groce, his Security on the Stay of Execution, Who Each Acknowledge themselves jointly and Severally bound for the true payment of the Eventual Condemnation Money according to the Statute in Such Case Made and provided. Given under our hands & seals This 31st day of May 1828.

                                 Samuel Gillespie
                                 S. Groce

Georgia   }
Bibb County } In Chambers June 2nd 1828

Present, their honors   Timothy Mathews   }
                             Tarpley Holt   }
                             Mathew Robertson } J. I. C.
                             Robert Birdsong   }
                             David Ralston   }

The following Jury were Drawn to Serve at November Term 1828, viz.

    1. William Folds　　　　　19. Tyra Parriot
    2. William Hatcher 1　　　20. Whitmill Williams
    3. Benjamin McKiney　　　 22. Caleb Smith
    4. George A. Rodgers　　　23. Josiah Swearingin
    5. Elbert Crew 1　　　　　24. Lewis Hammock
    6. Council Briant gm　　　25. Whitmill Hardy

7. Addison Ellis 1 gm
8. Thoˢ Dickson 1
9. Joseph Wiggins inst [blot]
10. Elijah Mathews 1
11. John Chapman 1
12. Silas Carter
13. Reddin Rutland
14. William Ross
15. James Holensworth
16. Ephram Jones
17. John Johnston
18. Thoˢ Taylor

26. William P. Harris
27. Stephen Menard
28. Murdock Ray
29. William L. Edwards
30. John Bridges
31. Benjamin Lacy
32. Mathew Berry
33. Thoˢ Crawford
34. Nathaniel Enis
35. John Scully
36. Maston Whitehead
21. omitted James Jones

Test. Martin Simmons, Clk I. C.

November Term 1828

Georgia } The Honorable the Inferior Court in & for Said County
Bibb County } Meet November 24ᵗʰ 1828 Agreeable to adjournment

Present, their Honors

Timothy Mathews }
David Ralston }
Reubin Turner } J. I. C.
Luke Ross & }
Rene Fitzpatrick }

The following Jury Were Sworn to Serve at this Term, viz.

Jury Nº 1

1. George A. Rodgers
2. Lewis Hammock
3. Whitmill Hardy
4. Calub Smith
5. Nathaniel Enis
6. Mastern Whithead

7. Ephriam Jones
8. William Harris
9. Thomas Dixson
10. James Holeyworth
11. Benjamin McKiney
12. William Folds

Napier, Munroe &c }
    vs } Debt
Reddin Rutland }

I Confess Judgment in favour of the plaintiff for Three Hundred & fifty Seven dollars & fifty Cents, With interest & Cost.

        Reddin Rutland

Thomas Victery, adm[r] }
of Tho[s] A. Billups, dec[d] }
  vs   } Assumpsit
George A. Rodgers }

I hereby Confess Judgment To the plaintiff for the Sum of one hundred & Sixty five Dollars, With Interest & Cost, Saving the right of Appeal.

        George A. Rodgers

Anselm Bugg }
 vs   } Assumpsit
John D. Walker }

We, the jury, find for

The plaintiff the Sum of one Hundred and ten Dollars, With interest & Cost.

        George A. Rodgers, forman

James Herring }
 vs   } Assumpsit
Isaac M. Tate }

On Motion of Plff Counsel, it is ordered that they have Leave To take out of the office the Note on Which the Above Action is founded to persue his remedy Against the Executors of Zenire Tate, the Maker, on leaving in The office a Correct Copy of the Said Note.

Burton Hepburn }
 vs   } Debt
Addison Mandell }

I Confess judgment the plaintiff for the Sum of one hundred & Six dollars & Eighty Six Cents, With Cost of Suit.

        Campbell & Seymour, Def[ts] Att[ys]

Hollaway & Danforth }
     vs   } Assumpsit
J. D. & A. Chapman }

We, the jury, find for Plff the Sum of Two hundred and Sixty Eight Dollars & twelve Cents, With interest & Cost.

                              George A. Rodgers, forman

Masten Whitehead }
for the use of   }
John McAlister   }
     vs   } Assumpsit
Daniel Wardworth }
& John McMurrian }

We, the jury, find for Plff the Sum of Sixty Dollars, besides interest & Cost.

                              George A. Chapman, forman

Kimberly & Chisholm }
     vs   } Assumpsit
John Loving   }

We, the Jury, find for Plff the Sum of Sixty one Dollars, besides interest & Cost.

                              George A. Rodgers, forman

Kimberly & Chisholm }
     vs   } Assumpsit
Alexander McGregor }

We, the jury, find for Plaintiff the Sum of one hundred & Eleven dollars and fifty Six Cents, Besides interest & Cost.

                              George A. Rodgers, forman

Joseph Collins, bearer }
     vs   } Assumpsit
Daniel B. Worsham }

We, the Jury, find for the Plff the Sum of one hundred And Eighty Dollars, With interest & Cost.

George A. Rodgers, forman

Thomas Ellis, Indorsee }
      vs   } Assumpsit
Coffin & Clark   }

We Confess Judgment to the Plaintiff the Sum of two Hundred & Eighty three Dollars & Sixty two Cents, Besides interest & Cost.

Campbell & Seymour, Def^d Att^y

Robertson & Granberry }
for the use of   }
M. Lesuar   }
     vs   } Assumpsit
Philip Powledge   }

I hereby Confess Judgment to the Plff in the Sum of one hundred and Seventy five Dollars, besides interest & Cost.

P. Powledge

James Pearson & }
Samuel Stanford }
    vs   } Assumpsit
Reddin Rutland }

I Confess Judgment to the Plaintiff for the Sum of one hundred & Sixty three Dollars & thirteen Cents, With interest & Cost of Suit.

Reddin Rutland

James A. Everett }
    vs   } Assumpsit
Ambrose Baber }

We Confess Judgment to the Plff in the Sum of two Hundred dollars, besides interest & Cost.

Campbell & Seymour, Def^t Att^y

Anson Kimberly }
    vs   } Assumpsit
James W. Alston }

We, the Jury, find for Plff the Sum of one Hundred & thirty one dollars and Sixty five Cents, Besides interest & Cost.

                              George A. Rodgers, forman

Devenport Lawson }
    vs   } Assumpsit
John M. Shelman }

We, the jury, find for Plff the Sum of four Hundred & Thirty Dollars, besides interest & Cost.

                              George A. Rodgers, forman

Haines H. Magie }
    vs   } Assumpsit
George A. Smith }

We, the Jury, find for the Plff the Sum of Forty two Dollars and twelve & one half cents, besides interest & cost.

                              George A. Rodgers, forman

———

John Kirkpartrick }
    vs   } Assumpsit
John M. Shelman }

We, the Jury, find for The Plff the Sum of Fifty Eight Dollars, besides interest & Cost.

                              George A. Rodgers, forman

William G. Springer }
    vs   } Assumpsit
Solomon Groce   }

Judgment Confessed for the plaintiff for the Sum of Eighty Eight Dollars & fifty Cents, With interest & Cost.

Tracy & Butler, Att^{ys} for Def^d

Cornelius Watkins }
     vs   } Attachment
George Lacklain   }

We, the Jury, find for the Plff the Sum of Sixty Dollars, with Cost of Suit.

George A. Rodgers, forman

John Rushin   }
for the use of   }
Robert Collins   }
     vs   } Assumpsit
Williamson Smith }
James H. Rodgers }
& John C. Rodgers }

~~We hereby Acknowledge~~ We, the Jury, find for Plff the Sum of fifty Dollars, besides interest & Cost.

George A. Rodgers, forman

William J. Danelly & Co }
     vs   } Debt
Elijah Cotton   }

We, the Jury, find for The plaintiff the Sum of one Hundred & forty two Dollars and three Cents, With interest & Cost.

George A. Rodgers, forman

Thomas Napier   }
     vs   } Case
Edward W. Wright }
Jeremiah Smith & }
John S. Childers   }

We, the Jury, find for the Plff Six hundred & Sixty Six dollars & Sixty two Cents, With interest & Cost.

George A. Rodgers, forman

Thomas Napier }
    vs   } Case
Austin Janes }
Robert Collins }
John D. Chapman }
& Abner Chapman }

We find for the plaintiff one hundred & twenty five Dollars fifty Cents, With interest & Cost.

George A. Rodgers, forman

Thomas Napier }
    vs   } Case
Jeremiah Smith }
John S. Childers & }
Edward W. Wright }

We find for the plaintiff two hundred & twenty five Dollars & Ninety & one half Cents, With interest & Cost.

George A. Rodgers, forman

Thomas Napier }
    vs   } Case
Jeremiah Smith }
John S. Childers & }
Edward W. Wright }

Same }
  vs }
Same }

It Appearing to the Court That Daniel Pratt is an Indorser on the Note on Which the Above Suits Were Commenced. Ordered that Plff have leave to With Draw the Said Notes to Pursue his Remady vs Said Pratt, The Clk retaining a Copy of Each.

Goddard & Langdon }
    vs } Assumpsit
Addison Mandell }

I Confess to the plff the Sum of one hundred and Sixty Seven dollars and fifty Six Cents, Besides interest & Cost.

                          Campbell & Seymour, Def[t] Att[y]

Drury M. Leseur }
Guardian of Mary Nunn }
    vs } Assumpsit
Charles Bullock }

We, the jury, find for Plff the Sum of two Hundred and Ninety nine Dollars and forty Nine Cents, besides interest & Cost.

                          George A. Rodgers, forman

Roger Macarthy }
    vs } fifa
James Thompson }

On Motion of Counsel, it is Ordered that Spencer Riley, Sheriff, do return the above Statted fifa into Court, With his Actings and doings thereon, on to Morrow Morning at the opening of the Court, or So Soon thereafter as Consell Can be heard, & further Shew Cause Why he will Not pay over The Money to plff[s] attorney.

Jesse Bell }
    vs } Assumpsit
Cornelius Townsend }

We, the jury, find for the Plff the Sum of two hundred and thirty dollars & twelve Cents, besides interest & Cost.

                          George A. Rodgers, forman

Marine & fire }
insurance Bank }
    vs } Assumpsit
Alexander McGregor }

We, the Jury, find for Plff the Sum of five Hundred Dollars, besides interest & Cost of Suit.

        George A. Rodgers, forman

Napier, Munroe & C° }
   vs   } Case
Young Johnson & }
Mathew Robertson }

We, the Jury, find for the Plff Sixty one dollars & fifty Cents, with interest & Cost.

        George A. Rodgers, forman

Drury M. Leseur }
   vs   } Assumpsit
Mathew Robertson }

We, the jury, find for the Plff the Sum of one hundred and Seventy five dollars, besides interest & Cost.

        George A. Rodgers, forman

Thomas Battle }
  vs   } Assumpsit
Uriah Perkins }

We, the Jury, find for plff the Sum of Seventy Six dollars, Besides interest & Cost.

        George A. Rodgers, forman

Marine & Fire   }
Insurance Bank }
   vs   } Assumpsit
Smith & Childers }

We, the jury, find for plff The Sum of five hundred Dollars, besides interest & Cost.

        George A. Rodgers, forman

Jewett Abell }
   vs   } Assumpsit
Israel Keith }

We, the Jury, find for the Plff the Sum of Seven Hundred & Seventy Eight Dollars & Seventy three Cents, besides interest & Cost.

                                      George A. Rodgers, forman

John Rushin }
   vs   } Case
Rodger McCall }

We, the Jury, find for the Plaintiff one hundred & Sixteen Dollars & Eighty one Cents, With Cost of Suit.

                                      George A. Rodgers, forman

---

David Ralston }
   vs   } Casa from justice Bates' Court
David F. Wilson }

Same }
   vs   } Casa from justice Bates' Court
Same }

It appearing to the Court that David F. Wilson, defendant in the foregoing Cases, Was bound for his appearance at the Last term of this Court to take the benefit of the Honest Debtors Act, and that his Security, Alexander McGregor, at Said Term of This Court delivered the Said David F. Wilson into the Custody of Spencer Riley, Esqr, Sheriff of Bibb County, And that the Sheriff has Suffered the Said Wilson to go at Large. It is therefore Ordered that the Sheriff pay over the amount of Said Casa to the Plaintiff, or his Attorney, or Shew Cause at The opening of this Court to Morrow Morning Why he Should not be attached as for Contempt.

Pearson & Stanford }
   vs   }
Thomas Knight }

It appearing to the Court that the defendant, Thomas Knight, has been arrested at the instance of Pearson and Stanford and that he has Appeared & Complied With the requisits of the Honest Debtors act. It is therefore ordered That the Said Thomas Knight be admitted to all the Benefits of Said Act and that he be discharged from Custody.

The Court Adjourned untill Moring at 9 O'clock A. M.

          Timothy Mathews, J. I. C.
          Luke Ross, J. I. C.
          Reuben Turner, J. I. C.
          Rene Fitzpatrick, J. I. C.

November 25th 1828. The Honorable the Inferior Court in and for the County of Bibb Meet agreeable to adjournment.

Present, their Honors   Timothy Mathew }
            David Ralston } J. I. C.
            Rene Fitzpatrick }
            Reuben Turner }

John Rushin }
  vs   } Case
Roger McCall }

Came into office Roger McCall, the defendant in the above Case, Who being disatisfied With the Verdict of the Jury, paid the Cost and Entered an appeal. Also, at the Same time, Came Eleazer McCall, His Security in the Appeal, Who Each Acknowledge Themselves jointly and Severally bound for the true payment of the Eventual Condemnation Money According to the Statute in Such Case Made and Provided. Given under our hands & Seals the 25th Day of November 1828.

Test. Martin Simmons, Clk   Roger McCall
                Elezer McCall

William Mackey, Plaintiff }
& John G. Polhill, Defendant }
& Robert Collins, Claimant }

We, the Jury, find the Property Subject to the Plaintiff Execution, with Cost of Suit.

George A. Rodgers, forman

The following Jury N° 2 Were Sworn to Serve at this Term.

1. William Bass
2. Whitmill Williams
3. James Fergerson
4. Elias Harris
5. George A. Smith
6. John Molsby
7. William Hatcher
8. Thompson Powell
9. Leonard Adams
10. Thos Bush
11. Thos Moor
12. Josiah P. Smith

James H. Rodgers }
    vs   } Casa
James Gamble }

The defendant having been Arrested in the foregoing Casa and giving bond with Alexander Richards, Security, for his appearance to take the benefit of The Honest Debtors Act and the Said Security Having Surrendered his principal, the Said James Gamble, into Court. It is therefore ordered that Said Security be released from His bond and the said James Gamble is ordered into the Custody of the Court.

David Ralston }
    vs   } Casa from Justice Bates' Court
David F. Wilson }

Same }
  vs } Casa from Justice Bates' Court
Same }

Motion to Shew Cause why the Shff Should not be attached for Contempt, Who for Cause Sheweth that at The Last Term of this Court the defendant, David F. Wilson, paid me the amount of Said Cases and there Having been a fifa of an older Date In My hands, I therefore paid the Money over to the Said older fifa and Have Taken on Said fifa the Recept of the

---

Holder thereof for the Same, which is now in Court.

David Ralston }
    vs   } Casa from Justice Bates' Court
David F. Wilson }

Same }
  vs } Casa from Justice Bates' Court
Same }

upon hearing of a Rule Nisi against Spencer Riley, Esqr, Sheriff of Bibb County, To Shew Cause Why he Should not pay over the amount of the foregoing Casas to plaintiff, or His attorney, and the Sheriff having Made a Shewing Which the Court adjudged insufficient. It is therefore ordered that the Said Rule be Made Absolute & that the Sheriff pay over the amount of Principal, interest, & Cost of Said Casas tomorrow Morning at the opening of the Court according To the Exegeneis of the Rule Aforesaid or that He be Committed to the Common jail of this County for Contempt of this Court.

L. Atkinson, Surviver }
    vs   } Debt
Timothy Brewin   }

Jury N° 2

We find for the plaintiff one Hundred and Sixty Eight Dollars Ninety Eight Cents, with interest & Cost.

                                                Whitmill Williams, forman

L. Atkison, Surviver }
    vs   } Debt
William Bivins   }

Jury N° 2

We find for the plaintiff thirty Seven dollars thirty one Cents, With interest & Cost.

                                                Whitmill Williams, forman

The Court adjourned untill the Morning at 10 O'clock AM.

Rene Fitzpatrick, J. I. C.
Luke Ross, J. I. C.
R. Turner, J. I. C.

November 26th 1828

The Honorable the Inferior Court in and for Bibb County Meet agreeable to adjournment.

Present, their Honors   Luke Ross   }
            Rene Fitzpatrick } J. I. C.
            Reuben Turner }

Bank of Darien   }
   vs   } Assumpsit
A. G. Clopton &   }
Ambrose Baber, adm^{rs} }
of Joseph Morgan, dec^{d}}

Judgment Confessed to The plaintiff for the Sum of two hundred Dollars, with interest & Cost.

Albert G. Clopton, Att^{y}
for administrators of
Joseph Morgan

Wafford & Caldwell }
   vs   } Casa from Justice Court
Henry B. Hill   } The 564 Company dist

It Appearing to the Court That the foregoing Capias ad Satisfacendum has Been fully paid off and discharged & that the Defendant appears before the Court According to the Provisions of the Honest Debtors act, under bond & Security. It is therefore ordered that the Appearance Bond be Canceled and the Said Hill be Discharged without any further proceeding on Said Case.

Henry P. Cutler, Surviver }
   vs   } Case
George A. Smith   }

I hereby Confess Judgment To plaintiff for fifty Eight Dollars & Seventy two Cents, with Cost of Suit, Saving the right of appeal.

George A. Smith

Imlay & C° }
    vs } Debt
James Langford }

Jury N° 1

We find for the plaintiff the Sum of three hundred & forty four Dollars and ten & one half cents, With Interest & Cost of Suit.

George A. Rodgers, forman

Mortimer R. Wallis }
    vs } Garnishment in Bibb Inferior Court
John B. Cumming & } Novr Term 1828
Roger McCall, Garnishee }

Rule Nisi

It appearing to the Court by the return of the Sheriff that summons of garnishment has been served upon said garnishee and he having failed to appear and depose. It is therefore ordered that unless said garnishee and depose by the next Term of this court and shew cause why execution shall not issue for principal, interest, & Cost that this rule be made absolute.

John Loving }
    vs } Assumpsit
Samuel Gillespie }

We, the Jury, find for the Plaintiff Three hundred and Twenty nine dollars and Eighty Cents, With Cost of Suit.

George A. Rodgers, forman

Georgia }
Bibb County } Inferior Court November Term 1828

James H. Rodgers }
    vs   } Casa from Justis Court
Johnson Hammock }

It appearing to the Court That Said defendant has been arrested upon the above Casa and has given bond & Security to appear at the Inferior Court of this County to Take the benefit of the act under the Statute passed for

---

The relief of Honest Debtors, Wherefore the Said Johnson Hammock as Well as his Security on Said Bond, Elijah Cotton, having been Called & failing To Appear, it is therefore ordered that Said James H. Rodgers Enter up judgment for the Principal, interest, & Cost Specified in Said Casa against Said defendant and Elijah Cotton, his Security.

Gillespie & Birdsong }
for the use of   }
Samuel Gillespie   }
    vs   } Case
John Loving   }

I Confess Judgment to The plaintiff for the Sum of Seventy five Dollars Eighty Eight & three Quarter Cents, With Cost of Suit.

                              Polhill & Cole, Att^y for Def^t

Enoch T. Bowers }
    vs   } Case for Rent
Owen Brown   }

We, the Jury, find for the plaintiff three hundred Dollars, with interest & Cost of Suit.

                              W. Williams, forman

Bullock & Wells   }
    vs   } Case
Ambrose Baber &   }
Albert G. Clopton, adm^r }
of Joseph Morgan, dec^d }

We, the Jury, find for the plaintiff Fifty Dollars, with Cost of Suit.

Wittmill Williams, forman

Ordered that Spencer Riley, Sheriff, be paid the Sum of three hundred & fifteen Dollars & forty Eight Cents, the am^t of his acc^t as Jailer & Sheriff fees up to date.

Roger McCarthy }
     vs   } fifa from the Inferior Court
James Thompson }

It appearing to the Court That the foregoing Execution issuing out of this Court has been Satisfied. It is therefore ordered By the Court that Satisfaction thereof be Entered of record on the Minutes of this Court and The Said Execution filed away in the Sheriff's office.

Whitmill Williams }
     vs   } Casa
Hampton B. Wats }

It appearing to the Court That the Defendant Entered into a bond, Rene Fitzpartrick Security, to Appear at the present term of this to take the benefit of the Act promising relief for honest Debtors as to abide by Such dissions as Might be had By the Court in the premises & it Appearing to The Court that Said defendant has failed to Appear in Violation of his Said obligation. On Motion of Counsel, it is ordered that Judgment be Entered against the Said Defendant & his Security in the above Case.

We Confess Judgment to the plaintiff in The Above Case for twenty dollars principal & Three Dollars an Seventy three Cents interest, with Cost of Casa & all other Costs in this behalf Expended.

H. B. Watts, by his agent
R. Fitzpartrick
Rene Fitzpartrick

November Term 1828

Enoch T. Bowers }
    vs   } Case & Judgment
Owen Brown   }

Came into office Owen Brown, the Defendant in The Above Case, Who being disatisfied with The Verdict of the Jury, paid the Cost and Entered an appeal. also, at the Same time, Came Henry H. Cone, his Security on the Appeal, Who Each Acknowledge themselves jointly and Severally bond for the for the true payment of the Eventual Condemnation Money according to the Statute in Such Case Made and provided. Given under our hands & Seals this 26th Day of November 1828.

Test. M. Simmons, Clk   Owen Brown
                                      H. H. Cone

William Mackey, Plaintiff   }
& John G. Polhill, Defendant } Judgment against Claimant
& Robert Collins, Claimant   }

Came into office Robert Collins, the Defendant in the Above Case, Who being Disatisfied with the Verdict of the Jury, paid the Cost and Entered an appeal. Also, at the Same time, Came Mortimer R. Wallis, his Security on the appeal, Who Both Acknowledge themselves jointly and Severally bound for the true payment of the Eventual Condemnation Money According To the Statute in Such Case Made & provided. Given under our hands & Seals this 26th Day of November 1828.

                                                    Robt Collins
                                                    Mortimer R. Wallis

Thomas Victery   }
administrator of   }
Thomas A. Billups, Dec^d }
    vs   } Assumpsit & Judgment
George A. Rodgers   }

Came into office George A. Rodgers, the defendant in the Above Case, Who being disatisfied With The Verdict of the Jury, paid the Cost and Entered an Appeal. also, at the Same time, Came James H. Rodgers, his

Security on the Appeal, Who both Acknowledge themselves jointly and Severally bound for the true payment of the Eventual Condemnation Money according to the Statute in Such Case Made and provided. Given under our hands & Seals this 26th day of November 1828.

George A. Rodgers
Ja^s H. Rodgers

Mastern Whithead }
for the use of }
John McAllister }
    vs } Assumpsit & Judgment
Daniel Wadsworth }
& John McMarrian }

Came into office John McMarrian, one of the Defendant in the Above Case, Who being disatisfied With The Verdict of the Jury, paid the Cost and Entered an Appeal. also, at the Same Time, Came Thomas McMarrian, his Security on The Appeal, Who both Acknowledge them Selves jointly and Severally bound for the true payment of the Eventual Condemnation Money According To the Statute in Such Case Made and provided. Given under our hands & Seals this 26th day of November 1828.

Test. M. Simmons, Clk   John McMarrian
                                                  Thomas McMarrian

---

November Term 1828

Mathew Robertson }
for the use of }
M. Lesuar }
    vs } Assumpsit & Judgment
Philip Powledge }

Came into office Philip Powledge, the defendant in this Case, Who being Disatisfied with the Verdict, paid the Cost and Entered a Stay of Execution. Also, at The Same time, Came Reubin Turner, his Security on the Stay, Who Each Acknowledge Themselves jointly & Severally bound for the true Payment of the Eventual Condemnation Money

According to the Statute in Such Case Made and provided. Given under our hands & Seals this 26th day of November 1828.

            P. Powledge
            R. Turner

William G. Springer }
  vs   } Assumpsit & Judgment
Solomon Groce   }

Came into office Solomon Groce, the defendant in The Above Case, Who being disatisfied With The Verdict of the Jury, paid the Cost and Entered an Appeal. Also, at the Same time, Came Lewis J. Groce, his Security on the Appeal, Who Each Acknowledge themselves jointly and Severally bound for the true payment of the Eventual Condemnation Money according to The Statute in Such Case Made and Provided. Given under our hands & Seals this 26th Day of November 1828.

            S. Groce
            Lewis J. Groce

John Loving   }
  vs   } Assumpsit & Judgment
Samuel Gillespie }

Came into office Samuel Gillespie, the defendant in The Above Case, Who Being Disatisfied With The Verdict of the Jury, paid the Cost and Entered an Appeal. Also, at the Same time, Came Solomon Groce, his Security on the Appeal, Who Each Acknowledge themselves jointly and Severally bound for the true payment of the Eventual Condemnation Money according to The Statute in Such Case Made and Provided. Given under our hands & Seals this 26th Day of November 1828.

            Saml Gillespie
            S. Groce

Adams & Fessendon }
  vs   } Debt
Coffin & Clark   }

Judgment Confessed for Plaintiff one hundred & Ninety Two Dollars and Seventy one Cents principal, With interest & Cost.

Tracy & Butler, Att^y for Defn^t

E. W. Wright }
    vs } Case
Cornelius Townsend }
& Tuttle H. Moreland }

We, the Jury, find for plaintiff Seventy Nine Dollars and thirty Seven Cents principal, interest, and Cost.

W. Williams, forman

Oliver Sage }
    vs } Case
Z. Sims }

We, the Jury, find for plaintiff fifty Dollars principal, interest, and Cost.

W. Williams, forman

William J. Danelly & Co }
    vs } Debt & Judgment
Elijah Cotton }

Came into office Elijah Cotton, the Defendant in the above Case, Who being disatisfied With The Verdict of the Jury, paid the Cost and Entered a Stay of Execution. Also, at the Same time, Came Came Benjamin Allen, his Security on the Stay of Execution, Who both acknowledge themselves jointly and Severally bound for the true payment of the Eventual Condemnation Money According to The Statute in Such Case Made and Provided. Given under our hands & Seals this 26th Day of November 1828.

E. Cotton
Ben^j Allen

Oliver Sage }
    vs } Debt
Israel Keith }

We, the Jury, find for plaintiff Seven hundred & forty Nine Dollars principal, with interest & Cost.

         W. Williams, forman

Commissioners of }
the Town of Macon }
  vs   } Case
Samuel Gillespie }

Judgment Confessed for Eighty Dollars principal, interest, and Cost.

         S. Gillespie, Security

Fairchild, Lyon & C°}
  vs   }Assumpsit for rent
Tuttle H. Moreland }
William Harrison }
& Harvey Kendrick }

We, the Jury, find for Plaintiff one hundred and fifty Dollars against Tuttle Moreland & William Harrison, With interest & Cost.

         W. Williams, forman

Hugh Loving & C° }
  vs   } Debt
Jonathan T. Meeker }

We hereby Confess Judgment to the plaintiff in The Sum of one hundred & twenty Six Dollars & Ninety five Cents, with interest & Cost.

         Tracy & Butler, Att^y for Def^t

Charles S. Lewis }
  vs   } Garnishment
Moreland & Townsend }

Isaac G. Seymour, one of the Garnishees in Said Case, Having Made oath that he is indebted to Said Defendant twenty Six Dollars. It is ordered that Said plaintiff enter up judgment Against Said Seymour instanter for Said Amount.

Ellis, Shotwell & C° }
     vs   } Garnishment
Thomas Campbell }
& John D. Walker }

Thomas Campbell, one of the above Garnishees, in Conformity With Said Summons, Appeared & Acknowledged himself indebted to Moreland and Townsend, the defendants in the original Action, in the Sum of fifty Six $^{17}/_{100}$ Dollars. it is Ordered That Said plaintiff Enter up Judgment instanter for Said amount & that Moreland & Townsend be [illegible] in Cost of Suit.

Charles S. Lewis }
     vs   } Debt
Moreland & Townsend }

We, the Jury, find for plaintiff One hundred and thirty Nine Dollars & 62 Cents principal, With interest & Cost.

                          George A. Rodgers, forman

Ellis, Shotwell & C° }
     vs   } Case
Moreland & Townsend }

We, the Jury, find for plaintiff one hundred & twenty Nine Dollars and Sixty Six Cents principal, With interest And Cost.

                          W. Williams, forman

Lewis Fitch & C° }
     vs   } Case
Solomon Groce }

We, the Jury, find for plaintiff Thirty four Dollars and Ninety Cents principal, With interest & Cost.

                          George A. Rodgers, forman

J. & C. Nichols & C° }
     vs   } Case
Absolom Brown }

We, the jury, find for plaintiff against defendant Seventy four Dollars and Seventy five Cents principal, interest, & Cost.

George A. Rodgers, forman

Daniel Oakley }
    vs } Debt
Jonathan T. Meeker }

Judgment Confessed for one hundred & twenty Six Dollars & Ninety five Cents principal, With interest & Cost.

Tracy & Butler, Att[ys] for Def[t]

Bailey Goddard }
for the use of }
W. H. & E. P. Hagen }
    vs } Debt
John M. Shelman }

We Confess for plaintiff one hundred & Eighty Eight Dollars principal, interest, and Cost.

Polhill & Cole, att[ys] for def[t]

———

Bailey Goddard }
for the use of }
W. H. & E. P. Hagen }
    vs } Debt
Robert B. Shelman }

We Confess for plaintiff Two hundred & three Dollars and thirty Nine Cents principal, With interest & Cost.

Polhill & Cole, att[ys] for defen[t]

Thomas A. Ranolds }
    vs } Case & Bail
Coffin & Clark }

Judgment Confessed for plaintiff two hundred ~~Eighty Seven~~ Dollars Eighty Seven Cents principal, with interest and Cost.

Tracy & Butler, att^{ys} for defendant

Anson Kimberly }
     vs   } Debt
Francis H. Hickenburg }

We, the Jury, find for Plaintiff two hundred and five Dollars and Eight Cents principal, with interest And Cost.

George A. Rodgers, forman

W. & H. Rose }
     vs   } Case
Alex^r Merewether }

We, the Jury, find for plaintiff one hundred & forty Dollars Thirty two Cents principal, with interest & Cost.

George A. Rodgers, forman

Solomon D. Chapman }
     vs   } Debt
Henry Crew }

We, the Jury, find for plaintiff two hundred & fifty one Dollars and Sixty Cents principal, With interest and Cost.

George A. Rodgers, forman

Philander Judson }
     vs   } Case
Beverly Rew }

We, the jury, find for plaintiff forty five Dollars and Seventy five Cents principal, with interest and Cost.

George A. Rodgers, forman

Philander Judson }
     vs   } Case
Solomon D. Chapman }

We, the jury, find for plaintiff against Solomon D. Chapman, indorsee, forty five Dollars and Seventy five Cents principal, with interest and Cost.

                           George A. Rodgers, forman

Gillespie & Birdsong }
     vs   } Case
Joseph Folker   }

We, the jury, find for plaintiff fifty Eight & fifty Cents principal, with interest & Cost.

                           George A. Rodgers, forman

J. C. Rodgers, adm^r }
of Rushing   }
     vs   } Case
R. D. Beall   }

We, the Jury, find thirty Dollars & fifty five Cents for plaintiff, With Cost.

                           W. Williams, forman

W. F. Scott }
     vs   } Case
A. Mandell }

We, the jury, find for plaintiff thirty one $^{87}/_{100}$ Dollars principal, with interest & Cost.

                           George A. Rodgers, forman

Bailey Goddard   }
for the use of   }
W. H. & E. P. Hagen }
     vs   } Case
Spencer Riley   }

Judgment Confessed for forty one Dollars and ninety one Cents principal, with interest and Cost.

        Spencer Riley

———

The following Jury Were Drawn to Serve at May Term 1829, Viz.

  1. Henry Abott   19. Robert Smith
  2. Abraham P. Partrick 20. Allen Buzby
  3. Stephen Williams   21. Charles Crawford
  4. Samuel Slate   22. Leroy Watson
  5. James S. Weeks   23. John Tucker
  6. Reubin Williams   24. Thomas Brigman
  7. Oliver Sage   25. Watson Coutch
  8. John Elsworth   26. Gillis Wright
  9. Zackariah Williamson 27. Wm F. Brown
  10. Wiley Dorman   28. Martin L. Harding
  11. John James   29. Andrew Collins
  12. John Allen   30. Jerdon Ivey
  13. George Collins   31. Green Wilder
  14. James Brigham   32. David Burks
  15. John Holezworth   33. Jeremiah Patterson
  16. John Tompkins   34. Edmund Nobles
  17. Abner Hammond   35. Moses Anderson
  18. Thomas Williams   36. Elijah Etheredge

The Court then adjourned untill Court in Course.

        Lu Ross, J. I. C.
        David Ralston, J. I. C.
        R. Turner, J. I. C.

———

      November Term 1828

Joseph Collins, bearer }
  vs   } Assumpsit & Judgment
Daniel B. Worsham }

Came into office Daniel B. Worsham, the defendant in the Above Case, Who being disatisfied With The Verdict of the jury, paid the Cost and Entered an appeal. Also, at the Same time, Came John D. Chapman, his Security on the appeal, Who Each acknowledge themselves jointly & Severally Bound for the true payment of the Eventual Condemnation Money According to the Statute in Such Case Made and Provided. Given under our hands & Seals this first day of December 1828.

D. B. Worsham
J. D. Chapman

Henry P. Cutler, Survivor &c }
         vs   } Case and judgment
Ge° A. Smith   }

Came into office George A. Smith, the defendant in the Above Case, Who being disatisfied with the Verdict of the jury, paid the Cost and Entered an appeal. Also, at the Same time, Came Edward W. Wright, his Security on the appeal, Who Each acknowledge themselves & Severally bound for the true payment of the Eventual Condemnation Money according to The Statute in Such Case Made and Provided. Given under our hands & Seals this first day of December 1828.

Ge° A. Smith
Edwd W. Wright

April Term 1829

Georgia   } the honorable the Inferior Court in And for the County
Bibb County } of Bibb Meet Agreeable to adjournment

Present, their honors   Luke Ross   }
                                            Reuben Turner } J. I. C.
                                              Samuel B. Hunter }
                                              Timothy Mathews }

Ordered that John T. Rowland, Thomas P. Bond, and Isaac G. Seymour be Appointed Notory Public for the County of bibb by their taken the usual oath.

Ordered that Van Swearingin be paid Eighteen Dollars and Seventy five Cents in full of his account as Corroner.

Ordered that the Clk of this Court pay Spencer Riley, Sheriff, Seventy Eight Dollars and twenty One Cents, in full of his Account up to the 23rd January last.

Ordered that Thos J. McCluskie be paid five dollars for two Coffins, one for Cynthia and the other for Boyd's Child.

Ordered that M. Bartlett be paid fifty one Dollars, in full of his Account for printing up to 6th September 1828.

Ordered that Richard W. Ellis Be paid two Dollars for Centering public Square for Court House.

Ordered that Mortimer R. Wallis Be paid twenty Dollars for rent of Grand jury Room for two terms.

Ordered that Henry B. Hill be Appointed Constable for the 716 dist.

April Term 1829

William J. Danelly & Co }
      vs   }
John J. Kaigler   }

It Appearing to the Court that the Defendant has been Arrested at the Instance of William J. Danelly & Co & that he has Appeared and Complied With the requisits of the honest Debtors Act. It is Therefore ordered that the Said John J. Kaigler be Admitted to the benefit of Said Act & that he be Discharged from Custody.

Jeremiah Smith }
      vs   } Casa from Justice Court
Hiram Vines   }

John James, the Security on this Case, Came in to Court and delivered up the defendant. It is therefore ordered that he be discharged from the Bond.

The Court then adjourned Untill the first Monday in May next.

          R. Turner, J. I. C.
          D. Ralston, J. I. C.
          Saml B. Hunter, J. I. C.

April Term 1829

Georgia   } The honorable the Inferior Court
Bibb County } In and for the County of Bibb
May 4th 1829} Meet agreeable to adjournment

Present, their honors   Timothy Mathews }
           Reubin Turner } J. I. C.
           Luke Ross   }
           Samuel B. Hunter }

The following Jury were Sworn to Serve at this Term.

Jury N° 1

1. Allen Busbee   4. Martin L. Harding
2. Charles Crawford 5. Green Wilder
3. Thomas Brigman   6. John H. Kimbro

April Term 1829

7. Henry Abott   10. Samuel Slate
8. Abraham P. Partrick 11. Reubin Williams
9. Stephen Williams 12. John Elsworth
    James Thompson in place of the above

Benjamin Allen }
for the use of   }
John S. Childers }
  vs   } Debt
Joshua Jordon }

We find for the plaintiff Seventy five Dollars, with Interest & Cost of Suit.

            A. P. Partrick, forman

The Bank of Darien }
     vs   } Case
George Stovall   }

We find for the plaintiff One hundred and twenty five Dollars, With interest & Cost of Suit.

                                         A. P. Partrick, forman

Williamson Mims   }
     vs   } Debt
Richmond Bosworth }

We find for the plaintiff Two hundred & four Dollars Eighty four Cents, With interest & Cost of Suit.

                                         A. P. Partrick, forman

Ordered that Messrs Smith, Davidson, and Alexander be paid Seven hundred and fifty Dollars for part of the Court house Contract.

Thomas N. Pullain   }
     vs   } Debt
Jeffrey E. Thompson }
& Tabitha, his wife   }

We, the Jury, find for The plaintiff the Sum of Thirty Seven dollars fifty Six & a Quarter Cents, With interest & Cost.

                                         A. P. Partrick, forman

---

                                April Term 1829

John B. Gaudry   }
     vs   } Assumpsit
Jonathan A. Hudson }
& James Fitzgarrald }

We, the jury, find for plaintiff the Sum of Sixty Six Dollars & thirty Cents, With Interest & Cost.

                                         A. P. Partrick, forman

C. W. Rockwell & C° }
    vs   } Assumpsit
James Alston   }

We, the jury, find for plaintiff the Sum of Four hundred & thirty Dollars and thirty Cents, With interest & Cost.

                                     A. P. Partrick, forman

John L. Hodges }
    vs   } Assumpsit
Ralston & Jones }

We hereby Confess Judgment to the plaintiff In the Sum of five hundred & forty One dollars & Seventy two Cents, With interest & Cost, reserving the right of appeal.

                                     Polhill & Cole, Def[t] att[ys]

W. H. & E. P. Hegen, bearer }
    vs   } Case
Elam Alexander   }

We, the Jury, find for The plaintiff fifty Dollars Twelve and a half Cents, With interest & Cost.

                                     A. P. Partrick, forman

Benjamin Baird   }
    vs   } Assumpsit
Jeffrey E. Thompson }

We, the jury, find for the plaintiff the Sum of forty Eight dollars and fifty One Cents, With interest & Cost.

                                     A. P. Partrick, forman

April Term 1829

Ellis, Shotwell & C° }
    vs   } Assumpsit
William Cumming }

We, the jury, find for The plaintiff the Sum of Thirty One Dollars and fifty Cents, With interest and & Cost.

                                                                              A. P. Partrick, forman

B. W. Dalamaten & Cº }
        vs   } Debt
Hezekiah Douglass   }

We, the Jury, find for the plaintiff fifty Three Dollars & twenty one Cents principal, With Interest & Cost.

                                                                              A. P. Partrick, forman

James M. Milner   }
        vs   } Assumpsit
Albert G. Clopton }

I hereby Confess Judgment to the plaintiff in the Sum of Ninety Eight dollars & Eighty One & a Quarter Cents, With interest & Cost.

                                                                              Albert G. Clopton

John B. Gaudry }
        vs   } Assumpsit
Robert S. Patton }

We, the Jury, find for Plaintiff the Sum of Eighty five Dollars, With interest and Cost.

                                                                              A. P. Partrick, forman

Willis F. Colt   }
        vs   } Debt
Thomas J. McCluskie }

We, the Jury, find for The plaintiff fifty one Dollars Eighty one fourth Cents, With interest & Cost.

                                                                              A. P. Partrick, forman

April Term 1829

John B. Gaudry }
    vs   } Assumpsit
Rufus K. Evans }

Judgment Confessed to Plaintiff the Sum of Ninety Dollars, With interest & Cost.

                        Albert G. Clopton, def^t att^y

Martha Legueux }
    vs   } Assumpsit
Cornelius Townsend }

We, the jury, find for Plaintiff the Sum of Sixty Nine Dollars, With interest & Cost.

                        A. P. Partrick, forman

Inspectors of Penitentiary }
    vs   } Debt
Moreland & Townsend }

We, the jury, find for plaintiff One Hundred & fifty Dollars principal, With interest & Cost.

                        A. P. Partrick, forman

Imlay & Co }
    vs   } Judgment in Bibb Inferior Court
James Langford }

It appearing to the Court that there was an Error in entering up Judgment in the foregoing Case in the amount of Interest. Ordered that The Judgment & Execution be Amended So as to Insert the Correct Amount of Interest.

J. C. Rodgers, adm^r }
of Rushin }
    vs   } Case
F. H. Godfrey }

We, the Jury, find a Verdict for the Plaintiff for Sixty five Dollars principal & Cost of Suit.

          A. P. Patrick, forman

      April Term 1829

John Rushing }
  vs   } Assumpsit
John Loving }

We hereby Confess judgment To plaintiff in the Sum of three Hundred Dollars, With Interest & Cost, reserving the right to appeal. 4th May 1829

         Polhill & Cole, Deft[ds] Att[ys]

The Court then adjourned till tomorrow Morning at 9 O'clock.

         R. Turner, J. I. C.
         Lu Ross, J. I. C.
         Sam B. Hunter, J. I. C.

Georgia } The honorable the Inferior Court In and for the
Bibb County } County of Bibb Meet agreeable to adjournment

Present, their honors   Reubin Turner }
           Luke Ross   } J. I. C.
           Samuel B. Hunter }
           Timothy Mathews }

John Scully }
  vs   } Assumpsit
Charles Bullock }

We, the Jury, find a Verdict in favour of plaintiff for Thirty five Dollars, With Cost of Suit.

          A. P. Patrick, forman

April Term 1829

John Scully }
    vs   } Assumpsit & Judgment
Charles Bullock }

Came into open Court Charles Bullock, the defendant In the Above Case, who being disatisfied with The Verdict of the jury, paid the Cost and Entered an appeal. also, at the Same time, Came Mortimer R. Wallis, his Security on the Appeal, who both acknowledge themselves jointly And Severally bound for the true payment of the Eventual Condemnation Money According To the Statute in Such Case Made and provided. Given under our hands and Seals This 5th day of May 1829.

Test. Martin Simmons, Clk   Chas Bullock
                                             M. R. Wallis

Isham Woodward }
    vs   } Debt
Archibald R. Woodson }

I Confess judgment To the plaintiff in the Sum of one hundred and Seventeen Dollars & Seventy five Cents, With interest & Cost.

                                       Albert G. Clopton, def^t att^y

Ordered That Guy Champion be appointed Notory Public for the County of Bibb.

Mortimer R. Wallis, plff in Ex }
    vs   } Rule absolute
John B. Cumming, def^t in Ex } Bibb Inferior Court
& Roger McCall, Garnishee } April Term 1829

It appearing by the Records of this Court that a Rule Nisi Was granted at the last term of this Court ordering

———

That unless the Said Garnishee Appear and Depose By the Next term of this Court & Shew Cause Why Execution Should Not issue against him for Principal, interest, & Cost in the above Suit & The Said Garnishee having failed to appear and Depose. It is therefore Ordered that

Attachment do Issue against Said Roger McCall for Contempt of this Court.

James H. Rodgers }
    vs } Capies ad Satisfaciendum
James Gamble }

On Motion, it is ordered That the Sheriff Shew Cause as Soon as Counsel Can be heard Why he Should Not Pay to the plaintiff, or his Attorney, the Amount Due upon the Said Casa.

Nathan Brady, Junr }
    vs }
John R. Jones }

It appearing to the Court from the Superior Court of Jones County Was directed to John G. Polhill & Carlton B. Cole, Esq^{rs} Authorising them to take the deposition of one Thomas Miller and other Witnesses therein Named. And It also Appearing that the Said Miller refused to Appear before the Said Commissioners and That a Subpoena issued from the Clerk of this Court under the attestation of Reubin Turner, Esqr, One of the Honorable Justices of Said Court, Requiring the Said Miller to appear before the Said Commissioners at a Certain time & place Therein Specified to testify in the foregoing Case in Behalf of the defendant. and it also Appearing That Notwithstanding the Subpoena Aforesaid the Said Miller Still Stands out in Contempt of the process of this Court. It is therefore Ordered that the

---

Sheriff do by two o'clock this Afternoon bring the Said Thomas Miller before this Court to Shew Cause, if any he have, Why he Should Not be Attached for a Contempted & undergo the Pain & penalties to Which Witnesses are Subject Who refuse to obey the process of the Court.

Ordered that James S. Weeks, John Hollingsworth, Jordon Ivy, and Jeremiah Patterson, Severally And Each of them, be fined in the Sum of Ten Dollars for their Non Appearance as Jurors at Said Court And that the Clerk of Said Court do after four days adjournment of Said Court do issue Execution for Said fines.

Samuel Gillespie }
    vs   } Case
John Loving   }

We, the Jury, find a Verdict for ten Dollars in favour of the plaintiff, With Cost.

                        A. P. Patrick, forman

Littleton Atkison }
    vs   } Claim
William Bivins }

We, the Jury, find the Property Not Subject.

                        A. P. Patrick, forman

William J. Danelly & Co }
    vs   } Assumpsit & Bail
Addison Mandell   }

We Confess Judgment To the plaintiff in the Sum of two hundred & Eighty Six dollars and Sixty Cents principal, With interest & Cost.

                        Campbell & Seymour, Deft^d Att^{ys}

The Court adjourned untill tomorrow Morning at ten O'clock.

                        Timothy Mathews, J. I. C.
                        Lu Ross, J. I. C.
                        R. Turner, J. I. C.
                        Saml B. Hunter, J. I. C.

Georgia   } The honorable the Inferior Court
Bibb County } In & for the County of Bibb
May 6th 1829   agreeable to adjournment

Present, Their honors   Timothy Mathews }
                                Luke Ross   } J. I. C.
                                Reubin Turner }

Ordered that Richard W. Ellis be paid Eight Dollars for Laying out the Road from Macon to Walnut Creek.

George B. Wardlaw }
      vs   } Case from Magistrate Court
Patrick Cunningham }

It appearing To The Court that Patrick Cunningham has been Arrested by Virtue of the Said Casa Now in file in this Court & that Solomon Groce became Security for the Appearance of the Said Patrick at this Court under The pervissions of the act for the relief of honest Debtors. Now the Said Patrick having been Called & Making default. It is ordered and adjudged by the Court that the plaintiff recover from the Court that the plaintiff recover from the Said Patrick Cunningham and the Said Solomon Groce the Sum Nine Dollars & fifty Cents principal, With interest from the 11th October 1828, and the further Sum of [blank] dollars and [blank] Cents Cost, & that Execution issue forthwith

―

April Term 1829

against the Said Patrick & the Said Solomon for The amount aforesaid.

Mortimer R. Wallis   }
      vs   } Assumpsit
Thomas J. McCluskey }

We, the Jury, find for the plaintiff The Sum of one hundred & fifty Dollars, With interest And Cost.

                                                    A. P. Patrick, forman

Jacob Danforth   }
      vs   } Debt for Rent
John G. Polhill & }
John W. Campbell }

We Confess judgment to the plaintiff Thirty Seven Dollars $^{69}/_{100}$ principal, With interest & Cost.

                                                   E. D. Tracy, for defd^{s}

Edward W. Wright }
       vs   } Assumpsit for Rent
Williamson Smith }
James H. Rodgers }
& Rufus K. Evans }

We, the jury, find for the plaintiff Seventy five Dollars Principal, With interest & Cost.

                                                   A. P. Patrick, forman

James Gillespie }
       vs   } Assumpsit
John Corbett }

We, the jury, find for Plaintiff the Sum of four Hundred & thirty three Dollars & Seventy one Cents, With interest and Cost.

                                                   A. P. Patrick, forman

---

John K. Boyd   } Casa from Justices Court
       vs   } & Bond for taking
Joseph Folker &   } Benefit of Honest Debtors Act
Robert Collins, Security }

It appearing that Joseph Folker, the Defendant, has failed to Appear & file his Schedule & Notify his Creditors in terms of the Law. It is therefore ordered by the Court That Judgment be entered up instanter Against The Said Joseph Folker and Robert Collins, his Security on the Bond aforesaid, for the principal, Interest, & Cost in Said Case.

~~Mortimer R. Wallis, Plff in Ex~~ }
             vs   } ~~attachment in Bibb Inferior Court~~
~~John B. Cumming, Deft &~~ } ~~April Term 1829~~
~~Roger McCall, Garnishee~~ }

~~To the sheriff~~

It appearing to the Court that a Casa issued at The Suit of Moreland & Townsend against Joseph Folker from the justices Court of the five hundred and Sixty fourth Company district, Upon Which Casa the Said Joseph Folker Was arrested and Whereas Robert Collins became

Security on a bond For the Said Joseph Folker's Appearance at the Last term of this Court to Comply With & take The benefit of the Act for the relief of honest Debtors. And the Said Joseph Folker having failed to Appear According to the requisitions of The bond given in terms of the Law in Such Case Made & provided, it is therefore ordered That Judgment be entered against the Said Joseph Folker and the Said Robert Collins, his Security, for principal, interest, & Cost due on Said Casa.

April Term 1829

Nicholas Wagner }
  vs   } Casa
Charles Pearson }

It appearing to the Court that George Micklejohn Was Security for the Appearance of the above defendant at the present term of This Court to take the benefit of an Act passed for the relief of Honest Debtors And to abide Such decisions as might be Made by the Court. And It appearing to the Court that Said Defendant Has failed to Appear in Violation of Said Obligation. On Motion of Counsel, it is ordered That the plaintiff has leave to Enter up judgment Against Said Charles Pearson & George Micklejohn for the full Amount of the principal, interest, & Cost due the plaintiff in the Above Case.

Bank of Darien   }
  vs   } Debt
Albert G. Clopton & }
Ambrose Baber, adm^{rs} }
of Joseph Morgan & }
Ezekiel Wimberly }
Benjamin Bryan & }
James Wimberly   }

Same }
vs } Debt
A. G. Clopton & }
Ambrose Baber, adm^{rs} }
of Joseph Morgan, dec^d }
& Ezekiel Wimberly }
Rogers Lawson & }
W. W. Williamson }

In these Cases exceptions Was taken by the defendants' Counsel in Each at April term 1829 of the Inferior Court of Bibb County (being the Appearance term) That the Suits, When brought in the Name of the

---

Bank of Darien, the Defendants' Counsel intending That the Bank of Darien being a Corporation Cannot Sue in any other Manner or form but By & in the name of their Attorney in fact. And thereupon the defendants' Counsel Moved The Court that Nonsuits be entered. Which Exceptions Was Overruled by the Court and The Motion for a Nonsuit refused.

James H. Rodgers }
vs } Casa & rule against the Sheriff
James Gamble }

In obediance to the foregoing rule, this respondent answers that He has always Kept the defendant in prison according to Law & that he has Never been Without the Jail limits, except in one instance Where He was taken out by Habeas Corpus to testify In one of the Courts of this County.

Spencer Riley, Sheriff

The Court heard the argument on the foregoing Rule & being of the opinion that the Shewing of the Sheriff is Sufficient & No Contempt has been Committed. Ordered that the rule be discharged At the Cost of the plaintiff, James H. Rodgers.

Ordered, that Henry B. Hill be paid three dollars for three days Services as Bailiff at this term of this Court.

Norman Wallace }
     vs   } Assumpsit
Samuel Gillespie }

I Confess judgment to the plaintiff in the Sum of Three hundred & thirty Seven Dollars and twenty five Cents, With interest & Cost.

                        Samuel Gillespie

April Term 1829

Low, Taylor & C° }
     vs   } Assumpsit
Samuel Gillespie }

I Confess judgment to the plaintiff in the Sum of one thousand Nine hundred & four Dollars & forty Nine Cents, With interest & Cost.

                        Samuel Gillespie

The Court adjourned untill tomorrow Morning at 9 O'clock.

                        Timothy Mathews, J. I. C.
                        Lu Ross, J. I. C.
                        R. Turner, J. I. C.
                        Saml B. Hunter, J. I. C.

Georgia   } The honorable the Inferior Court In and for the
Bibb County } County of Bibb Meet agreeable to adjournment
May 7th 1829

Present, their honors   Timothy Mathews }
                                   Luke Ross   } J. I. C.
                                   Reubin Turner   }

Ordered by the Court that in future No Bills or accounts Which May Accrue by The request or otherwise of the Grand Jury for the Publicity of their presentments Will Not be paid.

ordered that William Cumming Be paid forty two Dollars in full for Seven Coffins furnished by him for paupers as per bill.

ordered that William Cumming be paid Thirty Seven Dollars and Six & a Quarter Cents for funeral Expenses of James Bass and diging 8 Graves, as per Bill.

April Term 1829

Ordered that Lot Number one adjoining third and Mulberry Street in Square N° 19, being the Lot on Which the old Court house Now Stands and which was reserved from the former Sale Made of the Said Court house Square, together with the old Court house, be offered for Sale by public Outcry to the highest Bidder at the door of the old Court house on the first Tuesday in July Next at Eleven O'clock in the forenoon, terms to Be Made known on the day of Sale. And that The Clerk Give public Notice of Such Sale by advertisement at the Court house door & Elsewhere.

Fairchild, Lyon & C° }
      vs   } Debt for Rent
Tuttle H. Moreland }
William Harrison }
Harvy Kendrick }

We Confess judgment to the plaintiff for One Hundred & fifty Dollars Principal, With interest & Cost.

                                Moreland & Harrison

The following Jury Were Drawn to Serve at October Term 1829, Viz.

1. Thomas J. Biddle
2. Mathew Hughs
3. Hiram Walker
4. Thomas Howard
5. Alexander D. Brown
6. John Brady
7. William B. Cone
8. Lewis Gregory
9. Edmond Jones
10. Lewis B. Langford
11. Lewis Collins
12. David Kid
13. Henry Johnston
14. John Killingworth
15. John Rowlan
16. Samuel Chamberless
17. John Douglass
18. John T. Cox
19. Needham Huff
20. John Hughs
21. Joseph Boren
22. Carter B. Langford
23. James Douglass
24. John Jones

April Term 1829

25. Robert Roffe
26. Thomas Rowlan
27. Alexander Adams
28. Mathew Carter
29. Thomas Sacrey
30. Patrick Cunningham
31. Daniel Smith
32. Thomas Knight
33. Samuel Berry
34. Zackariah Cowart
35. Nicholas Wagner
36. Drury Thompson

The Court adjourned Untill Court in Course.

R. Turner, J. I. C.
Timothy Mathews, J. I. C.
Saml B. Hunter, J. I. C.

John L. Hodges }
  vs } Assumpsit & Judgment
Ralston & Jones]

Came into office David Ralston & John L. Jones, the Defendants in the above Case, Who being Disatisfied with the Verdict of the Jury, paid the Cost and Entered an appeal, also at the Same time, Came Marmaduk J. Slade, their Security on the Appeal, Who Each Acknowledge themselves jointly and Severally bound for the true ~~Eventual~~ payment of the Eventual Condemnation Money According to the Statue in Such Case Made and provided. Given under our hands and Seals this 11th May 1829.

David Ralston
By Jno L. Jones
Jno L. Jones
M. D. J. Slade

April Term 1829

John C. Rodgers }
adm^{rs} of Rushin }
  vs } Case & Judgment
F. H. Godfrey }

Came into Office Francis H. Godfrey, the defendant in the Above Case, Who being disatisfied with the Verdict of The Jury, paid the Cost and Entered an Appeal, also at the Same time, Came Luke Ross, his Security on the Appeal, Who both Acknowledge Themselves jointly and Severally bound for the true payment of the Eventual Condemnation Money According to the Statute in Such Case Made And provided. Given under our hands and Seal this 11th day of May 1829.

Test. M. Simmons, Clk   F. H. Godfrey
                             [cross-out]
                             Lu Ross

Georgia   } In Chambers September 10th 1829
Bibb County }

Present, their honors   Timothy Mathews }
                             Luke Ross   } J. I. C.
                             David Ralston   }
                             Reubin Turner   }

Georgia   } To the honorable a Justice of the
Bibb County } Inferior Court for Said County

The petition of John Mills Sheweth That Thomas Moore has been taken out of his Custody Now Confined in the Jailer of Said County and Your petitioner avers that Said Confinement is Illegal and prays that Your honor Will grant To him the Writ of Habeas Corpus to be directed To Said Jailor requiring him to bring up the body

---

of Said Thomas Moore before the proper tribunal, With the Cause of his Caption and detainment.

                             John Mills, by his
                             Attys Prince & Poe

Georgia   }
Bibb County } To the Jailer of Said County, Greeting

You are hereby Commanded To bring before a Majority of the Justices of The Inferior Court of Said County at Nine O'clock A. M. of this day the body of Thomas Moore, Who is Now Confined in Your Custody, together With the Cause of his Caption and detainer, in Order that the Court May do in his behalf as to Justice May Appertain. Witness My hand & Seal This 10th day of September 1829.

David Ralston, J. I. C.

Georgia }
Bibb County } In Obediance to the Within process, I have brought forward the body of the Within Name Thomas Moore, Who is Now in My Custody, together With a Capias ad Satisfacendum Eminating from the Justice Court for the 716 district Georgia Milittia in favour of James J. Erby for the use of William Tarpley vs Said Moore, Which is the Cause of his Caption & detention, Returned to me by H. B. Hill, Constable, This the 10th of September 1829.

Young Johnston, D. Shff

September 10th 1829. It is upon full hearing adjudged that the Habeas Corpus be Sustained and that the Said Thomas Moore be delivered to John Mills, his bail, upon payment of Cost.

———

Timothy Mathews, J. I. C.
R. Turner, J. I. C.
Luke Ross, J. I. C.

Georgia } October 19th 1829 The Honorable the Inferior Court
Bibb County } In and for the County of Bibb meet this day agreeable to adjournment

Present, Spencer Riley, Shff & M. Simmons, Clk

The Court was then adjourned untill the first Monday in November Next.

Test. Martin Simmons, Clk

Georgia } November 2nd 1829. The honorable The Inferior Court
Bibb County } in and for Said County Meet this Day agreeable to adjournment

Present [blank]

October adjourned Term 1829

The Honorable the Inferior Court of Bibb County met agreeable to adjournment, present their Honors Timothy Mathews, Reuben Turner, and Saml B. Hunter. November 2nd 1829

The Sheriff returned the Veneri and the following persons were Sworn on Jury N° 1.

1. Mathew Hughes
2. Thomas Howard
3. Alex^a D. Brown
4. Wm B. Cone
5. Edmund Jones
6. Lewis B. Langford
7. Saml Chambless
8. Joseph Boren
9. James Douglass
10. Saml Berry
11. Zach^a Cowart
12. Nicholas Wagner

Vincent R. Porter }
    vs   } Debt
George A. Smith }

I confess Judgment to the Plaintiff for thirty five Dollars, with interest and Cost. 2 Novr 1829

                                 Ge° A. Smith

Thomas Carter }
    vs   } Debt
C. B. Strong }

I confess Judgment to the plaintiff for Ninety four Dollars & Eighty nine cents, with interest and Cost.

                              Henry G. Lamar, Def^{ts} At^y

Thomas Hardeman, adm^r }
of Josephus Levi, Dec^d }
    vs   } Assumpsit
Zebulon Veasey &   }
Absalom Echols   }

Jury N° 1

We, the Jury, find for plaintiff one hundred and fifty four Dollars & fifty cents, with interest and Cost.

Wm B. Cone, Form

William Hogan }
  vs   } Debt
Charlton Thompson }

I Confess Judgement to the Plaintiff in the Sum of Thirty five Dollars, with interest and Cost, reserving the right of Appeal.

C. Thompson

Parish, Corning & C° }
  vs   } Assumpsit
Rene Fitzpatrick }

I hereby Confess Judgement to the plaintiffs in the Sum of One thousand and Twenty Seven Dollars and thirty three cents, with interest and Costs.

Rene Fitzpatrick

Kimberly & Chisholm }
  vs   } Assumpsit
Jeffrey E. Thompson }

I hereby Confess Judgement to plaintiff the Sum of Forty five Dollars and Seventy two cents, with interest and Costs.

J. E. Thompson

Bailey Goddard, for the }
use of James Goddard }
  vs   } Assumpsit
John G. Polhill }

I hereby confess Judgement to plaintiff in the Sum of One Hundred and thirty Dollars and Ninety two cents, with interest and Cost.

C. B. Cole, Att^y for Def^t

Hatch, Porter & C⁰ }
    vs   } Assumpsit
Ralston & Jones }

We Confess Judgement to the plaintiff in the Sum of One Thousand three hundred and forty two Dollars & Sixty three Cents, with interest and Costs.

                                      Ralston & Jones, Pr
                                      Campbell & Seymour, Att[ys]

October adjourned Term 1829

Thomas Napier   }
    vs   } Case
William P. Harris }
Henry Newsom & }
James Flewellen   }

I Confess Judgement to the Plaintiff in the Sum of Hundred and Twenty five Dollars, with interest & Cost.

                                      Charles J. McDonald, Def[ts] Att[y]

Gordon C. Coit }
    vs   } Assumpsit
John Corbett   }

I confess Judgement to the plaintiff the Sum of Two Hundred and Twenty Eight Dollars and Sixty nine Cents, with interest and Cost.

                                      Prince & Poe, Def[ts] Att[ys]

Otis Johnson }
    vs   } Assumpsit
John Corbett }

I confess Judgement to Plaintiff the Sum of Three Hundred and thirty Eight Dollars and twenty one cents, with interest and Costs.

                                      Prince & Poe, Def[ts] Att[ys]

Lay & Hendrickson }
    vs   } Assumpsit
John Corbett   }

I confess Judgement to plaintiff the Sum of Fifty Seven Dollars and fifty three cents, with interest and Costs.

                                  Prince & Poe, Def^{ts} Att^{ys}

Ambrose Baber }
    vs   } Debt
A. D. Brown   }

Judgement Confessed to the plaintiff for Thirty Six Dollars & fifty Cents, with interest and Cost.

                                    A. D. Brown

October adjourned Term 1829

Thomas Hardeman, Adm^r }
of Josephus Levi, Dec^d }
    vs   } Assumpsit
Abraham Echols &   }
Zebulon Veasey   }

We, the Jury, find for the Plaintiff the Sum of Forty nine Dollars and fifty Cents, with interest and Costs.

                                    Wm B. Cone, Form

Burton & Roffe, for the   }
use of Benjamin B. Lamar   }
Executor of Robert Burton, Dec^d }
    vs   } Debt
Mark Don^l Clark   }

                          Jury N° 1

We, the Jury, find for the defendant, with Costs of Suit.

                                      Wm B. Cone, Fm

M. Hoag & Co }
    vs   } Assumpsit
John Corbett }

I confess Judgement to plaintiff the Sum of One Hundred and twenty five Dollars & Seventy five cents, with interest and Costs.

                      Prince & Poe, Def^ts Att^ys

Allford Clopton }
    vs   } Assumpsit
William Harrison }
& Isaac Kendrick }

Judgement Confessed to the Plaintiff in the Sum of Four Hundred Dollars, with interest & Cost.

                      Campbell & Seymour, Def^ts Att^ys

John Victery }
    vs   } Assumpsit
James Pearson }
Solomond Bond }
& E. T. Bowers }

Judgement Confessed to the plaintiff for One Hundred and Sixty Three Dollars and Eighty five cents, with interest and Cost. 2 Novr 1829

                      C. B. Cole, Def^ts Att^y

October adjourned Term 1829

Ambrose Baber }
    vs   } Debt
John Holzendorf }

Judgement Confessed to the plaintiff in the Sum of Forty three Dollars and Twenty five cents, with interest and Cost.

                      C. B. Cole, for Def^t

Baber & Rodgers }
     vs   } Assumpsit
Thomas Rowland }

Judgement Confessed to the Plaintiff for the Sum of Thirty nine dollars and fifty Cents, with interest and Costs.

                            Thomas Roland

David Crockett   }
     vs   } Judgement & Stay of Execution
William Tapley & wife }

came into office the defendant, William Tapley, who wishing the stay of Execution in Terms of the Law, paid all Costs and Entered a Stay of Execution for Sixty days. And, at the same time, Came Arthur Foster, his Security, and they, the Said William Tapley, acknowledge themselves jointly and severally bound for the payment of said Judgement & all future Costs at the Expiration of Sixty days in terms of the Law. In witness whereof, they have hereunto set their hands and Seals this 2 Novr 1829.

Test. Martin Simmons, Clk   William Tapley
                                     Arthur Foster

October adjourned Term 1829

Lucius Q. C. Lamar }
     vs   } Assumpsit
James Thompson }

I confess Judgement to the plaintiff for thirty five Dollars Principal, with interest and Cost.

                            James Thompson

Wm J. Danelly & Co }
     vs   } Debt
James Thompson }

I confess Judgement to the plaintiff for One Hundred $^{44}/_{100}$ Dollars Principal, with interest & Cost.

Ja^s Thompson

Wm J. Danelly }
     vs   } Case
Elijah Cotton }

I confess Judgement to the Plaintiff for fifty Dollars principal, with interest and Costs.

E. Cotton

Ambrose Baber }
     vs   } Debt
John D. Chapman }

I confess Judgement ~~for~~ to plaintiff for fifty three Dollars & fifty Cents principal, with interest and Costs.

J. D. Chapman

James Marshall }
     vs   } Assumpsit
John Corbett & }
Keeland Tyner }

Jury N° 1

We, the Jury, find for plaintiff One Hundred & fifty Dollars principal, with interest and Cost.

Wm B. Cone, Fm

J. Freeman & Co }
     vs   } Debt
Albert G. Clopton }

I confess Judgement to the Plaintiff for One Hundred and forty one Dollars, with interest & Cost.

Albert G. Clopton

Court adjourned till tomorrow morning at 9 O'Clock Novr 2nd 1829.

R. Turner, J. I. C.
Saml B. Hunter, J. I. C.
Timothy Mathews, J. I. C.

Tuesday Morning Novr 3rd 1829 The honorable the Inferior Court met agreeable to adjournment. Present, their Honors Timothy Mathews, Reuben Turner, & Saml B. Hunter.

Ordered, that Henry G. Ross, Deputy Clerk of the Superior Court, be paid Sixteen Dollars and fifty cents for costs.

Zachariah Cowart and Saml Chambless being absent from Jury N° 1, Nathan Carter and John Hollingsworth were empanelled and sworn in their stead.

Ambrose Baber }
    vs   } Assumpsit
Samuel Gillespie }

I confess Judgement to plaintiff for thirty four Dollars, with interest and Cost.

Saml Gillespie

Ambrose Baber }
    vs   } Debt
William Cumming }

I Confess Judgement to the plaintiff for fifty five Dollars and fifty cents, with interest & Cost.

Wm Cumming

Henry F. Young, for the }
use of Saffold & Porter }
    vs   } Assumpsit
Washington Poe   }

I hereby Confess Judgement to the plaintiff for One Hundred and Seventy five dollars, with interest and Cost.

Washington Poe

October adjourned Term 1829

It appearing to the Court that Edmund C. Beard has been arrested by virtue of Two writs of Capias as Satisfaciendum issued at the instance of Harrison Smith from the Justices Court of Captain Brown's District on the Sixteenth day of April Eighteen Hundred and twenty nine. and it appearing to the Court that the said Edmund C. Beard gave bond and Security for his appearance at this Term of the Court to take the benefit of the act entitled an act for the relief of Honest Debtors, and the said Edmund C. Beard not having filed a Schedule or notified the Creditor at whose instance he was arrested in Terms of said act. And the said Edmund C. Beard having Surrendered himself in Court in discharge of said obligation, it is ordered and adjudged by the Court that the said Edmund C. Beard be imprisoned untill he shall make a full and fair disclosure of all his property, money, and effects, and untill he shall give the necessary notice to his Creditor aforesaid to be judged of by the Court.

Lewis J. Groce was empanelled and Sworn on Jury N° 1 in place of William B. Cone.

Bartholomew Harrison, for } \
the use of Robert H. Benton } \
    vs } Debt \
Lewis Foy }

I confess Judgement to plaintiff for the Sum of Sixty Eight Dollars principal, with interest and Cost.

                              Tracy & Butler, Att^{ys} for Def^t

Thomas Parker, Indorsee } \
    vs } Case \
Daniel B. Worsham }

                        Jury N° 1

We, the Jury, find for plaintiff Fifty one Dollars, with interest and Cost.

                                   Wm B. Cone, F^m

October adjourned Term 1829

William Moore, for the }
use of William B. Cone }
     vs   } Debt
Young Johnston   }

                    Jury N° 1

We, the Jury, find for the Plaintiff Forty One Dollars and Eighteen and three fourth Cents, with interest and Cost.

                    N. Wagner, F^{m}

Benjamin B. Lamar, Executor }
of Robert Burton, Dec^{d} }
     vs   } Assumpsit
John Loving   }

I confess Judgement to the plaintiff for One Hundred $^{15}/_{100}$ Dollars principal, with interest and Cost.

                  C. B. Cole, Def^{ts} Att^{y}

Daniel Smith   }
     vs   } Assumpsit
John M. Shelman }

I hereby Confess Judgement to the plaintiff in the Sum of Seventy five Dollars, with interest & Cost.

                  Jn° M. Shelman

John Warren   }
     vs   } Assumpsit
Nicholas ~~Wagner~~ }
    Childers }

I hereby Confess Judgement to the Plaintiff in the Sum of Seventy four Dollars ~~& Eighty one Cents~~, with interest and Cost.

                  N. Childers

James C. Watkins}
    vs   } Debt
Nicholas Childers}

I hereby Confess Judgement to Plaintiff in the Sum of four Hundred and Eighty six Dollars, with interest and Costs.

                        N. Childers

Wm B. Cone took his seat on Petit Jury N° 1 in place of Lewis J. Groce.

October adjourned Term 1829

Jury N° 2

1. David Kidd
2. Thomas Sacrae
3. Zachariah Cowart
4. Lewis Collins
5. John Bryan
6. James Gamble

7. Torrance C. Conner
8. John Flowers
9. ~~Richard Lee~~
    George Powell
10. ~~Thomas Mussellwhite~~
    Samuel Chambless
11. John Smith
12. John Briggs

L. Newcomb }
    vs   } Debt
A. McGregor }

I Confess Judgement to the Plaintiff for Forty Dollars & thirteen Cents principal, with interest and Costs.

                        Alex^a McGregor

Alexander McGregor having been the Surety in a Bond taken under the provisions of the Honest Debtors act for the appearance of Christopher Lynch at this Court to answer upon a Casa in which Nicholas Wagner is plaintiff. And the said Alexander McGregor now producing the body of the said Lynch in Court. It is ordered that the said Lynch be taken into the Custody of the Sheriff. And that the said McGregor be and he is hereby discharged from his Bond.

Joshua Jordan }
    vs } Assumpsit
Josiah H. Carter }
& Seaborn Jones }

                    Jury N° 2

We, the Jury, find for Plaintiff the Sum of Thirty five Dollars, with interest & Cost.

                                    John Bryan, Form

Hubbard Williams, Indorsee }
    vs } Case
Benjamin Russell }

                    Jury N° 2

We, the Jury, find for the plaintiff fifty One Dollars, with interest and Costs.

                                    John Bryan, Form

October adjourned Term 1829

Arthur Ginn }
    vs } Case
James P. Ward }
Richard W. Ward }
& Alex^a D. Brown }

                    Jury N° 2

We, the Jury, find for the Plaintiff Thirty Six $^{6\frac{1}{4}}/_{100}$ Dollars principal, with interest and Costs.

                                    John Bryan, Foreman

William Belknap }
    vs } Assumpsit
Isabella Clark }

Jury N° 1

We, the Jury, find for the Plaintiff fifty three Dollars.

Wm B. Cone, F^m

Alexander D. Brown, one of the Jury, being Called & He Not appearing, ordered that he be fined in the Sum of five dollars for his Non attendance.

James Freeman }
    vs   } Debt
Nicholas Childers }
& William F. Scott }

Jury N° 2

We, the Jury, find for the plaintiff the Sum of Three Hundred & thirty Seven dollars, With interest & Cost.

James Bryan, forman

Alex McGregor }
    vs   } Assumpsit
James Flewellen }

Jury N° 1

We, the Jury, find for the plaintiff The Sum of Seventy dollars, With interest & Cost. Oct Term 1829

Wm B. Cone, forman

Alex McGregor }
    vs   } Assumpsit
Lewis Foy }

I Confess Judgement to plaintiff for the plaintiff for the Sum of Seventy dollars, With Interest & Cost. Oct Term 1829

Tracy & Butler, def^t Att^{ys}

———

<u>October adjourned Term 1829</u>

Benjamin Pickart }
    vs   } Assumpsit
David Dalmeyda }

I Confess Judgement To plaintiff for One hundred and Eight Dollars and Nine Cents, With interest & Cost.

                        Tracy & Butler, Att^{ys} for Def^t

Arther Foster, bearer }
    vs   } Assumpsit
John Scott }

I Confess judment To plaintiff for forty Dollars, With interest & Cost.

                        William Scott

Napier, Munroe & C° }
    vs   } Debt
James Alston }

                Jury N° 1

We, the jury, find for the plaintiff one hundred dollars, With interest & Cost.

                        Wm B. Cone, forman

William B. Cone }
    vs   } Case
Henry Milburn & }
Charles J. McDonald }

We Confess judgment To the plaintiff in the Sum of One hundred & twenty dollars, With interest & Cost, reserving the right of Appeal.

                        Charles J. McDonald
                        for Self & att^y for Milburn

John Stokes }
    vs   } Debt
T. C. Conner }

jury Nº 1

We, the jury, find for the plaintiff fifty Eight Dollars and fifty Cents, With interest & Cost.

Wm B. Cone, forman

Thomas King }
    vs   } Bail in Bibb Inferior Court
David Burks }

James H. Rodgers, Bail of David Burks in the Above Case, brings Said Burks into open Court & Surrenders Him to the Court & prays his Bond May be Canceled.

October adjourned Term 1829

Bank of Darien   }
    vs   } Debt
A. G. Clopton &   }
A. Baber, adm^{rs}   }
of Joseph Morgan, dec^d}
E. Wimberly   }
Roger Lawson &   }
W. W. Williamson }

jury Nº 2

We, the jury, find for the defendants Cost of Suit.

Jnº Bryan, forman

The Court adjourned till tomorrow Morning at 9 O'clock.

R. Turner, J. I. C.
Timothy Mathews, J. I. C.
Saml B. Hunter, J. I. C.

Wednesday Morning November 4th 1829 The honorable The Inferior Court in & for Bibb County Meet agreeable to adjournment.

Present, the honors   Timothy Mathews }
                                        Samuel B. Hunter } J. I. C.
                                        Reubin Turner   }

Thomas Howard being Called and do Not Appear as a Juror, ordered that he be fined in the Sum of five dollars.

Edmund C. Beard having been brought into Court Upon a Writ of Habeas Corpus and that the Jailor having Returned that he detained him in Custody by Virtue of an order of this Court remanding him to Jail for failing To Comply With the provisions of the Honest Debtors Act. The Court, after hearing argument, Ordered the Said Edmund C. Beard to be remitted to the Common jail.

October adjourned Term 1829

William Lanford   }
      vs   } Debt
Alexander Merrewether }

I Confess judment to the Plaintiff the Sum of five Hundred & Ninety Six dollars & Sixty Six Cents, With interest & Cost.

                                              Prince & Poe, deft attys

Nathan C. Munroe }
      vs   } Case
James Alston   }

Judgment Confessed to The plaintiff for one hundred and Seventy dollars, with interest & Cost.

                                              C. J. McDonald, Deft atty

Mortimer R. Wallis   }
      vs   } Assumpsit
Richmond Bosworth }
Williamson Mims &   }
Michael W. Perry   }

Jury Nº 1

We, the jury, find for the Plaintiff three hundred dollars, with interest & Cost.

Wm B. Cone, forman

Nathan C. Munroe }
     vs   } Case
James W. Alston }

Judgment Confessed to the plaintiff for One hundred & Seventy Dollars, With interest & Cost.

Charles J. McDonald, def^{ts} att^y

Walter L. Campbell }
     vs   } Assumpsit
Stephen Manard }

Jury Nº 1

We, the Jury, find for plaintiff The Sum of Ninety five Dollars, with interest & Cost.

Wm B. Cone, forman

Anson Kimberly }
     vs   } Assumpsit
James W. Alston }
& Wiley Dorman]

Jury Nº 1

We, the jury, find for plaintiff The Sum of three hundred & fifty Dollars, With interest & Cost of Suit & protest.

Wm B. Cone, forman

October adjourned Term 1829

Lewis Fitch }
    vs   } Case
Young Johnston & }
William Cumming }

Jury N° 1

We, the Jury, find for the plaintiff Sixty Dollars principal, With interest & Cost.

Wm B. Cone, forman

Anson Kimberly }
    vs   } Assumpsit
James W. Alston }

I hereby Confess judgment to the plaintiff in the Sum of Eighty Dollars, with interest & Cost.

Charles J. McDonald, Def^{ts} att^y

Smith & Childers, bearer }
    vs   } Case
Thomas Howard }

I Confess judgment To the plaintiff for the Sum of thirty five dollars, with interest & Cost.

Thomas Howard

Charles Woodruff }
    vs   } Case
Joshua Jordan }

Jury N° 1

We, the Jury, find for the plaintiff One hundred and Ninety three dollars $^{84}/_{100}$ principal, with interest & Cost.

Wm B. Cone, forman

Thomas Napier }
    vs   } Case
Thomas Howard }

I Confess judgment to The plaintiff in the Sum of Five hundred and Sixty two Dollars & thirty four Cents Principal, with interest & Cost.

$$\text{Thomas Howard}$$

John M. Shelman }
    vs   } Debt
Elam Alexander }

Judgment Confessed to The the plaintiff for forty one Dollars, With interest & Cost.

$$\text{Campbell \& Seymour, Def}^{t}\text{ att}^{ys}$$

October adjourned Term 1829

Oliver Sage, for the use }
    vs   } Debt
John Corbett   }

I Confess judgment to the plaintiff to the for one hundred & twenty two $^{12}/_{100}$ Dollars principal, with Interest & Cost.

$$\text{Prince \& Poe, def}^{t}\text{ att}^{ys}$$

Henry Crew }
    vs   } Assumpsit for Rent
James Willson }

Jury N° 1

We, the Jury, find for the Defendant, with Cost of Suit.

$$\text{W}^{m}\text{ B. Cone, F}^{m}$$

J. W. Marshall }
    vs   } Case
M. D. J. Slade }

I Confess Judgement to the Plaintiff for One Hundred and fifty Dollars principal, with interest and Cost, with right of appeal.

Prince & Poe, Def^s Att^y

Edward W. Wright }
    vs   } Debt
James Langford }

Jury N° 2

We, the Jury, find for the plaintiff Forty One Dollars principal, with interest and Cost.

John Bryan, Form

Philip Powledge & }
Gideon Powledge }
    vs   } Debt
Samuel Gillespie }

Judgement Confessed to the plaintiff for forty five Dollars and twenty cents, with interest and Cost, reserving the right of appeal.

Campbell & Seymour, Def^s Att^{ys}

Ralston & Jones }
    vs   } Debt
Philip Cook   }

Jury N° 2

We, the Jury, find for the plaintiff Two hundred and Sixty two Dollars and twenty cents principal, with interest & Cost.

John Bryan, form

<u>October adjourned Term 1829</u>

Executors of Baldwin Fluker, Dec^d }
           vs   } Assumpsit
Hardeman Owen   }

Jury 2

We, the Jury, find for Plaintiffs the Sum of Sixty five Dollars, with interest & Cost.

John Bryan, Foreman

The Bank of Macon }
    vs   } Assumpsit
Thomas Lundy   }

I Confess Judgement to the Plaintiff for Eleven Hundred and thirty four Dollars, with interest & Cost.

Thomas Lundy

John S. Childers }
    vs   } Debt
Lewis Foy   }

I Confess Judgement to the Plaintiff for Fifty five Dollars and fourteen Cents, with interest & Cost.

Tracy & Butler, Def[ts] Att[ys]

David Crocket   }
    vs   } Debt
Winefred King, formerly }
now Winefred Tapley   }
& William Tapley   }

I Confess Judgement to the plaintiff for Six Hundred Dollars, with interest and Costs of Suit.

William Tapley

John S. Childers   }
    vs   } Debt
Jeffry E. Thompson }

I confess Judgement to plaintiff for Sixty five Dollars & fifteen Cents, with interest & Cost.

J. E. Thompson

John S. Childers, bearer }
       vs   }
Moreland & Harrison }
& Nimrod W. Long }

[blank]

October adjourned Term 1829

Elias Bliss, bearer }
      vs   } Case
Redden Rutland }

I confess Judgement to Plaintiff for Two Hundred and ninety Dollars, with interest and Cost.

                                    Redden Rutland

Roger Macarthy }
      vs   } Fifa in Bibb Inferior Court
James Thompson }

It appearing to the Court that an affidavit of Illegality has been filed & returned to this Court of the above Execution and it appearing to the Court that the said affidavit has been lost. It is ordered that a copy be established in lieu thereof instanter.

The Bank of Macon }
      vs   } Assumpsit
Rice Durrett }

I hereby Confess Judgement to the Plaintiff for Eleven Hundred and thirty four Dollars principal, with interest and Cost. October Term 1829

                                    R. Durrett

Martin Simmons }
      vs   } Case
P. R. Clements }
A. D. Brown }

Jury Nº 1

We, the Jury, find for Plaintiff Thirty one 87½ Dollars principal, with interest & Cost.

Wm B. Cone, F^m

Arthur Ginn   }
    vs   } Case
P. R. Clements   }
A. D. Brown   }

Jury Nº 1

We, the Jury, find for the Plaintiff Eighty Dollars principal, with interest and Cost.

Wm B. Cone, F^m

October adjourned Term 1829

Andrew Cumming   }
    vs   } Debt
Alexander McDonald }

I Confess Judgement to the Plaintiff for thirty one Dollars, with interest and Cost.

Charles J. McDonald, Def^{ts} Att^y

John S. Childers, bearer }
    vs   } Case
Tuttle H. Moreland   }
William Harrison &   }
Nimrod W. Long   }

Settled.

John S. Childers }
    vs   } Debt
Thomas Howard   }

I confess Judgement to the Plaintiff for the Sum of Seventy four Dollars Principal, with interest and October Term 1829.

Thomas Howard

Thomas Napier }
    vs   } Debt
Enoch Byne & }
Bullock & Wells }

Jury N° 1

We, the Jury, find for the Plaintiff against Enoch Byne & Nicholas W. Wells, the Surviving defendants, the Sum of One Hundred & Sixty Seven Dollars Eighty Eight Cents, with interest and Costs.

Wm B. Cone, F^m

Thomas Napier }
    vs   } Case
Samuel Tompkins }

Jury N° 1

We, the Jury, find for the Plaintiff the Sum of Four Hundred Dollars, with interest & Costs.

Wm B. Cone, F^m

<u>October adjourned Term 1829</u>

James Martin }
    vs   } Assumpsit
Reason D. Beall }

I confess Judgment to the Plaintiff in the Sum of Five Hundred and Twenty three Dollars, with Costs of Suit, reserving the right of appeal.

Prince & Poe, Def^{ts} Att^y

Thomas King }
    vs   } Assumpsit
David Burks }

I Confess Judgement to Plaintiff the Sum of One Hundred Dollars, with interest and Cost, reserving the right of appeal.

       David Burks

E. E. Slade   }
  vs   } Debt
A. R. Woodson }

Judgement Confessed to the Plaintiff for Ninety Dollars, with interest and Costs.

      Albert G. Clopton, Def[ts] Att[y]

The Bank of Darien }
  vs   } Debt
Albert G. Clopton & }
Ambrose Baber, Adm[rs] }
of Joseph Morgan & }
Ezekiel Wimberly   }
Benjamin Bryan &   }
James Wimberly   }

We confess Judgement for Defendant, with right of Appeal.

      Henry G. Lamar, Plff[s] Att[y]

John S. Childers }
  vs   } Debt
Moreland & Harrison }

Judgement Confessed to the Plaintiff for Forty nine Dollars, with interest & Cost.

      Albert G. Clopton, Att[y]
      for W[m] Harrison, Survivor

<u>October adjourned Term 1829</u>

Roger McCarthy }
  vs   } Affidavit of Illegality &c
James Thompson }

Upon hearing Evidence and Argument on the above affidavit, the Court order it to be dismissed & that the Execution proceed.

Georgia }
Bibb County } To the Justices of the Inferior Court of said County

The petition of William Adams, a free man of Colour residing in said County, prays that he may have Jacob Shotwell, of said County, appointed his Guardian according to the Laws of said State in Such Cases made and provided.

Albert G. Clopton, Att°
for Williams Adams

William Adams having applied to this Court to have a Guardian appointed under the laws of this State. It is ordered that Jacob Shotwell, he having consented in writing to be come his Guardian, be and is hereby appointed his Guardian, with all the rights, priviledges, and liabilities imposed by the Statute ~~Laws~~ of this State and that the said Shotwell give bond and security for the faithful Execution of his trust in the Sum of five Hundred Dollars.

James Douglass having failed to appear on ~~Pet~~ Jury N° 1, Clement Echols was sworn & empanelled in his Stead.

James Douglass being Called and he not appearing as a Juror. Ordered that he be fined the Sum of Five Dollars.

<u>October adjourned Term 1829</u>

Thomas King }
    vs   } Assumpsit
David Burks }

Jury N° 1

We, the Jury, find for the Plaintiff in the Sum of Forty two Dollars, with interest and Costs.

Wm B. Cone, F^m

James R. Turner }
    vs   } Debt
Sir James Pittman }

Jury N° 1

We, the Jury, find for the Plaintiff in the Sum of Sixty dollars, with interest and Costs.

Wm B. Cone, F^m

Smith & Wright }
    vs   } Debt
Bailey Goddard }

Jury N° 1

We, the Jury, find for the Plaintiff the Sum of three Hundred and Sixty five Dollars and thirteen Cents, with interest and Cost.

Wm B. Cone, F^m

Henry B. Hill }
    vs   } 5 Casas from Justices' Court
Peter M. Curry }

The Same }
    vs   } 2 Casas from Justices' Court
Peter M. Curry & }
John Hollingsworth }

Benjamin Russell, the Security for the appearance of Peter M. Curry under the Insolvent Debtors act, having brought the said Curry into Court and delivered him into the hands of the Sheriff. It is ordered that the said Benjamin Russell be discharged and that an exonater be entered on the Bond.

October adjourned Term 1829

Goddard & Langdon }
    vs } Assumpsit
George H. Bryan }
& Solomon Groce }

Jury N° 1

We, the Jury, find for Plaintiff the Sum of Two Hundred and Fifty three Dollars and fifty Cents, with interest and Costs.

Wm B. Cone, F^m

Rufus K. Evans }
    vs } Assumpsit
Isaiah E. Thompson }

Jury N° 2

We, the Jury, find for the plaintiff Fifty nine Dollars Seventeen and a half Cents, with interest from the Seventh day of February 1829.

John Bryan, Foreman

Joel Rushin }
    vs } Fifa from Inferior Court
Mary Minor & }
Thomas Blancet }

It appearing to the Court that the above fifa has been paid off and that the Sheriff has failed to make his return, it is ordered that the Sheriff shew Cause why he does not return said fifa, with his actings and doings thereon.

Benjamin F. Harris, bearer }
    vs } Assumpsit
John D. Chapman & }
Alexander McGregor }

Confess Judgement to the plaintiffs for Eight Hundred and Ninety Seven $^{89}/_{100}$ Dollars, with interest and cost, reserving right of Appeal.

Campbell & Seymour, Def^{ts} Att^y

Kimberly & Chisholm }
    vs   } Assumpsit
Joshua Jordan }

Jury N° 2

We, the Jury, find for Plaintiff the Sum of Two Hundred and fifty Seven Dollars and thirty Seven Cents, with interest and Cost.

John Bryan, Form

October adjourned Term 1829

Benjamin W. Rodgers }
    vs   } Assumpsit
Philip Cook }

Jury N° 2

We, the Jury, find for Plaintiff the Sum of One Hundred and ninety Seven Dollars, with interest and Costs.

John Bryan, Foreman

Hungerford & Stoddard }
    vs   } Assumpsit
Philip Cook }

Jury N° 2

We, the Jury, find for Plaintiff the Sum of One Hundred and fifty Seven dollars and Sixty four cents, with interest and Costs of Suit.

John Bryan, Form

John Redding & C° }
    vs   } Debt
Robert Warren }

Jury N° 2

We, the Jury, find for Plaintiffs the Sum of Fifty five Dollars, with interest and Costs.

John Bryan, foreman

Ordered that John C. Caldwell, together with his Bail, be discharged from the Custody of the Constable and Exonerated from all further proceedings, upon The ground that the Casa which arrested the Said John C. Caldwell is fatally defective, because the Casa Was Made returnable to 716 district Magistrates Court, when it ought to have been Made returnable to the 513 district from whence it Issued.

L. Q. C. Lamar }
     vs   } assumpsit
Solomon Groce }

I Confess judgment to the plaintiff for Sixty dollars principal, with interest & Cost, & right of appeal.

Charles J. McDonald, Def^t Att^y

October adjourned Term 1829

The Court adjourned till tomorrow Morning 9 O'clock.

R. Turner, J. I. C.
Timothy Mathews, J. I. C.
Saml B. Hunter, J. I. C.

Thursday Morning November 5th 1829

The honorable the Inferior Court in and for the County of Bibb Meet agreeable to adjournment.

Present, their honors   Timothy Mathews }
                                       Reubin Turner   } J. I. C.
                                         Samuel B. Hunter }

It is ordered that the fine imposed on John Hollingworth at the last term of this Court be and the Same is hereby Remitted and that further ordered that the Execution issued against him be Cancelled.

Henry Mitchel }
    vs } Case
Jesse L. Owens, adm^r }
of Jesse Robenett, Dec^d }

Jury N° 1

We, the Jury, find for the plaintiff five hundred Thirty three Dollars & fifty Cents.

Wm B. Cone, foreman

Spencer Riley }
    vs } Case &c
James H. Rodgers }

Jury N° 1

We, the Jury, find for the plaintiff Fifty Six dollars & forty five cents, with interest and Cost of suit.

Wm B. Cone, F^m

Henry S. Cutler }
    vs } Assumpsit
John T. Lamar }

I Confess Judgement to the Plaintiff for two Hundred and forty three Dollars $^{97}/_{100}$, with right of appeal.

John T. Lamar by his
Att^{ys} Tracy & Butler

<u>October adjourned Term 1829</u>

Henry S. Cutler, Survivor &c }
    vs } Assumpsit
John T. Lamar }

I Confess Judgement to the Plaintiff for Sixty Eight $^{47}/_{100}$ Dollars, with right of appeal.

John T. Lamar by his
Att^{ys} Tracy & Butler

Ordered by the Court that the Several fines imposed upon diferent individuals acting as Jurors during this Term be and they are hereby remitted.

James H. Rodgers }
  vs   } Casa
James Gamble }

A rule nisi having been taken against the Sheriff requiring him to Shew Cause why he should not pay to the plaintiff the amount of principal, interest, and Costs on the above Casa and no Sufficient Cause being Shewn, it is ordered that the said Sheriff pay over to the said Plaintiff the amount of principal, interest, and Costs on said Casa.

James J. Earby for the }
use of William Tapley }
  vs   } Casa from 716 Dis^t Georgia Militia
Arthur Sherrod   }

It appearing to the Court from the return of the officer that the above defendant was taken upon the said Casa, and that said officer (to wit, George Vigal) has taken an insufficient bond for the release of the said Defendant from his Custody, Conditioned for said Defendant's appearance at this time of our Court, & Said Defendant not appearing. It is ordered that said George Vigal ~~shew cause by tomorrow morning why he should not~~ pay the amount of plaintiff's Debt.

October adjourned Term 1829

Kimberly & Chisholm }
  vs   } Casa from Justices' Court and Bond to take
Hiram Mann &   } the benefit of Insolvent Debtors act
Luke Ross, Security   }

It appearing to the Court that Hiram Mann is bound to appear at this Court to take the benefit of the act for the relief of Honest Debtors, and that he has failed to return a Schedule of his property and notify his Creditors in terms of the Law, and his Security, Luke Ross, having failed to Surrender his body into open Court. On motion, it is ordered by the Court that the plaintiffs do enter up Judgement against the said Hiram Mann and his Security, Luke Ross, for the amount of said Casa, with interest and Cost.

James Tobin }
    vs } Casa from Justices' Court &
Francis Willey, principal & } Bond to take the benefit of
Alexander McGregor, Security } Insolvent Debtors act

It appearing to the Court that Francis Willey is bound to appear at this Court to take the benefit of the act for the relief of Honest Debtors, and that he has failed to return a Schedule of his property and notify his Creditors in terms of the Law. And his Security, Alexander McGregor having failed to Surrender his body into Court. On motion, it is ordered by the Court that the plaintiff do enter up Judgement against the said Willey and his Security, McGregor, for the amount of said Casa, with interest and Cost.

October adjourned Term 1829

David Ralston }
    vs } Garnishment
William J. Danelly }
I. B. Rowland }
Keeland Tyner & }
Joseph Washburn }

David Ralston }
    vs } Garnishment
Mortimer R. Wallis }

The Garnishees having failed at this term of the Court to answer on said Garnishment. It is ordered by the Court that they come in and answer at the next Term of this Court, in default of being Considered in Contempt.

James H. Killen }
    vs   } Four Casas from the Justices' Court
John Philpot   } of 516 District of Georgia Militia

The defendant, John Philpot, having been arrested under the above Casas and having given bond with William Cumming, Security for his appearance at this Court to take the benefit of the act for the relief of honest debtors, and the said Philpot having failed to Comply with the provisions of said act. It is therefore adjudged and ordered that the plaintiff do recover of said John Philpot & William Cumming, his Security, the Sum of One Hundred and twenty dollars principal, and the further sum twenty three dollars and Sixty Eight Cents interest, and the further Sum of [blank] for his Costs and Charges in this behalf laid out and expended.

October adjourned Term 1829

James H. Killan }
    vs   } Four Casas from the 564th district
John Philpot   } Georgia Militia

The defendant, John Philpot, having been Arrested Under the above Cases and having bond with William Cumming, Security for his appearance at this Court to Take the benefit of the act for the relief of Honest Debtors act, and the said Philpot having to Comply with the provisions of said act. It is therefore adjudged and ordered that the plaintiff do recover of Said John Philpot & William Cumming, his Security, The Sum of One Hundred and twenty dollars principal, & The further sum of twenty three dollars & Sixty Eight Cents for his interest, & also the further Sum of [blank] for his Cost & Charges in this Behalf laid out and Expended.

The Court adjourned till Saturday Morning the 7th at 9 O'clock.

                              Timothy Mathews, J. I. C.
                              R. Turner, J. I. C.
                              Saml B. Hunter, J. I. C.

Henry Mitchell }
    vs } Case & Judgment
Jessee L. owens, adm^r }
of Jessee Robinett }

Came into office Jessee L. Owens, the defendant in the above Case, who being disatisfied With the Verdict of the Jury, paid the Cost and Entered and appeal, Who Acknowledge himself firmly bound for the true Eventual Condemnation Money according to the Statute in Such Case Made & provided. Given under My hand & Seal this 7th day of November 1829.

M. Simmons, Clk   J. L. Owens, adm^r of the
                                            Estate of J. Robinett

---

October adjourned Term 1829

H. S. Cutler }
   vs } Assumpsit & Judgment
J. T. Lamar }

Came into office John T. Lamar, The defendant in the above Case, By his attorney David B. Butler, Who being disatisfied with the verdict, paid the Cost and Entered an appeal, also, at the Same time, Came Charles A. Higgins, the Security on the appeal, Who both acknowledged themselves jointly & Severally bound for the True payment of the Eventual Condemnation Money according to the Statute in Such Case Made and Provided. Given under our hands & Seals this 7th day of November 1829.

Test. M. Simmons, Clk   John T. Lamar
                                        by his Attorney at Law
                                        D. B. Butler
                                        C. A. Higgins

H. S. Cutler, Survivor }
    vs } Assumpsit & Judgment
John T. Lamar }

Came into office David B. Butler, attorney for John T. Lamar, The defendant in the above Case, Who being Disatisfied with the verdict, paid the Cost and Entered an appeal, also, at the Same time, Came

Charles A. Higgins, the Security on the appeal, Who Both acknowledged themselves jointly & Severally bound for the true payment of the Eventual Condemnation Money According to the Statute in Such Case Made & Provided. Given under our hands & Seals this 7th day of November 1829.

Test. M. Simmons, Clk   John T. Lamar
                              by his Attorney at Law
                              D. B. Butler
                              C. A. Higgins

October Adjourned Term 1829

The Honorable the Inferior Court in and for the County of Bibb Meet this day agreeable to adjournment Monday Morning 9th November 1829. Present, Reubin Turner, J. I. C., Young Johnston, D. Shff.

Test. Martin Simmons, Clk

The Court then adjourned untill Thursday Morning the 12th at 8 O'clock.

John S. Childers }
       vs   } Debt & Judgment
Thomas Howard   }

Came into office Thomas Howard, the Defendant in the Above Case, Who being disatisfied With the Verdict, paid the Cost and Entered a Stay of Execution. Also, at the Same time, Came Solomon D. Chapman, his Security on the Stay of Execution, who both Acknowledged themselves jointly and Severally bound for the True payment of the Eventual Condemnation Money According to the Statute in Such Case Made and provided. Given under our hands & Seals this 9th day of November 1829.

Test. Martin Simmons, Clk   Thos Howard
                                  S. D. Chapman

W. J. Danelly & Co }
        vs   } Judgment & Stay of Execution
E. Cotton   }

Came into office the defendant, Elijah Cotton, Who Wishing the Stay of Execution in Terms of the Law, paid all Cost and Entered a Stay of

Execution for Sixty days, and, at the Same time, Came William Finch, his Security, and they, the Said Elijah Cotton & William Finch, Acknowledged themselves jointly & Severally bound for the payment of Said judgment & all further Cost at the Expiration of Sixty days in Terms of the Law. In Witness Whereof, they have

---

October Adjourned Term 1829

hereunto Set their hands & seals this 9th day of November 1829.

Test. M. Simmons, Clk   E. Cotton
                                         William X Finch, his mark

James Martin   }   Assumpsit & Verdict for the plaintiff for five
      vs   }   hundred & twenty three Dollars, With
Reason D. Beall }   interest & Cost

The Defendant, Reason D. Beall, being Disatisfied with the Verdict of the Jury rendered in the above Cause, and having paid All Costs, and demanded an appeal, Brings Eason Smith and tenders him as his Security, and they, the Said Reason D. Beall & Eason Smith, acknowledge themselves jointly & Severally Bound to James Martin, the plaintiff, for the payment of The Eventual Condemnation Money in Said Cause. In Testamony Whereof, they have hereunto Set their hands & Seals This 9th day of November 1829.

Test. Martin Simmons, Clk   Ren D. Bealle
                                         Eason Smith

Bank of Darien   }
      vs   }   Debt & Verdict for Defendant
A. G. Clopton   }   Cost thirteen Dollars &
Ambrose Baber, adm^{rs} }   twelve & a half Cents
of Joseph Morgan, dec^d }
E. Wimberly   }
Roger Lawson   }
& W. W. Williamson   }

the plaintiff, Being disatisfied With The Verdict of the jury Rendered in the above Case, paid all Cost and demanded an appeal, brings Harrison Smith & tenders him as his Security, and they, the Said Bank of Darien, by their attorney, Charles J. McDonald, and Harrison Smith, acknowledge themselves jointly and Severally bound to A. G. Clopton, Ambrose Baber, adm^r of Joseph Morgan, dec^d, E. Wimberly, Roger Lawson, & W. W. Williamson, the defendants, for the payment of the Eventual

---

<u>October adjourned Term 1829</u>

Condemnation Money in Said Cause, in testamony Whereof, they have Set their hands & Seals this 10th Day of November 1829.

Test. M. Simmons, Clk   Bank of Darien
            by their attorney at Law
            Charles J. McDonald
            Harrison Smith

Bank of Darien   }
  vs   } Debt & Verdict for defendant
Albert G. Clopton & } for eleven dollars and
Ambrose Baber, adm^{rs} } fifty Cents Cost
of Joseph Morgan, dec^d }
Ezekiel Wimberly }
Benjamin Bryan & }
James Wimberly

The plaintiff, being disatisfied With the Verdict in the Above Cause, and having paid all Cost and demanded an appeal, Brings Scott Cray and tenders him as his Security. And they, the Said Bank of Darien, by their attorney in fact, Robert Collins, and Scott Cray, Acknowledge themselves jointly & Severally Bound to Albert G. Clopton & Ambrose Baber, adm^{rs} of Joseph Morgan, dec^d, Ezekiel Wimberly, Benjamin Bryan, & James Wimberly, the defendants, for the true payment of the Eventual Condemnation Money in Said Cause. In Testimony Whereof, they have hereunto Set their hands & Seals this 10th day of November 1829.

Test. M. Simmons, Clk   Robt Collins
               Scott Cray

Thursday Morning November 12th 1829, The honorable The the Inferior Court in and for the County of Bibb meet this day agreeable to adjournment.

Present, Their honors   Timothy Mathews }
           Samuel B. Hunter } J. I. C.
           Reubin Turner }

October adjourned Term 1829

Bullock & Wells   }
  vs   } fifa from Bibb Inferior Court
A. G. Clopton &   }
Ambrose Baber, adm^{rs} }
of Joseph Morgan, dec^d }

the defendant in in the above Case, Having filed an affidavit of illegality to the Judgment, did Not pursue the Verdict and that Judgment Was entered up and Execution issued against The proper goods of their intestate and an agreement Having taken place between plaintiff and defendants that Said judgment be amended. It is ordered that Said Judgment & fifa be amended So as to Make the Same operative.

Ordered that Ralph O. Howard be paid four Dollars for Services as Bailiff to the Court.

Ordered that Henry B. Hill be paid Eleven Dollars and fifty Cents, the am^t of his bill as Bailiff and Guarding Negro Man Luke & Collins.

Ordered that William Cumming, over Seer of the Poor of Said County, be paid One hundred and Ten Dollars & Eighty One Cents, it being in full of his Account against the County as over Seer.

Ordered that Polhill & Cole be paid twenty Dollars, it Being in full for attending to the prosecution on the part of the State against a Negro Man Collins for Burglary.

Ordered that Spencer Riley be paid two hundred & Sixteen Dollars and Thirty four cents, it being in full of his account rendered to this date.

October Term 1829

Ordered, that Edwin E. Slade be paid thirteen Dollars, it being in full of his Account for attending to Luke While in jail.

Ordered that Neal Moses be paid [blank] it being the Neet proceeds of Estray Cattle Sold and Claimed by him According To Law.

The following Jury Were drawn to Serve at April Term 1830, to wit.

1. George Whitehead
2. John Roberts
3. Peter McCarthy
4. John Watson
5. William Strougher
6. William Johnson
7. Enoch Greene
8. Nathan Parker
9. William Harrilson
10. James Busby
11. William Bowden
12. Rufus K. Evans
13. Benjamin Smith
14. Benjamin Grubbs
15. Ellerson Summerlin
16. Stephen Atkison
17. Van Swearingin
18. Richard Jones
19. William Brinkley
20. Hezekiah Wattons
21. George Nothern
22. Daniel Henderson
23. John Wilson
24. James L. Eaton
25. John Reneid
26. Green Whatley
27. Oliver A. Stoors
28. Wade Harris
29. Timothy Reneid
30. Joseph H. Lee
31. Joshua Johnson
32. Davis B. Braswell
33. Solomon D. Chapman
34. Asa E. Earnest
35. Lewis Foy
36. Hampton B. Watts

The Court then adjourned untill Court in Course.

Timothy Mathews, J. I. C.
Luke Ross, J. I. C.
Saml B. Hunter, J. I. C.

October adjourned Term 1829

William BelKnap } Assumpsit & Verdict for the plaintiff
    vs   } for fifty three dollars & Cost
Isabella Clark   } thirteen dollars & Seven Cents

the defendant, being disatisfied with the verdict of the jury rendered in the above Case, And having paid all Cost and demanded an appeal, brings Scott Cray and tenders him as her Security, and the Said Isabella Clark, Scott Cray acknowledge themselves jointly and Severally bound To William BelKnap, the plaintiff, for the payment of the Eventual Condemnation Money in Said Cause. In testamony Whereof, they have hereunto Set their hands and Seals this 14th day of November 1829.

Test. M. Simmons, Clk   Isabella Clark
                                Scott Cray

L. Q. C. Lamar } assumpsit & verdict for the
     vs   } plaintiff for Sixty dollars principal
Solomon Groce   } with interest & Cost

The defendant, being disatisfied With the Verdict in the above Cause, and having paid all Cost & Demanded an appeal, brings Lewis J. Groce and tenders Him as Security, and they, the Said Solomon Groce & Lewis J. Groce, acknowledge themselves jointly & Severally bound To Lucius Q. C. Lamar, the plaintiff, for the payment of the Eventual Condemnation Money in Said Cause. In testamony Whereof, they have hereunto Set Their hands & Seals this 16th day of November 1829.

Test. M. Simmons, Clk   S. Groce
                                Lewis J. Groce

Thomas Napier   }
     vs   } Casa & Verdict for the plaintiff
William P. Harris   } for one hundred and twenty five Dollars
Henry Newsome   } With interest and Cost
& James Flewellen   }

The defendant, Being disatisfied With the Verdict, Paid all Cost and Entered a Stay of Execution of Sixty days, also at the Same time, Came William Wordsworth, his Security on the Stay, Who both acknowledge themselves jointly and Severally Bound for the true payment of the Eventual Condemnation Money in Such Case Made and provided. Given under our hands and Seals This 16th day of November 1829.

Test. M. Simmons, Clk   W. P. Harris
                                William Wordsworth

William Hogan } Debt & Verdict for the plaintiff
    vs } for thirty five Dollars
Charlton Thompson } With interest & Cost

the Defendant, Being disatisfied With the Verdict of the jury Rendered in the above Cause, and having paid All Cost and demanded an Appeal, brings James Thompson and tenders him as his Security, and they, The Said Charlton Thompson, Acknowledge themselves Jointly & Severally bound to William Hogan, the Plaintiff, for the payment of the eventual Condemnation Money in Said Cause. In Witness Whereof, they have Hereunto Set their hands & Seals this the 16th day of November 1829.

                              C. Thompson
                              James Thompson

Spencer Riley } Case & Verdict for the plaintiff
    vs } for fifty Six Dollars and
James H. Rodgers } forty five Cents, with Cost

The defendant, being disatisfied With the Verdict of the Jury rendered in the above Cause, and having paid all Cost and demanded an appeal, brings William Harris and tenders him as his Security, and They, the Said James H. Rodgers and William Harris, acknowledge themselves jointly and Severally bound To Spencer Riley, the plaintiff, for the payment of the Eventual Condemnation Money in Said Cause. In Testimony Whereof, they have hereunto Set their hands and Seals this the 16th day of November 1829.

Test. M. Simmons, Clk   Ja^s H. Rodgers
                                          W. P. Harris

Thomas Napier }
    vs } Judgment & Stay of Execution
Enoch Byne & }
Bullock & Wells }

Came into office Nicholas W. Wells, one of the defendants in the above Case, who wishing the Stay of Execution in terms of the law, paid all Cost and entered a Stay of Execution for Sixty days, and at the Same time, Came Archibald Darragh, his Security, and they, the Said Nicholas W. Wells and Archibald Darragh, acknowledge themselves jointly &

Severally bound for the true payment of Said Judgment & all further Cost at the Expiration of Sixty days in Terms of the Law. In Witness Whereof, they have hereunto Set their hand and Seals this 17th day of November 1829.

Test. Martin Simmons, Clk   Nicholas W. Wells
              A. Darragh

The Bank of Darien }
  vs   } Debt & Judgment for
Albert G. Clopton & } The defendant for
Ambrose Baber, adm^{rs} } Eleven Dollars & fifty
of Joseph Morgan, dec^{d}} Cents Cost
Ezekiel Wimberly }
Benjamin Bryan   }
& James Wimberly }

The plaintiff, being Disatisfied with the verdict in the above Cause, and Having paid all Cost And Demanded an appeal, Brings Scott Cray and Tenders him as their Security, and they, the Said Bank of Darien, by their attorney in fact, Robert Collins, & by their Attorney at Law, Henry G. Lamar, & Scott Cray Acknowledge themselves jointly and Severally bound To Albert G. Clopton & Ambrose Baber, adm^{rs} of Joseph Morgan, Dec^{d}, & Ezekiel Wimberly, Benjamin Bryan, and James Wimberly, the defendants, for the True payment of the Eventual Condemnation Money In Said Cause. In Witness Whereof, they have Hereunto Set their hands & Seals this 17th day of November 1829.

            Bank of Darien
            By att^{o} Robt Collins &
            Attorney at Law
            Henry G. Lamar
            Scott Cray

April Term 1830

Georgia   } April 19th 1830. The honorable the Inferior Court
Bibb County } in and for the County of Bibb Meet this day agreeable

to adjournment, present William B. Cone, Sheriff and Martin Simmons, Clk. The Court was adjourned over to the first Monday in May Next.

Test. Martin Simmons, Clk

Georgia } May 3rd 1830. The Honorable the Inferior Court for
Bibb County } Said County Meet this day agreeable to adjournment

present, their honors   Timothy Mathews }
                          Luke Ross } J. I. C.
                          Samuel B. Hunter }
                          & James Rodgers }

Alexander G. Raiford }
    vs } Assumpsit
Alexander Merrewether }

I Confess Judgment to the plaintiff for the defendants in the Sum of fifty three dollars & Ninety Six Cents, With interest & Cost, reserving the right of appeal.

       Polhill & Cole, Att^{ys} for Defendant

The following Jury Were Sworn to Serve at this Term.

   1. William Johnson   7. Joseph H. Lee
   2. William Bowden   8. Lewis Foy
   3. Stephen Atkison   9. Johnson Hammock
   4. Benjamin Smith   10. Hiram Man
   5. Rufus K. Evans   11. John Smith
   6. Asa E. Earnest   12. John Crowell

      April Adjourned Term 1830

James Earl & C° }
    vs } Debt
Meeker & Magee }

We, the Jury, find for the plaintiff Three hundred dollars principal, With Interest & Cost.

         A. E. Ernest, forman

James Earl & Cº }
  vs } Case 1
Meeker & Magee }

We, the Jury, find for the plaintiff Two hundred dollars principal, With interest & Cost.

         A. E. Ernest, forman

Henry S. Cutler }
  vs } Case
Beverly Rew }

I Confess judgment for the plaintiff Sixty Seven Dollars principal, With interest & Cost.

         Beverly Rew

Amory Sibley   }
  vs   } Assumpsit
Caleb Malden, jun, Senior }

We, the jury, find for the plff The Sum of two hundred and Seventy Eight Dollars Thirty two Cents, With interest & Cost.

         A. E. Ernest, forman

Robert Collins, for the }
use of David Henshaw }
& John Henshaw }
  vs   } Assumpsit
John Bailey   }

We, the Jury, find for the plaintiff the Sum of Eight Hundred & fifty dollars, With Interest & Cost.

         A. E. Ernest, forman

    April Term Adjourned 1830

Heard & Cook }
  vs   } Assumpsit
Rene Fitzpartrick }

I Confess Judgment to the plaintiff in the Sum of One Hundred and twenty Eight Dollars and Seventeen Cents, With interest & Cost

          Rene Fitzpartrick

William L. Sanders }
   vs   } Case & Bail
Edward Varner }
J. W. Campbell }

We, the jury, find for the plaintiff fifty five Dollars principal, With interest & Cost.

          A. E. Ernest, forman

Amon W. Langdon }
   vs   } Case
Charles S. Lewis }

We, the Jury, find for the plaintiff four hundred and Eleven Dollars & fifty five Cents, With interest & Cost of protest.

          A. E. Ernest, forman

John A. Jones }
  vs   } Assumpsit
John Bryan }

We, the Jury, find for the plaintiff One hundred Dollars principal, With Interest & Cost.

          A. E. Ernest, forman

Gordon C. Coit }
  vs   } assumpsit
A. Gillis & C° }

We, the Jury, find for the plaintiff the Sum of Fifty four Dollars and fifty Eight Cents, With interest & Cost.

          A. E. Ernest, forman

April Adjourned Term 1830

Amon W. Langdon for }
the use &c, Indorsee }
     vs   } Case
Job Magee and }
Charles S. Lewis, Indorsers }

We, the jury, find for the plaintiff four hundred and Eleven Dollars & fifty five Cents, With interest & Cost.

                        A. E. Ernest, forman

The following Were Sworn to Serve as Jury N° 2.

1. Hampton B. Watts
2. Daniel Henderson
3. Solomon D. Chapman
4. Michiel Coxwell
5. Quinton Hoy
6. William Gamble
7. John Maulsby
8. Absolum Abney
9. Alfred Brady
10. Francis Willey
11. C. C. Wych
12. James Thompson

Douglass C. Watson }
     vs   } Case
Francis Willey & }
John Molesby }

                    Jury N° 1

We, the Jury, find for the plaintiff Eighty Nine dollars & Twenty five Cents and Cost.

                        A. E. Ernest, forman

Reazon D. Bealle }
     vs   } Assumpsit
William Williams }

It Appearing to the Court That the Original Declaration, of Which this is a Copy in Substance, Has been Lost and Washington Poe having Stated in his place That this Writ in the Same in Substance as the Lost Original. It is ordered that it be Substituted in Lieu of Said Lost Original.

A. Gillis & C⁰ }
    vs   } Attachment
Henry W. Conner }
& Joseph H. Towns }

We, the Jury, find for the plaintiff the Sum of Two hundred & Twenty One Dollars & thirty Seven Cents, with Cost of Suit.

James Thompson, forman

April Adjourned Term 1830

Henry B. Hill   } Rule Nisi against John Oliver
    vs   } Constable for the 514 Dis^t of
Ransom L. Bird } Georgia Militia

It appearing to the Court that the Said John Oliver, Constable as aforesaid, Arrested the Defendant on a Casa in favour of the plaintiff and That he took a bond With pretended Security for his Appearance at this Term of the Inferior Court to take the Benefit of the Honest debtors act, and it Appearing that the Securities are Wholly insolvent And are Not in terms of the Law good and Sufficient Security. It is on Motion ordered that The Said John Oliver do appear tomorrow Morning And Shew Cause Why he Should Not be held as Special Bail and also Why he Should Not pay to The plaintiff the Amount of Said Casa.

C. B. Cole, def^{ts} att^y

The Court adjourned till Tuesday Morning at 8 O'clock.

Saml B. Hunter, J. I. C.
Timothy Mathews, J. I. C.
Luke Ross, J. I. C.
Ja^s H. Rodgers, J. I. C.

Georgia } May 4th 1840 Tuesday Morning The honorable the Bibb County } Inferior Court in and for the County of Bibb Meet agreeable to adjournment.

Present, their honors Timothy Mathews }
　　　　　　　　　　　Luke Ross　　　 } J. I. C.
　　　　　　　　　　　Samuel B. Hunter }
　　　　　　　　　　　James H. Rodgers }

April Adjourned Term 1830

M. Pendergrast }
　　vs　　　　 } Debt
A. Gillis & C° }

We Confess judgment to plaintiff for Thirteen hundred & fifty Dollars & Sixty four Cents principal, with interest & Cost.

　　　　　　　　　　　Angus Gillis
　　　　　　　　　　　David Gregory

James Killin　　　}
　　vs　　　　　　} fifa Bibb Inferior Court
John Philpot &　　} Rule Absolute principal 150
William Cumming }

It appearing to the Court that the Sheriff of Said County having failed to Show Cause Why the Monies Collected upon above fifa Should Not be paid over to plaintiff, or his attorney, it is Hereby ordered that an Attachment issue against Said Sheriff in terms of the Law.

Patterson & Rhodes }
for the use &c　　　 }
　　vs　　　　　　　 } Debt
J. H. Hardeway　　　}

We, the Jury, find a Verdict for the defendant.

　　　　　　　　　　　A. E. Ernest, forman

Betheny Dismuke }
  vs   } Casa from 514 dis^t G. M.
C. C. Wych }

It appearance to the Court that The defendant, C. C. Wych, has been Arrested under & by Virtue of a Casa issued by Charles Ingram, a Justice of the Peace in & for the County of Bibb, on a Judgment rendered against the defendant in Capt Dennis' Dist of Jones County in Consequence of Which arrest the Defendant gave bond & Security for his appearance at this Term of this Court. On Motion, it is ordered that the defendant Be discharged from Liability on his bond, No Such Casa as that Described in the bond being in Court & Ingram having No authority to issue Said Casa.

April Adjourned Term 1830

Thomas Rod, John Scully, and Angus McCallum Were Sworn in place of David Harrison, Michiel Coxwell, & Francis Wily absent from Jury N° 2.

Charles S. Lewis }
  vs   } Case
Amon W. Langdon }

We, the jury, find for plaintiff Thirty one dollars & ninety two Cents principal, With interest & Cost.

            James Thompson, forman

A. R. Freeman }
  vs   } Declaration in attachment
Wm R. Smiley }

We, the Jury, find for plaintiff one hundred & Sixty one Dollars and fifty three Cents principal, with interest & Cost.

            James Thompson, forman

John Black }
  vs   } Debt & Bail
John Balton }

We, the Jury, find for plaintiff the Sum of three hundred & thirty dollars and twelve Cents, With interest & Cost.

A. E. Ernest, forman

David Ralston }
    vs   } Garnishment
M. R. Wallis }

It appearing to the Court that the Answer of the Garnishee is incompleat. It is ordered that he do by or before the next term of this Court amend his answer by answering More fully.

Amon W. Langdon, Indorsee }
        vs   } Case
Job Magie and }
Charles S. Lewis, Indorsers }

We, the Jury, find for the plaintiff four hundred & Eleven Dollars & fifty five Cents, With interest & Cost & three Dollars Cost of protest.

James Thompson, forman

April Adjourned Term 1830

William B. Cone }
    vs   } fifa in Bibb Inferior Court
Henry Melbourn & } April term 1830
Charles J. McDonald }

It appearing that Said fifa Was placed in the hands of Henry Carter, Coroner of Said County, and that he has Raised the Money on the Same but refuses to pay the Same To this plaintiff. It is ordered that the Said Coroner do Show Cause to Morrow Morning why he Should Not pay the Amount of Said Execution to the plaintiff, or his Attorney.

Thomas M. Ellis }
    vs   } Scire Facias
Isaac Winship & }
Henry H. Cone }

It appearing to the Court that a Scira Facias at the instance of Thomas M. Ellis, plaintiff, against Isaac Winship and Henry H. Cone, Bail for Ezekiel Coffin and George Clark, has issued from this Court returnable to the October Term 1829, Calling upon the Said Isaac Winship, Henry H. Cone To Shew Cause Why Judgment Should Not be Entered up Against the Said Isaac and the Said Henry H., as aforesaid, for the amount of the principal, interest, and Cost of the original Judgment recovered by the Said Thomas M. Ellis against the Said Ezekiel and George and also, for the Cost of the Said Scire Facias and this proceedings. And Now, at this term The Said Isaac and the Said Henry H. having failed to Shew Cause, it is ordered by the Court that the plaintiff's Attorney have Leave to Enter Judgment against the Said Henry H. and the Said Isaac, as aforesaid, and that the Clk of this Court issue Execution thereon.

Reason D. Bealle }
    vs   } Assumpsit
William Williams }

I Confess Judgment to the plaintiff in the Sum of Sixty Eight dollars & Cost of Suit, reserving the right of appeal. April 4th 1830

                                            William Williams

                          April Adjourned Term 1830

Reason D. Bealle }
    vs   } Assumpsit & Judgment for the plaintiff for Sixty
William Williams } Eight dollars and Cost

the Defendant, being Disatisfied With the Verdict in the above Cause, and Having paid all Cost and demanded an appeal, Brings John P. Smith and Tenders him as his Security. And they, the Said William Williams & John P. Smith, Acknowledge themselves jointly & Severally bound to Reason D. Bealle, the plaintiff, for the payment of the Eventual Condemnation Money in Said Case, in Witness Whereof, they have hereunto Set their hands & Seals this 4th day of May 1830.

Test. Martin Simmons, Clk   William Williams
                                            Jno P. Smith

John R. Wooton }
    vs   } fifa
James Butler   }

It appearing to the Court That the Sheriff has Collected the Sum of thirty five Dollars, inclusive of all Cost, on Motion ordered that he Shew Cause instanter, or as Soon as Counsel be heard, Why the Same Should Not be paid over to older fifas now in his hands & that the Shff have a Copy of this Nisi.

Charles McGregor }
    vs   } Assumpsit
George A. Smith }

We Confess Judgment To plaintiff for forty two Dollars and fifty Cents, With interest and Cost, Saving the right of appeal.

                        Prince & Poe, Def[ts] Att[y]

H. W. Harper   }
    vs   } Debt
Thomas Gardner }

We, the Jury, find for the plaintiff Ninety Six Dollars and Ninety four Cents principal, With interest & Cost.

                        A. E. Ernest, forman

            April Adjourned Term 1830

Robert Birdsong   }
    vs   } Debt
Moreland & Harrison }

We, the Jury, find for the plaintiff fifty two dollars principal, With interest & Cost.

                        A. E. Ernest, forman

Amon W. Langdon, for }
the use &c indorsee }
      vs   } Case
Charles S. Lewis   }

We Confess Judgment to the plaintiff in the Sum of five Hundred & twenty seven Dollars & Seventy seven Cents, With interest & cost of protest.

                              Campbell & Seymour, Def[ts] att[y]

Thomas Butler & C[o] }
      vs   } Assumpsit
Moreland & Harrison }

We, the Jury, find for the plaintiff The Sum of four hundred and Sixty Six dollars, With interest and Cost.

                              A. E. Ernest, forman

Thomas Butler & C[o] }
      vs   } Assumpsit
Young Johnston   }

We, the Jury, find for the plaintiff The Sum of four hundred and Sixty Six dollars, With interest & Cost.

                              A. E. Ernest, forman

John Larchan   }
      vs   } Debt
Martin Simmons   }

I Confess Judgment To plaintiff for three hundred Dollars, With interest & Cost.

                              Martin Simmons

Susan Wells   }
      vs   } Scire facias
Thomas P. Bond   }

We, the Jury, find for plaintiff One Hundred & Nineteen dollars & Seventy Two Cents, With interest & Cost.

          James Thompson, forman

     April Adjourned Term 1830

Zackariah Sims   }
Guardian of A. Sims }
   vs   } Trover
Joseph Washburn }

We, the Jury, find for the plaintiff Three hundred & Sixty dollars or the return of the negro to the plaintiff in fifteen Days, with Sixty Dollars hire.

          A. E. Ernest, forman

The Court adjourned till Wednesday Morning at 9 O'clock.

          Timothy Mathews, J. I. C.
          Luke Ross, J. I. C.
          Ja^s H. Rodgers, J. I. C.

Georgia   } Wednesday May 5th 1830
Bibb County } The honorable the Inferior Court In and for the County of Bibb Meet agreeable to adjournment

Present, their honors   Timothy Mathews }
              Luke Ross   } J. I. C.
              James H. Rodgers }

Thomas Tinsley Was Sworn to Serve on Jury N° 1 in place of Rufus K. Evans.

Lewis Foy   }
  vs   } Case and Bail
William Finch }

No Copy of the Affidavit to hold To bail having been attached to the Declaration, it is Ordered that the bail taken be Dischared.

John Loving }
    vs   } Assumpsit
Rufus K. Evans }

We, the Jury, find for the plaintiff fifty Dollars.

                                              A. E. Ernest, forman

---

April Adjourned Term 1830

Zackariah Sims }
Guardian of Amanda Sims } Trover and Verdict for The
    vs   } plaintiff for four hundred
Joseph Washburn } and twenty dollars And Cost

Joseph Washburn, The defendant, being dissatisfied With the Verdict of the Jury rendered in the above Cause, and having paid all Cost and demanded an appeal, brings Harrison Smith & Tenders him as his Security, and they, the Said Joseph Washburn and Harrison Smith, acknowledge themselves Jointly and Severally bound to Zackariah Sims, Guardian of Amanda Sims, the plaintiff, for the payment of the Eventual Condemnation Money in Said Cause. In testimony Whereof, they have hereunto Set their hands and Seals this 5th day of May 1830.

                                                J. Washburn
                                              H. Smith

Richard W. Ellis }
    vs   } Casa from 564 dis^t G. M.
Enoch Lunsford }

It appearing to the Court that The Said Defendant has been arrested by Virtue of Said Casa and Said defendant having given bond for his Appearance at the October Term 1829 of this Court then And there to be admitted to the benefit of the Act for the relief of Honest Debtors, and William Cumming having Become Security on Said Bond for the on Said Bond for the purformance of Said Condition, And Said Condition Not having been performed. It is Ordered that Judgment be Entered for principal, interest, and Cost on Said fifa against Said Security & his principal.

David A. Edgar }
    vs   } Assumpsit for rent
Hockey L. Towns}

We, the Jury, find for the Defendant, With Cost of Suit.

                                  James Thompson, forman

April Term 1830

Hatch, Porter & C°}
    vs   } fifa Returnable to this Court
Ralston & Jones }

Om Motion of plaintiff Counsel, Ordered by the Court that the Sheriff, William B. Cone, Esqr, Shew Cause Instanter, or So Soon as the he Can be heard by the Court, Why he Should Not pay over the Money required by Said Execution To the plaintiff Attorney.

Justices of the Inferior Court }
of Bibb County   }
          vs   } Fieri Facias
Benjamin Russell, tax Collector }
Stephen M. Ingersol   }
Rufus K. Evans   }
David F. Wilson, Securities   }

We, the Jury, find The defendant in debt five [blank] Dollars & Sixty two & half Cents, With Cost of Suit.

                                  James Thompson, form

Martin Simmons   }
Clerk of the Inferior }
Court of Bibb County }
    vs   } Rule Nisi
Spencer Riley   }

It appearing to The Court that Spencer Riley, Late Sheriff of Said County, has Collected & has now in his hands The amount of fifty Six dollars as Cost belonging To Said Clk, it is hereby ordered that Said

Riley Shew Cause instanter Why he Should Not pay over the above Cost to Clk.

Charles Woodruff } fifa Bibb Inferior Court
     vs   } April Term 1830
Joshua Jordon   } Prin^l 193.84 } Rule Nisi
                 } in^t 28.31   }

It appearing to the Court that Spencer Riley, late

April Adjourned Term 1830

Sheriff of Said County, has Collected the Money on The above fifa, it is hereby ordered that the Sheriff pay the above Monies to the plaintiff, or his Attornies, or Shew Cause instanter, or as Soon as Counsel May Be heard, Why a rule absolute for an Attachment Should Not be taken in terms of the Law & it is Hereby ordered that a Copy of this Rule be Served upon Said Spencer Riley.

Hatch, Porter & C°}
     vs   } fifa Returnable to this Court
Ralston & Jones }

The plaintiff attorney having by Rule Nisi Collected by Wm B. Cone, Shff of this County, To Shew Cause Why he Should Not pay over instanter To the plaintiff Attorney the principal, interest, & Cost required By the Said fifa, And, the Said Sheriff having failed to Shew Cause. It is Now ordered that the Said Rule Nisi be Made absolute and that the Sheriff, Wm B. Cone aforesaid, pay over Within One Week from The adjournment of this Court the Sum of One thousand Four hundred and Sixty Eight Dollars and thirty Six Cents, Being the Amount of the principal, Interest, & attorneys fees in Said Case, and that in default by Said Sheriff to pay over the Said Sum Within the time Specified Aforesaid, the Clk of this Court do issue an attachment against the Said Wm B. Cone directed to the Corner of this County of Bibb and Commanding him to Commit The body of the Said William B. Cone to the Common Jail of Said County, there to remain Without bail or Mainprise untill the payment by the Said Cone to the Attorney of the plaintiff of the Sum Aforesaid.

Ordered that the Clk of this Court pay Beverly Rew Three Dollars for his attendance as Bailiff at this Term.

April Adjourned Term 1830

Thomas King }
    vs   } Casa returnable to this Court
David Burks }

The defendant, David Burks, having been arrested under the Said Casa, and having given Bond in terms of the Statute for his appearance at this Court, and to Which Bond Robert Collins and Bennett S. Griffin are Sureties. Now the Said David Burks having been Called in open Court and failing to appear and the Said Robert Collins and the Said Bennett S. Griffin having Been Called and failing to produce the body of Said Burks. It is Ordered that the plaintiff's att^y have Leave to Sign Judgment according to the provisions of the Act of 1823.

James H. Rodgers, plff }
    vs   } Casa
Wilson H. Cay, Deft^d }

the defendant having been arrested by Virtue of the Above Casa & having given bond With C. C. Wych & Henry A. Candler as his Sureties for his appearance at the present term of this Court to take the Benefit of the Honest Debtors Act and the Said Wilson H. Cay Having failed to appear, it is therefore Ordered, Considered, and adjudged by the Court that the plaintiff do recover of Said Wilson H. Cay and C. C. Wych & Henry A. Candler the Sum of Eighteen Dollars for his principal Debt, and the further Sum of fifty Cents for his interest, And the Sum of one Dollar and fifty Six Cents for his on The Original Casa, and the further Sum of [blank] for his Cost in this behalf laid out and Expended, & the defendant in Mercy &c.

                                          Charles J. McDonald, plff Att^y

---

April Adjourned Term 1830

Spencer Riley }
    vs   } Ca Su
A. D. Brown }

It Appearing to the Court that Alexander D. Brown has Complied With the Terms of the law relating to relief of insolvent Debtors Applying for the benefit of the Act. It is herby Ordered That the benefit of Said Act be Extended to Said Brown & he is hereby discharged out of the Custody of the Sheriff.

Charles Woodruff }
    vs   } fifa returnable to Bibb Inferior Court
Joshua Jordon }

plaintiff's attornies having By rule nisi Called upon Spencer Riley, late Sheriff of Said County, to Shew Cause Why he Should Not pay over instanter To plaintiff attornies the principal, interest, and Cost required By Said fifa and Said Riley having failed to Shew Cause.

It is Now ordered that Said rule nisi by Made Absolute And that late Sheriff Riley Aforesaid pay over Within three Days from the adjournment of this Court the Sum of two Hundred & thirty four Dollars & Ninety Cents, being amount of Principal, interest, and Attornies fees due on Said fifa. And that in Default by Said Sheriff to pay over the Said Sum Within the time Specified, the Clerk of this Court do issue an attachment against Said Spencer Riley Directed To the Sheriff of Said County of Bibb Commanding him To Commit the body of Said Riley to the Without bail or Mainprise untill paid by Said Sheriff to plaintiff Attornies.

Ordered, that the Clerk of this Court pay to Charles J. McDonald fifty Dollars for professional Services Rendered in the Case of the Justices of the Inferior Court against Samuel Gillespie, late Treasurer.

April Term 1830

Martin Simmons }
Clerk of Inferior Court }
    vs } Rule Absolute
Spencer Riley }

plaintiff attornies having by rule nisi Called upon Spencer Riley, late Sheriff of Said County, To Shew Cause Why he Should not pay over to Said Simmons, or his attornies, the Sum of fifty Six dollars, the amount of Said Clerk's Cost And Which is Now in the hands of Said Riley and Said Riley having failed to Shew Cause, it is Now ordered that Said Rule Nisi be Made absolute And that Said Riley pay over within three days from The adjournment of this Court the Sum of fifty Six dollars, Being amount of Clerk's Cost in Said Riley hand, and That in default by Said Riley to pay over the Said Sum Within the time Specified, the Clerk of this Court do issue An Attachment against Said Spencer Riley directed to Shff of Bibb County Commanding him to Commit the body of Said Spencer Riley to the Jail of Said County, there to remain Without bail or Mainprise there to remain untill Said Sum Be paid by Said Riley.

Hatch, Porter & C° }
    vs } fifa from this Court
Ralston & Jones }

A Rule Absolute having been passed against The Sheriff ordering him to pay over The Monies in the Said Case to plff attorney & the Sheriff having fully Complied With the Said rule, it is ordered That the Said rule be and it is hereby discharged.

H. S. Stone }
    vs } Casa
Angus McCallum }

It appearing to the Court That Angus McCallum has Complied With the terms of the Law relating to relief of Honest Debtors applying for the Benefit of the Act, it is hereby ordered that the Benefit

April Adjourned Term 1830

of the Act be Extended to said McCallum and he is hereby discharged out of the Custody of the Sheriff.

Low, Taylor & C° }
      vs   } Rule against Spencer Riley, late Sheriff
William R. Smiley }

a rule Nisi having been granted at at the instance of the plaintiff Calling upon the Sheriff to Shew Cause Why he Should Not pay over to The plaintiff's attornies Certain Moneys Now in his hands Arrising from the Sale of the property of the Said William R. Smiley levied upon by Virtue of a process Attachment Sold Sold as perishable property. And the Said Spencer Riley having failed to Shew Cause, It is ordered that he pay over instanter to Tracy & Butler the Sum of [blank] and [blank] Cents, And that In Default thereof, the Said Spencer Riley be deemed and Held in Contempt of this Court.

Charles Collins }
      vs   } assumpsit for rent
Spencer Riley }

I Confess Judgment to the plaintiff in the Sum of thirty Seven Dollars Eighty One Cents, With interest & Cost. May 4th 1830

                                          Spencer Riley

Smith & Wright } Suit pending in this Court
      vs   } Summons of Garnishment
Keeland Tyner } for John T. Rowland Returnable to this Court

It appearing To the Court by the Return of the Sheriff that John T. Rowland Has been duly Served With a Summons of Garnishment at the Instance of the plaintiff in the above Case & the Said John T. Rowland having failed to Come into Court and answer According to the exigency of Such Summons. It is Now Ordered by the Court that the Said John T. Rowland answer on the first day of Next term of this Court and

April Adjourned Term 1830

That in Default thereof, an Attachment do issue in Terms of the Law. Ordered that the Sheriff have a Copy of this Rule on the Said John T. Rowland twenty days Before the Next term/

Henry S. Cutler }
     vs   } Suit pending in this Court
Beverly Rew   }

Summons of Garnishment returnable To the Last Term of this Court by the return of the Sheriff That John T. Lamar has been duly Served With a Summons of Garnishment at the instance of the plaintiff in above Case. And the Said John T. Lamar having failed to Come into Court and answer to the Exigency of Such Summons. It is now ordered by the Court that Said John T. Lamar answer on the first day of Next Term of this Court and that, in Default thereof, an Attachment do issue in terms of the Law. Ordered that the Sheriff Serve a Copy of this Rule on Said John T. Lamar Twenty days before Next term of this Court.

The Court then adjourned till Thursday Morning at 10 O'clock.

                                                    J. I. C.
                                                  J. I. C.
                                                  J. I. C.

Georgia   } May 6th 1830 Thursday Morning The honorable the Bibb County } Inferior Court in And for the County of Bibb Meet agreeable to adjournment

Present, their honors   Luke Ross   }
                                                David Ralston } J. I. C.
                                                James H. Rodgers }

Ordered, that Spencer Riley be paid Seventy Eight Dollars and fifty Eight Cents in full of his account rendered.

April Adjourned Term 1830

Thomas M. Ellis } Sci fa & Judgment for the plaintiff
  vs   } for two hundred and Eighty three Dollars
Isaac Winship & } and Sixty two Cents principal
Henry H. Cone } With interest & Cost

the defendant, being disatisfied With the Verdict rendered in the Above Cause, and having paid all Cost and demanded An appeal, and Brings Oliver Sage and tenders him Him as his Security. and they, the Said Isaac Winship and Oliver Sage, Acknowledge themselves jointly and Severaly Bound to Thomas M. Ellis, the plaintiff, for the payment of the Eventual Condemnation Money in Said Cause. in testimony Whereof, they have hereunto Sent their hands & Seals this 6th day of May 1830.

Test. M. Simmons, Clk   Isaac Winship
             Oliver Sage

Ordered that William P. Harris be paid One hundred and thirty One Dollars in full Satisfaction from the County for Building a Bridge Across Echeconna Creek at tharp's ford.

Ordered, that William Cumming be paid twenty four Dollars and fifty Cents in full of his bill rendered this day.

Ordered that Wiley, Baxter & Fort Be paid twenty five Dollars for a record Book for the Superior Court.

Ordered that Tracy & Butler be paid Twenty Dollars for his Services in The Case of the Court against B. Russell, tax Collector.

Ordered that Henry Carter, Coroner, Be paid twelve Dollars and fifty Cents for holding an inquest over E. Stringfield.

R. B. Harrison & Co }
  vs   } Assumpsit & Bail
John Strawbridge }

We Confess Judgment to plaintiff for thirty five Dollars four Cents, With Cost of Suit.

                Campbell & Seymour, def^t

April Adjourned Term 1830

Thomas Napier }
    vs   } Case & Bail in Bibb Inferior Court
James E. Jordon }

Elam Alexander, one of The Bail in the above Case, having brought James E. Jordon in open Court and Surrendered him to the Court in discharge of himself as Bail, It is ordered By the Court the Said Elam Alexander be discharged from all future liability on Said Bail Bond.

William B. Cone   }
    vs   } fifa in Bibb Inferior Court
Henry Melborn &   }
Charles J. McDonald }

It appearing to the Court That Charles J. McDonald Signed the Note upon Which the Judgment on Which the above fifa was issued as Security, and that he has paid the Same as Security, it is therefore ordered that the Verdict, Judgment, & fifa be So Amended as to Shew the Character in which the Said Charles J. McDonald Signed the Said Note & that the Said Charles J. McDonald have the Control of Said fifa to indemnify himself.

James H. Rodgers   }
    vs   } Casa from Justice Court
Wilson H. Cay &   }
Henry A. Candler &   }
Clark Wych, Securities }

I do releas Henry A. Candler from his obligation on the principal of the above Case.

6 May 1830   James H. Rodgers

Macon May 3rd 1830

To the honorable the judges of the Inferior Court of Bibb County. the undersigned humbly petitions your honors To Appoint Richard W. Ellis, Esqr Guardian for her and her four Children, viz. John McLaughlan,

Jared McLaughlan, William McLaughlan, and Rhoda McLaughlan. And as in duty bound, your petitioner Wil Ever pray &c.

Sally X McLaughlan, her mark

April Adjourned Term 1830

To the honorable the Judges of the Inferior Court of Bibb County Now in Session. I am Willing To Act as Guardian for the Above Named Sally McLaughlan, who is a free person of Color, & her four Children as above Named.

May 3rd 1830   Richard W. Ellis

on Motion being by Richard W. Ellis. It is ordered That the within petition and assent be Substituted in Lieu of the Original and that Letters of Guardianship Be granted to Said Richard W. Ellis for Sally McLaughlan only.

The following Jury Were Drawn to Serve at October Term 1830, Viz.

1. Joseph Parker	19. William Farington
2. Payton Vincent	20. Edward Montgomery
3. Shedrick Radford	21. John H. Kimbro
4. Emanuel Ezekiel	22. Jehu Hutcherson
5. Jeremiah Johnson	23. David Preston
6. James Hughes	24. John H. Powledge
7. William Dunn	25. John Ellsworth
8. Willis Pitts	26. William Blancett
9. James Smith	27. A. D. Goulding
10. William Johnson (Shiney)	28. Jered Smith
11. Elerson Sumerlin	29. Hezekiah McKiney
12. John P. Vance	30. John Molsby
13. Absolom Brown	31. Charles McCardle
14. Absolom Jackson	32. John Singer
15. George Whitehead, Jun	33. William Coopie
16. Mitchell Coxwell	34. Leonard Adams
17. Charles ingham	35. Philander Judson
18. Williamson Smith	36. Benjamin A. Sims

April Adjourned Term 1830

The Court adjourned till Court in Course.

Luke Ross, J. I. C.
Timothy Mathews, J. I. C.
Saml B. Hunter, J. I. C.
Ja^s H. Rodgers, J. I. C.

A. Gillis & C°　　　} Declaration in attachment & Verdict for the
　　vs　　　　　　} plaintiff for two hundred and twenty one
Henry W. Conner　 } dollars thirty one & a half Cents
& Joseph H. Towns} principal and Cost

The Defendants, being Disatisfied With the Verdict of the Jury rendered in the above Cause, and having paid all Costs, and Demanded an appeal, Brings Littleton Atkison and tenders him as his their Security. And they, the Said Henry W. Conner & Joseph H. Towns, by their Attornies, Campbell & Seymour, acknowledge themselves jointly and Severally bound to A. Gillis & Co, the plaintiff, for the payment of the Eventual Condemnation Money in Said Cause. In testimony Whereof, they have hereunto Set their hands & Seals this 10th day of May 1830.

Test. M. Simmons, C. I. C.　　　Henry W. Conner
　　　　　　　　　　　　　　　Joseph H. Towns, by their
　　　　　　　　　　　　　　　Att^y at Law I. G. Seymour
　　　　　　　　　　　　　　　Littleton Atkison

David A. Edger　　}
　　vs　　　　　　} Assumpsit for Rent & Verdict for the
Hockey L. Towns}　Defendant for Cost

the plaintiff, Being disatisfied With the verdict of the Jury rendered in the above Cause, and having paid all Cost and demanded an Appeal, brings Lemuel Newcomb and tenders him as his Security, and they, the Said David A. Edger, by his attornies Campbell & Seymour, Acknowledge themselves jointly and Severally bound to Hockey L. Town, the defendant, for the True payment of the Eventual

Condemnation Money in Said Cause. In testamony Whereof, hey have hereunto Set their hands & Seals this 10th May 1830.

Test. Martin Simmons, C. I. C.   David A. Edgar
                                                        his Att^y at Law
                                                       Isaac G. Seymour
                                                       Lem Newcomb

---

April Adjourned Term 1830

Charles Collins }
      vs   } Judgment & Stay of Execution
Spencer Riley   }

Came into Office the defendant Spencer Riley, Who Wishing the Stay of Execution in terms of the Law, paid all Cost and Entered a Stay of Execution Sixty Days, and at the Same Time Came Hockey L. Towns, his Security, and they, The Said Spencer Riley and Hockey L. Towns, Acknowledge Themselves jointly & Severally bound to the plaintiff for the payment of Said Judgment and all further Cost at the Expiration of Sixty days in terms of the Law. In Witness Whereof, they have hereunto Set their hand & Seals this 11th May 1830.

Test. Martin Simmons, Clk   Spencer Riley
                                                H. L. Towns

Charles McGregor }
      vs   } Assumpsit & Judgment for the plaintiff for forty
George A. Smith   } two Dollars & fifty Cents, With interest & Cost

the Defendant, being disatisfied With the Verdict of the Jury rendered in the above Cause, and having paid all Cost and demanded an Appeal, Bring Jacob Shotwell and tenders him as his Security, and They, the Said George A. Smith and Jacob Shotwell, acknowledge Themselves jointly and Severally bound to Charles McGregor, the plaintiff, for the payment of the Eventual Condemnation Money in Said Cause. In testimony Whereof, they have hereunto Set their hands and Seals this 11th day of May 1830.

Test. Martin Simmons, Clk   Geo A. Smith
                                                Jacob Shotwell

[blank page]

October Term 1830

Georgia } The Honorable The Inferior Court in and for the
Bibb County } County of Bibb Meet this day agreeable to adjournment October 18th 1830

Present, their honors   Timothy Mathews }
                                   Samuel B. Hunter } J. I. C.
                                   James H. Rodgers }

The following Jury Were Sworn to Serve at This Term.

Jury N° 1

1. John Malsby
2. William Blancet
3. William Farington
4. Williamson Smith
5. John Singer
6. John Elsworth
7. James Summerlin
8. William Johnson
9. Shadrick Radford
10. William Dunn
11. Thomas Brigman
12. Caleb Condon

Jury N° 2

1. Jehu Hutcherson
2. Willis Pitts
3. Hezekiah McKinney
4. John Darnell
5. James Hughs
6. Charles McCardle
7. John H. Kimbro
8. George Whitehead
9. Leonard Adams
10. William Johnson (Shiney)
11. Benjamin A. Sims
12. Asalom Abney

B. G. Walker }
Executor of }
John D. Walker, dec^d }
     vs   } Sci fa
Henry G. Lamar }

We Confess judgment To plaintiff in the Sum of One hundred & twenty five Dollars, With interest & Cost

Campbell & Seymour, Def^{ts} Att^y

October Term 1830

Benjamin G. Walker }
Executor of }
John D. Walker }
    vs } Sci fa
A. R. Woodson }

We Confess judgment to the plaintiff in the Sum of hundred & Twenty five Dollars, With interest & Cost.

Campbell & Seymour, Def^t Att^y

Kimberly & Chisholm }
    vs } Casa
George W. Jackson & }
Lewis Collins & }
D. Smith }

The Securities on the Bail Bond in the above Case having Surrendered the body of George W. Jackson to the Court, it is ordered That the bond in Said Case be Cansield.

William Bivins }
    vs } Debt
D. J. Holt }

We, the Jury, find for the plaintiff Eighty one Dollars, With interest & Cost.

J. W. Hutcherson, forman

Thomas Napier }
    vs } Case
Keeland Tyner }

We, the Jury, find for the plaintiff the Sum of Two hundred & Ninety Two Dollars & Sixty Cents, With interest & Cost.

          John Elsworth, forman

Thomas Napier }
  vs   } Case
Marmaduke J. Slade }

We, the Jury, find for The plaintiff the Sum of five hundred Dollars, With interest & Cost.

          John Elsworth, forman

October Term 1830

Thomas Napier }
  vs   } Case
Samuel Tompkins }

We, the Jury, find for the plaintiff the Sum of Three hundred & forty Dollars & forty one Cents, interest & Cost.

         J. W. Hutcherson, forman

Thomas Napier }
  vs   } Case
Absolum Jordon }

I Confess Judgment To the plaintiff in the Sum Eighty three Dollars & thirty Three & a Third Cents, With interest & Cost

          Absolum Jordon

Thomas Napier }
  vs   } Case
Alexander McGregor }

I Confess Judgment to the plaintiff in the Sum of Sixty Eight Dollars & Seventy three Cents, With interest & Cost

          Alex^r McGregor

Thomas Napier }
    vs   } Case
Elijah Cotton }

I do Confess judgment to the plaintiff in the Sum Sixty Nine Dollars & Ninety four Cents, With interest & Cost

                        E. Cotton

Thomas Napier }
    vs   } Case
Keeland Tyner }

We, the Jury, find for the plaintiff the Sum of Two hundred & Ninety Six Dollars & Seventy three Cents, With inert & Cost.

                        John Elsworth, forman

Thomas Napier }
    vs   } Case
Cyrus Cotton }

We, the jury, find for The plaintiff the Sum of five hundred Dollars, With interest & Cost.

                        John Elsworth, forman

October Term 1830

Shadrick F. Slatter }
    vs   } Case
William Harrison }
Survivor &c }
& Y. Johnston }

We Confess judgment to plaintiff for Sixty Dollars, With interest & Cost of Suit.

                        Tracy & Butler, Att[ys] for Def[ts]

Thomas Victery, adm^r }
of Thos A. Billups }
    vs } Assumpsit
Solomon Groce, principal }
& George Vigal, Security }

We, the jury, find for the plaintiff Sixty Eight dollars and Twelve Cents, With interest & Cost.

                                            John Elsworth, forman

Thomas Napier }
    vs } Case
Daniel B. Worsham }

We, the jury, find for the plaintiff the Sum of Sixty Dollars, with interest & Cost.

                                            John Elsworth, forman

Thomas Napier }
    vs } Case
Hockey L. Towns }

We, the jury, find for the plaintiff the Sum of Sixty Dollars, with interest & Cost.

                                            John Elsworth, forman

Thomas Napier }
    vs } Case
Vance & Knox }

We, the jury, find for the plaintiff the Sum of Eighty Six Dollars, with interest & Cost.

                                           J. W. Hutcherson, forman

---

October Term 1830

Towns & Riley }
    vs } Bail in justice Court & application to take the
Mary Frederick } Benefit of the Insolvent Law

Mary Frederick having appeared in open Court & having taken the oath prescribed by Law for the relief of Honest Debtors, on Motion. It is ordered that the Said Mary Frederick be Discharged from further Confinement & that the Sheriff be Autherised to discharge her from Jail Instanter.

John Philpot }
    vs   } Case
Owen Brown }

We, the jury, find for the plaintiff fifty Dollars, With Cost of Suit.

                                                  John Elsworth, forman

Kimberly & Chisholm }
    vs   } Assumpsit
Alexander McGregor }

I Confess Judgment to plaintiff in the Sum of fifty Dollars & Sixty five Cents, with interest & Cost.

                                          Campbell & Seymour, Def.t Att.y

Susan Wells, Extr.x   }
    vs   } Assumpsit
Noel Clark, principal   }
Thomas Campbell &   }
Edwin E. Slade, Securities }

We, the jury, find for The plaintiff in the Sum of fifty three Dollars & twelve Cents, with interest & Cost.

                                            J. W. Hutcherson, forman

W. J. Wayman }
    vs   } Trover
John T. Lamar }

We, the jury, find for the defendant Cost of Suit.

                                                John Elsworth, forman

October Term 1830

Low, Taylor & C᠊ᵒ }
    vs   } Assumpsit
Keeland Tyner }

I hereby Confess Judgment to the plaintiff in the Sum of One hundred and two Dollars & Seventy five Cents & one dollar for Noting, With interest & Cost.

                          K. Tyner

Low, Taylor & C᠊ᵒ }
    vs   } Assumpsit
Keeland Tyner }

I hereby Confess Judgment to plaintiff in the Sum of five Hundred & Seventy three dollars & three Cents, With interest & one Dollar for Noting, Besides Cost of Suit.

                          K. Tyner

Susan Wells, Extr[x] }
    vs   } Assumpsit
Keeland Tyner }

I hereby Confess judgment to plaintiff in the Sum of one hundred & thirty Seven dollars & Seventeen Cents, With interest & Cost.

                          Keeland Tyner

James A. Blanton   }
    vs   } Assumpsit
Alexander McGregor }

I hereby Confess judgment in The Sum of Seventy Six Dollars & Seventy Eight Cents, With interest & Cost.

                          Alex[r] McGregor

D. &. T. Parrish & C᠊ᵒ }
    vs   } Assumpsit
Alexander McGregor }

I Confess Judgment to the plaintiff The Sum of one hundred & thirteen Dollars, With Interest & Cost of Suit.

Alex[r] McGregor

October Term 1830

Isaac Norton }
    vs   } assumpsit
Keeland Tyner }

I hereby Confess judgment to plaintiff in the Sum of Three Hundred & Sixty eight dollars & fifty four Cents, With interest & Cost of protest & Cost of Suit.

Keeland Tyner

William C. Butler }
    vs   } assumpsit
Keeland Tyner }

I hereby Confess Judgment to plaintiff in the Sum of Two hundred & thirty Nine Dollars & forty Eight Cents, with interest & Cost of Suit & three dollars Cost of protest.

Keeland Tyner

George W. Smith & C[o] }
    vs   } Assumpsit
Keeland Tyner }

I hereby Confess judgment to plaintiff in the Sum of Two hundred & Seventy Six Dollars & Sixty four Cents, With interest & Cost of Suit & Cost of protest.

Keeland Tyner

Low, Taylor & C[o] }
    vs   } Assumpsit
Keeland Tyner }

I hereby Confess judgment To plaintiff in the Sum of One Thousand & three dollars & Seventy Six Cents, with interest & Cost of protest & Cost of Suit.

K. Tyner

Smith & Wright }
    vs   } Assumpsit
Keeland Tyner }

I hereby Confess Judgment to plaintiff in the Sum of two hundred & Eighty Eight Dollars & fifty Cents, With interest & Cost of Suit & Cost of protest.

K. Tyner

October Term 1830

The Court adjourned till tomorrow Morning at 9 O'clock.

Timothy Mathews, J. I. C.
Saml B. Hunter, J. I. C.
Ja^s H. Rodgers, J. I. C.

Georgia   } Tuesday Morning October 19th 1830 The honorable the
Bibb County } Inferior Court in and for the County of Bibb Meet agreeable to adjournment.

Present, their honors   Timothy Mathews }
                                       Samuel B. Hunter } J. I. C.
                                         James H. Rodgers }

Thomas Napier }
    vs   } Case
Keeland Tyner }

We, the jury, find for The plaintiff the Sum of Six Nine Dollars and twenty four Cents, With interest & Cost.

J. W. Hutcherson, forman

Gordon C. Coit }
    vs } Debt
John D. & A. Chapman }

We Confess judgment To the plaintiff for two Hundred & Seventy two Dollars, With interest & Cost.

                      Tracy & Butler, att[ys] for Def[t]

Gordon C. Coit }
    vs } Debt
J. D. & A. Chapman }

We Confess judgment To the plaintiff for two hundred & twenty five Dollars, With interest & Cost.

                      Tracy & Butler, Att[ys] for Def[t]

October Term 1830

Wiley, Baxter & Fort }
    vs } Assumpsit
Young Johnston }

I Confess judgment To the plaintiff for fifty dollars & fifty four Cents, With interest & Cost.

                      Young Johnston

N. B.& H. Weed }
    vs } Assumpsit
Keeland Tyner }
and Simri Rose }

We hereby Confess judgment to the plaintiff in the Sum of Eighty Nine dollars & Sixty five Cents, besides interest & Cost.

                      Keeland Tyner
                      Simri Rose by
                      Campbell & Seymour, att[ys]

Luke Reed & C° }
     vs   } Assumpsit
Robert Birdsong }

We, the jury, find for the plaintiff in the Sum of One hundred & Eighty Nine Dollars & Eighty Cents, With interest & Cost.

                               John Elsworth, forman

Wiley, Baxter & Fort }
     vs   } assumpsit
Henry Milburn   }

We, the jury, find for the plaintiff the Sum of One hundred and two Dollars & Eighty three Cents, With Interest & Cost.

                               John Elsworth, forman

Wiley, Baxter & Fort }
     vs   } assumpsit
John Loving   }

We, the jury, find for the plaintiff the Sum of Ninety four Dollars fifty Six Cents, With Interest & Cost.

                               John Elsworth, forman

B. S. Griffin }
     vs   } assumpsit
M. Robertson }

We, the jury, find for The plaintiff One hundred & Sixty One Dollars and thirty three Cents.

                               J. W. Hutcherson, form

<u>October Term 1830</u>

Rob Bledsor   }
     vs   } Case
Daniel B. Worsham }

We, the jury, find for The plaintiff the Sum of five Hundred and fifty two Dollars and Ninety two Cents, With Interest and Cost of protest & Suit.

           J. W. Hutcherson, form

Robert Bledsor   }
 vs   } Case
Alexander McGregor }

We, the jury, find for The plaintiff in the sum of Five hundred & fifty two dollars and Ninety two Cents, With Interest and Cost of protest & Suit.

           J. W. Hutcherson, forman

Thomas Napier   }
 vs   } Debt
Alexander McGregor }

We, the jury, find for the plaintiff the Sum of one hundred & thirty dollars Sixty two & a half Cents, With interest & Cost.

           J. W. Hutcherson, forman

Kimberly & Chisholm }
 vs   } Assumpsit
James W. Alston }

We, the jury, find for plaintiffs the Sum of One hundred & Sixty Two dollars & five Cents, With Interest & Cost.

           John Elsworth, forman

Owen Brown   }
 vs   } Assumpsit
William P. Tompkins }

We, the jury, find for plaintiff thirty Eight Dollars & twenty five Cents, With interest & Cost of Suit.

           John Elsworth, forman

James A. Blanton }
 vs   } assumpsit Judgment
J. D. & A. Chapman }

Confessed to plaintiff the Sum of Seven hundred & Seventeen Dollars & forty four Cents, With interest & Cost of Suit.

        C. B. Cole, Def^t att^y

October Term 1830

Nicholas Wagner }
  vs   } assumpsit
James L. Blanton }

We, the jury, find for the plaintiff the Sum of forty Six dollars Sixty two & a half Cents, With Cost of Suit.

        J. W. Hutcherson, forman

Daniel Barringer }
  vs   } Debt
Elam Alexander }

We hereby Confess Judgment to the plaintiff in the Sum of Seventy five dollars and Seventy five Cents, With interest & Cost.

        Elam Alexander by
        Campbell & Seymour, att^y

Robert H. Benton }
  vs   } Assumpsit
Nicholas Wagner }

We, the jury, find for the plaintiff one hundred & Two Dollars, With Cost of Suit.

        John Elsworth, forman

George Newhall }
  vs   } Assumpsit
Hockey L. Towns}

Judgment Confessed for plaintiff the Sum of Six hundred and Twenty Seven dollars & Seven Cents, With interest & Cost.

        C. B. Cole, Def^{ts} att^y

George Newhall }
    vs   } Assumpsit
Solomon D. Chapman }

Judgment Confessed the Sum of Six hundred and Twenty Seven dollars & Seven Cents, With interest & Cost of protest & Cost of Suit.

                                        C. B. Cole, def^{ts} att^y

Spear & Patton }
    vs   } Assumpst
J. D. & A. Chapman }

I Confess judgment for plaintiff the Sum of Nine Hundred dollars & Eighty five Dollars & Eighty five Cents, With interest & Cost of protest & Cost of Suit.

                                        C. B. Cole, Def^{ts} att^y

---

October Term 1830

George Newhall }
    vs   } Assumpsit
J. D. & A. Chapman }

I hereby Confess judgment to plaintiff in the Sum of Six hundred and twenty Seven Dollars & Seven Cents, With interest & Cost.

                                        C. B. Cole, att^y for def^t

Thomas Napier }
    vs   } Case
James E. Jordon }

I do Confess judgment To the plaintiff in the Sum of one hundred dollars, With interest & Cost.

                                        James E. Jordon

Thomas Napier }
    vs   } Case
Keeland Tyner }

We, the jury, find for the plaintiff the Sum of Sixty Eight Dollars & Seventy three Cents, With interest & Cost.

         J. W. Hutcherson, forman

Anson Kimberly }
  vs   } Assumpsit
James Alston }

We, the jury, find for plaintiff in the Sum of Two hundred & twenty five Dollars, With interest & Cost.

         J. W. Hutcherson, forman

N. B. & H. Weed }
  vs   } Assumpsit
James Alston }

We, the jury, find for plaintiff in the Sum of three Hundred & Eighty Eight Dollars & Sixty Eight Cents, With interest & Cost.

         J. W. Hutcherson, forman

Mark H. Wakeman }
  vs   } AAssumpsit
James W. Alston }

We, the jury, find for plaintiff the Sum of Sixty Seven Dollars & thirty Cents, Besides interest & Cost of Suit.

         J. W. Hutcherson, forman

October Term 1830

Wiley & Baxter }
  vs   } Assumpsit
William J. Danelly }
Guardian of   }
James M. Danelly }

We, the jury, find for plaintiff the Sum of one hundred & fifty Dollars & Thirty four Cents, With Interest & Cost.

J. W. Hutcherson, forman

Wiley & Baxter }
    vs } Assumpsit
Wm J. Danelly }
Guardian of }
Louisa B. Danelly }

We, the jury, find for plaintiff the Sum of three hundred & fifty Two Cents, With Interest & Cost.

J. W. Hutcherson, forman

Wiley & Baxter }
    vs } Assumpsit
Wm J. Danelly }
Guardian of }
Maria P. Danelly }

We, the jury, find for plaintiff the Sum of Two hundred & fifty Six Dollars & forty Eight Cents, With Interest & Cost.

J. W. Hutcherson, forman

Wiley & Baxter }
    vs } Assumpsit
William J. Danelly }

We, the jury, find for plaintiff the Sum of Eighty Dollars, With Interest & Cost.

J. W. Hutcherson, forman

Bank of Darien }
    vs } Assumpsit
Alexander McGregor }

We Confess judgment To plaintiff for four hundred & fifteen Dollars, With interest and Cost & three Dollars for Noting protest.

Tracy & Butler, Att^{ys} for Def^t

Griffin & Welch }
    vs   } Assumpsit
James A. Blanton }

We, the jury, find for the plaintiff Two hundred Twenty Nine Dollars forty five Cents.

                                        J. W. Hutcherson, forman

---

October Term 1830

Anson Kimberly }
    vs   } Debt
George B. Wardlaw }

I Confess judgment To the plaintiff for Eighty Dollars & twenty Cents, With interest & Cost of Suit.

                                Tracy & Butler, Att^{ys} for plff

Marine & Fire Insurance   }
Bank of the State of Georgia }
    vs   } Assumpsit
Spencer Riley   }

I hereby Confess judgment to the plaintiff in the Sum of five hundred & Eighty Seven Dollars & thirteen Cents, With interest & Cost, and three Dollars Cost of protest.

                                          Spencer Riley

Campbell & Seymour }
    vs   } Case
Spencer Riley   }

I Confess judgment to plaintiff for one hundred and twenty two Dollars & twelve Cents principal, With Interest & Cost.

                                          Spencer Riley

Thomas B. Stubbs, Ex^{trix} &c }
    vs   } Assumpsit
Calton B. Cole   }

I Confess judgment to plaintiff for four hundred Dollars principal, With interest & Cost.

         C. B. Cole

M. F. Freeman }
Survivor &c   }
  vs   } Assumpsit
John M. Shelman }

I Confess judgment The plaintiff fifty four Dollars and Six Cents principal, besides interest & Cost.

         John M. Sanders

Campbell & Seymour }
   vs   } assumpsit
J. D. & A. Chapman }

We Confess judgment for plaintiff five hundred Dollars principal, With interest & Cost.

         C. B. Cole, Def^{ts} att^y

October Term

Mathew F. Freeman }
Survivour &c   }
  vs   } Debt &c
William Hoge }

We, the jury, find for The plaintiff Sixty Seven Dollars and thirty four [blot] one Quarter Cents principal, With interest & Cost.

         John Elsworth, forman

Mathew F. Freeman }
Survivour &c   }
  vs   } Assumpsit
William Cumming }

I Confess judgment for the plaintiff forty Dollars & Ninety five Cents, With interest & Cost.

        William Cumming

Thomas B. Stubbs }
  vs   } Assumpsit
Robert Coleman }

I Confess judgment for the plaintiff four hundred Dollars principal, With interest & Cost.

        C. B. Cole, Def[ts] att[y]

Edward W. Wright }
  vs   } Debt
C. B. Strong   }

We, the jury, find for the plaintiff One hundred And Seventy Nine Dollars and thirty Seven Cents principal, With interest & Cost.

        John Elsworth, forman

Isaiah Chapman }
  vs   } assumpsit
J. D. & A. Chapman }

I Confess judgment To the plaintiff for four hundred & Seventy five Dollars principal, With interest and Cost.

        C. B. Cole, att[y] for Def[t]

Isaiah Chapman }
  vs   } assumpsit & Bail
Keeland Tyner }

I Confess Judgment to the plaintiff for five hundred & Seventy five Dollars, With interest & Cost.

        Campbell & Seymour, Def[ts] att[y]

October Term

Wm J. Danelly & C° }
for the use &c }
    vs } Case
Spencer Riley }

We, the Jury, find for the plaintiff fifty Six dollars and Eighty Seven cents, With interest And Cost of Suit.

                          J. W. Hutcherson, forman

Susan Wells, Executrix }
of N. W. Wells, dec^d }
    vs } assumpsit
Young Johnston }

We, the jury, find for the Defendant Twenty Eight Dollars Six and a Quarter Cents, With ~~interest~~ Cost of Suit.

                          John Elsworth, forman

The Bank of Darien }
    vs } Case
Charles S. Lewis }

We, the jury, find for the plaintiff four hundred & fifteen Dollars principal debt, & three Dollars for Noting & protest, With Cost of Suit.

                          J. W. Hutcherson, forman

Wiley & Baxter }
    vs } Debt
Francis A. Manard }

We, the jury, find for the plaintiff forty two Dollars & thirty one Cents, with interest & Cost of Suit.

                          J. W. Hutcherson, forman

Wiley & Baxter }
    vs } Debt
Stephen Manard }

We, the Jury, find for the plaintiff fifty Eight Dollars & thirty Eight Cents, with interest & Cost.

J. W. Hutcherson, forman

Abraham C. Byrd }
  vs   } Trover
George A. Smith }

We, the Jury, find for the defendant, With Cost of Suit.

John Elsworth, forman

October Term 1830

Wm J. Danelly & Co }
for the use of   }
Wiley & Baxter }
  vs   } Debt
John M. Sanders }

I confess judgment to the plaintiff for the Sum of Eighty four Dollars & Sixty five Cents, With interest & Cost of Suit.

John M. Sanders

Philip Cook, for the use }
of the penitentiary }
  vs   } Assumpsit
Hugh Knox   }

We Confess judgment to the plaintiff for fifty Dollars, With interest & Cost, With right of appeal.

McDonald & Franklin, Def^{ts} att^{ys}

Q. & T. Parrish &c }
  vs   } Assumpsit
Vance & Knox }

We, the jury, find for plaintiff the Sum of Seventy Seven Dollars & Eighty one Cents, With interest & Cost.

J. W. Hutcherson, forman

Thomas B. Stubbs }
Executor &c }
    vs } Assumpsit
J. D. & A. Chapman }

We Confess Judgment for the plaintiff four hundred Dollars principal, With interest & Cost.

C. B. Cole, Def^t att^y

Napier & Rilander }
    vs } Assumpsit
Elijah Cotton }

We, the jury, find for the plaintiff the Sum of forty Seven Dollars & Sixty Cents, With Cost of Suit.

John Elsworth, forman

Kimberly & Chisholm }
    vs } Assumpsit
Sir James Pitman }

We, the jury, find for plaintiff the Sum of Thirty Two Dollars & Eighty three Cents & Cost.

John Elsworth, forman

October Term 1830

Bank of State }
of Georgia }
    vs } Assumpsit
Simri Rose, indorser }

We, the jury, find for the plaintiff five Hundred dollars principal, With interest & Cost.

         John Elsworth, forman

Marine & Fire }
Insurance Bank }
  vs } Assumpsit
Nathaniel Barker }

I hereby Confess Judgment to plaintiff in the Sum of five hundred & Eighty Seven Dollars and thirteen Cents, With interest & Cost.

         Nathaniel Barker

Campbell & Seymour }
  vs } Assumpsit
Alexander McGregor }

We, the jury, find for plaintiff five hundred Dollars principal, with interest & Cost.

         J. W. Hutcherson, forman

Isaac Norton }
  vs } Assumpsit
Nicholas Childers }

We, the jury, find for the plaintiff in the Sum of Fifty Eight Dollars, with interest & Cost.

         J. W. Hutcherson, forman

Mathew F. Freeman }
  vs } Debt
Alexander McGregor }

We Confess Judgment for the plaintiff Sixty three Dollars & thirty four Cents principal, with interest & Cost.

         Tracy & Butler, att[ys] for Def[t]

Bigelow & Birch & C° }
     vs   } Case
David Dalemyda &   }
Keeland Tyner, indorsee}

Judgment Confessed for the plaintiff thirty three Dollars & two Cents principal, With interest & Cost.

                                  Tracy & Butler, Def[ts] att[y]

October Term 1830

Robert Collins   }
     vs   } Assumpsit
Hockey L. Towns}

We, the jury, find for the plaintiff one hundred and Ninety four Dollars, with interest & Cost.

                                    John Elsworth, forman

Jeremiah Smith }
     vs   } Debt
Keeland Tyner }

I Confess judgment for the plaintiff Sixty three Dollars principal & Cost.

                                    K. Tyner

Bigelow, Birch & C° }
     vs   } Case
David F. Wilson & }
Keeland Tyner   }

We Confess for the plaintiff Eighty Six Dollars & Eighty Seven Cents principal, With interest & Cost.

                                    David F. Wilson
                                    & K. Tyner

Campbell & Seymour }
     vs   } Assumpsit
Chapman & Arnett   }

We Confess Judgment for the plaintiff five hundred Dollars principal, with interest & Cost.

C. B. Cole, Def[ts] att[y]

Robert Collins }
    vs   } Assumpsit
Chapman & Arnett }

We, the Jury, find for the plaintiff One Hundred and Ninety four Dollars, With interest & Cost.

J. W. Hutcherson, forman

Jeremiah Smith }
    vs   } Assumpsit
John M. Sanders }

We, the jury, find for the plaintiff Two hundred thirty Dollars principal, With interest and Cost.

J. W. Hutcherson, forman

October Term 1830

John Oler }
    vs   } Case
Zackariah Sims }

We, the jury, find for The plaintiff fifty dollars, With interest & Cost of Suit.

J. W. Hutcherson, forman

Kimberly & Chisholm }
    vs   } assumpsit
Thomas McMurrian }

We, the jury, find for plaintiff The Sum of Eighty One Dollars & twenty Six Cents, With interest & Cost.

John Elsworth, forman

William J. Danelly & C°}
for the use &c   }
    vs   } Debt
Robert S. Patton   }

We, the jury, find for The plaintiff forty Dollars & fifty Cents, With interest & Cost of Suit.

                                        J. W. Hutcherson, forman

The Court adjourned till Wednesday Morning at 8 O'clock.

                                        Timothy Mathews, J. I. C.
                                        Saml B. Hunter, J. I. C.
                                        Ja^s H. Rodgers, J. I. C.

Georgia   } Wednesday Morning
Bibb County } October 20th 1830

The Honorable the Inferior Court In and for the County of Bibb Meet agreeable To agreeable to adjournment. present their honors

                                      Timothy Mathews }
                                      Samuel B. Hunter } J. I. C.
                                      James H. Rodgers }

James Tobin   } Fifa returnable to April Term
    vs   } 1830 Bibb Inferior Court
Francis Willey & } Affidavit of Illegality
Alex McGregor   }

upon hearing the affidavit argument in the above Case, It is ordered that the

---

October Term 1830

above Case, It is ordered that the fifa be Set aside as Null & Void and no further proceedings be had under Said fifa against defendants.

Levi Eckly   }
    vs   } Assumpsit
John M. Sander   }

I Confess judgment To the plaintiff one hundred Dollars principal, With interest & Cost.

           John M. Sanders

Anson Kimberly }
  vs   } Assumpsit
James Alston }

We, the Jury, find for the plaintiff in the Sum of Two hundred and twenty five Dollars, With interest & Cost.

           J. W. Hutcherson, forman

Susan Wells, Extr^x }
of N. W. Wells }
  vs   } assumpsit
William Ward }

We, the Jury, find for plaintiff the Sum of Seventy Six Dollars & Eighty Cents, With Interest & Cost.

           J. W. Hutcherson, forman

Zackariah Lamar }
  vs   } Debt
Zackariah Sims }

We, the jury, find for the plaintiff One hundred Dollars, With interest & Cost.

           J. W. Hutcherson, forman

William Cumming, for }
the use of J. S. Childers }
  vs   } Casa from Magistrates Court
Micajah Williams   }

The defendant, having Been Arrested in Said Case, And having given bond & Security to appear at this Court and take the benefit of the Insolvent act, And Having been Called and not appearing, it is therefore Ordered that Said plaintiff enter up judgment against Said Defendant and his Security, William Riley, on the Bond for the principal, interest, & Cost of Said Execution.

October Term 1830

Thomas Napier }
  vs   } Case
Eaton Hollomon }

We Confess Judgment To the plaintiff for [blank]

Thomas Napier } In Bibb Inferior Court
  vs   } April term 1830 Case
Eaton Hollomon }

It appearing to the Court that an action has been Commenced on the note upon which the above Action is brought in Houston Superior Court against James Jarrett, the Maker of Said Note. It is therefore ordered by the Court that the plaintiff's Attorney have Leave to Withdraw Said original Note from this Court by filing a Copy of Said Note in this Court for the purpose of Maintaining the Action against the Maker in Houston Superior Court.

           George W. Gordon, plff att^y

William C. Powell was Sworn }
on Jury N° 1 in place of Wm Dun }

The Inspectors of }
The Penitentiary }
  vs   } Assumpsit
Hugh Knox }

      Jury N° 2

We, the jury, find for the plaintiff the Sum of Nine hundred Dollars & thirty Seven cents, With Cost of Suit.

           Leonard Adams, forman

Lewis Foy   }
  vs   } Case & Bail
William French }

We, the jury, find for the plaintiff forty Dollars, With interest & Cost of Suit.

         John Elsworth, forman

October Term 1830

B. S. Griffin } assumpsit and Verdict for the plaintiff
  vs   } for one hundred and Sixty one Dollars
M. Robertson } & thirty three Cents and Cost

The defendant, being dissatisfied With the Verdict of the jury rendered in the above Cause, and Having paid all Cost and demanded an appeal, by his Attorney at Law, Edward D. Tracy, brings Simri Rose and tenders him as his Security. And they, the Said Mathew Robertson, by his attorney, and Simri Rose acknowledge themselves jointly and Severally bound to Bennett S. Griffin, the Plaintiff, for the payment of the eventual Condemnation Money in Said Cause. In testimony Whereof, they have hereunto Set Their hands and Seals this 20th day of october 1830.

Test. M. Simmons, Clk   Mathew Robertson
           by his Attorney at Law
           Edwd D. Tracy
           Simri Rose

Griffin & Welch } Assumpsit & Verdict for the plaintiff for
  vs   } Two hundred and Twenty Nine dollars
James A. Blanton } & fifty five Cents & Cost

The defendant, being dissatisfied With Verdict of the jury rendered in the above Cause, and having paid all Cost and demanded an appeal, Brings John S. Childers and tenders him as his Security, and they, the Said James A. Blanton and John S. Childers, acknowledge Themselves jointly and Severally bound to Griffin & Welch, The plaintiff, for the true payment of the Eventual Condemnation Money in Said Cause. In testimony Whereof, they have hereunto Set their hands & Seals this 20th day of October 1830.

Test. M. Simmons, Clk   J. A. Blanton
           John S. Childers

October Term

Bank of Darien }
    vs } Sci fa
Robert Birdsong }
Executor of A. Jeter }

Jury N° 2

We, the jury, find for plaintiff the Sum of one Hundred & twenty five Dollars, With interest & Cost.

Leonard Adams, forman

Joel Bond }
    vs } Case &c
Mortimer R. Wallis }

We, the jury, find for the plaintiff one hundred Dollars, With Cost of Suit.

John Elsworth, forman

Thomas B. Stubbs, Ex &c }
    vs } assumpsit
Solomon D. Chapman }

I Confess Judgment to the plaintiff for four hundred & Eighty Seven Dollars principal, With interest & Cost.

C. B. Cole, Def^t att^y

Thomas Stubbs, Ex^r }
    vs } assumpsit
Luke Ross }

I Confess judgment To the plaintiff for four hundred & Eighty Seven Dollars principal, with interest & Cost.

C. B. Cole, Def^t att^y

Thomas Stubbs, Exr &c }
      vs   } assumpsit
Hockey L. Towns   }

I Confess Judgment to the plaintiff for four hundred & Eighty Seven Dollars principal, With interest & Cost.

                                      C. B. Cole, Defts atty

October Term 1830

Thomas B. Stubbs, Exr   }
      vs   } assumpsit
John D. & Abner Chapman }

I Confess judgment To plaintiff for four hundred & Eighty Seven Dollars principal, With interest & Cost.

                                      C. B. Cole, Deft atty

It appearing to the Court that a bond taken By a Magistrate of James Hall for the Maintainance & Support of a bastard Child is Not taken in the form prescribed by the law, it is ordered that the party applying for Said bond have leave to Institute proceedings (de Novo) anew.

Marine & Fire Insurance   }
Bank of the State of Georgia }
      vs   } Assumpsit
Hockey L. Towns   }

                                     Jury N° 2

We, the Jury, find for the plaintiff the Sum of Five hundred & Eighty Seven Dollars & thirteen Cents, With interest & Cost of protest & Cost of Suit.

                                      Leonard Adams, forman

Marine & Fire Insurance }
Bank of the State of Georgia }
      vs } Assumpsit
Solomon D. Chapman }
and Felix Arnett }

Jury N° 2

We, the Jury, find for the plaintiff the Sum of five hundred And Eighty Seven Dollars & thirteen Cents, With interest & Cost of protest & Cost of Suit.

Leonard Adams, form

Bank of State of Georgia }
      vs } assumpsit
Keeland Tyner }

We, the jury, find for The plaintiff five hundred Dollars principal, With interest & Cost.

John Elsworth, forman

<u>October Term 1830</u>

The Court adjourned till Thursday Morning at 10 O'clock.

Saml B. Hunter, J. I. C.
Ja^s H. Rodgers, J. I. C.
Timothy Mathews, J. I. C.

Georgia } Thursday Morning October 21st 1830 The honorable
Bibb County } the Inferior Court in and for said County Meet agreeable to adjournment

Present, their honors   Timothy Mathews }
                                       Samuel B. Hunter } J. I. C.
                                       James H. Rogers }

Alexander Richards } Bond to take the benefit
      vs } of the act for the relief
Jonathan Wilder & } of Honest Debtors
Harmon H. Howard, Security }

The defendant, Jonathan Wilder, having been arrested on three Casa in favour of plaintiff, Alexander Richards, and having given bond to Appear at this term of this Court to take the Benefit of the act for the relief of honest Debtors, & having failed to Appear When Called, & having failed to file his Schedule & Notify the Arresting Creditor in terms of the Law, on Motion, it is Ordered that judgment be entered up instanter Against The Said Jonathan Wilder & his Security, Harmon H. Howard, on their Said Bond.

David Smithheart, John Molsby, Ezekiel Smith, John Scully, Thomas Seacry were Sworn on Jury N° 2 in place Charles McCardell, Hezekiah McKinnie, Jehu W. Hutcherson, & William Johnson, & George Whitehead absent.

October Term

Arnold Johnson having been arrested on a Capias at the Suit of Precilla Good for a Debt of Six Dollars Besides interest & Cost & the Said Arnold Johnson having given bond in performance of the act in Such Case Made & provided to attend at the Last term of this Court to Take the benefit of the Honest debtors act and the Said Arnold Johnson having failed to appear at the Last term or the present, on Motion of Counsel for The plaintiff, Priscella Good. It is Ordered that they have Leave to enter up judgment in favour of the Said Priscella Good against the Said Arnold Johnson And William Cumming, his Security in Said bond, for the Sum of thirteen dollars and Sixty cents (the penalty Thereof) to be discharged upon payment of Said debt & Cost & that Execution issue accordingly.

Ordered that Beverly Rew be paid three dollars for three days Servis as Bailiff at this term.

Thomas B. Stubbs }
Executor &c }
      vs } Judgment & Stay of Execution
Luke Ross }

Came into office the Defendant by his attorney at Law, Calton B. Cole, Who Wishing the Stay of Execution in terms of the Law, paid all Cost and Entered a Stay of Execution for Sixty days and, at the Same time, Came Henry G. Ross, his Security, and they, the Said Luke Ross, by his attorney, & Henry G. Ross, acknowledge themselves jointly & Severally bound to the plaintiff for the payment of Said Judgment and all further Cost at the Expiration of Sixty Days in terms of the Law. In Witness Whereof, they have hereunto Set their hands & Seal This 21st day of October 1830.

Luke Ross, by his att^y
at Law, Carlton B. Cole
Henry G. Ross

October Term 1830

William Moore }
    vs } fifa
John J. Kaigler & }
David F. Wilson }
Def^{ts} in Ex and }
Sarah Q. Fluker }
Claimant }

We, the jury, find The property not Subject.

Leonard Adams, forman

John Smith   } Bond to take the benefit
    vs   } of the Honest Debtors act
Christopher Lynch }

The defendant, Christopher Lynch, having been arrested on a Casa issued from a justice Court in favour of John Smith & having given his bond for his appearance at this Term of this Court to Take the benefit of the act for the relief of honest debtors, With David F. Wilson as his Security, & having failed to file his Schedule & Notify the arresting Creditor in terms of the Law, & having failed to appear When Called. On Motion, it is ordered that Judgment be entered up instanter against the Defendants, Christopher Lynch & David F. Wilson, his Security on the bond.

David A. Edgar }
    vs   } assumpsit
Hockey L. Towns }

We, the jury, find for the plaintiff Thirty two Dollars and Eighty Cents, with interest & Cost.

                                            Leonard Adams, forman

Douglass C. Watson }
      vs   } fifa
Francis Willey &   }
John Molesby   }
Def^{ts} in Ex and   }
Alex^r McGregor   }
Claimant   }

We, the jury, find the property not Subject.

                                            Leonard Adams, forman

---

October Term 1830

John Smith   } fifa from justice Court Bond to take
     vs   } the Benefit of the Insolvent act
Christopher Lynch &   } Inferior Court
David F. Wilson, Security } October Term 1830

The Said Wilson, Security on Said bond, having Come into open Court and tendered his principal to Said plaintiff and the Officer of this Court In discharge of the Condition of a bond for his appearance at this Court to take the benefit of the Insolvent Debtors act, the Said Lynch is ordered into the Custody of the Sheriff and that Said Wilson be Considered as discharged from his Said Security Ship and that forasmuch as Said Wilson has before this adjournment of this Court tendered his Principal in discharge of Said bond, it is ordered and decreed that an order heretofore taken During the present Session of this Court in favour of Said plaintiff to enter up judgment upon Said bond from the Non appearance of Said Principal be wholly revoked and annulled.

ordered that Alfred Bady be paid five Dollars for his Services as Bailiff at this term.

Ordered that Rose & Slade be paid fifteen Dollars and Sixty two Cents for Stationary.

Ezekiel Smith }
for The use &c }
    vs } Assumpsit
Alex McGregor }

We find for the defendant.

                              Leonard Adams, forman

October Term 1830

~~The Inspectors of~~ }
~~The Penitentiary~~ } ~~Assumpsit & Verdict for the plaintiff~~
    ~~vs~~ } ~~for~~ [blank] ~~and Cost~~
~~Hugh Knox~~ }

~~the Defendant, being disatisfied With The Verdict of the jury rendered in the above Cause, Came and having paid all Cost and demanded an Appeal, by his attorney at Law, Charles J. McDonald, and Brings Archibald Darragh & Levi Eckly and tenders them as his S, Acknowledge Themselves jointly and Severally bound to the Inspectors of the Penitentiary, the plaintiff, for the payment of the Eventual Condemnation Money in Said Cause. In testimony Whereof, they have hereunto Set their hands~~

The Inspectors }
of Penitentiary } Assumpsit & Verdict for the plaintiff
    vs } for [blank] & Cost
Hugh Knox }

the defendant, by his attorney at Law Charles J. McDonald, being disatisfied With the Verdict of The jury rendered in the above Cause, and having paid all Cost and demanded an Appeal, Brings Archibald Darragh & Levi Eckly & tenders them as his Security, and they, the Said Hugh Knox, by his said attorney, & Archibald Darragh & Levi Eckly,

Acknowledge Themselves jointly and Severally bound to the Inspectors of the Penitentiary, the plaintiff, for the true payment of the Eventual Condemnation Money in Said Cause. In Testamony Whereof, they have hereunto Set their hands and & Seals this 21st day of October 1830.

Test. M. Simmons, Clk   Hugh Knox, by his
                                         attorney at Law
                                         Charles J. McDonald
                                         Levi Eckley

October Term 1830

The following Jury Was Drawn to Serve at April Term 1831.

1. George H. Grubbs
2. William R. Brown
3. William Bowden
4. Reubin Williams
5. Isaac Scott
6. Thomas Knowland
7. John Malloy
8. D. L. Harris
9. William Harris
10. Beverly Rew
11. Phillip Powledge
12. John W. Jackson
13. Charles Green
14. Benjamin Terry
15. Philander Judson
16. Alex^r McLaughlain
17. John W. Snow
18. Enoch Green
19. Ephram Jones
20. Lewis J. Groce
21. Joshua Johnson
22. Jesse Bateman
23. John Gamble
24. Peter P. Rockwell
25. John Bridges
26. Benjamin McSumner
27. Wm B. Jordon
28. Frederick B. Isler
29. Mathew Jones
30. Richard A. Cone
31. Henry Stewart
32. G. C. King
33. David Dean
34. Thomas McCarder
35. James Hammock
36. John McCarthy

The Court then adjourned till Court in Course.

Robert H. Benton } Assumpsit & Verdict for
      vs   } The plaintiff for one hundred
Nicholas Wagner } & ten dollars & Cost

the defendant, being Disatisfied With the Verdict of the jury rendered in the above Cause and having paid all Cost and demanded an appeal, brings Smith Bennett And tenders him as his Security, and they, the Said Nicholas Wagner and Smith Bennett, Acknowledge themselves jointly and Severally bound to Robert H. Benton, the plaintiff, for the true payment of the Eventual Condemnation Money in Said Cause. In testamony Whereof, they have hereunto Set their hands & Seals this 25th day of October 1830.

Test. M. Simmons, Clk   N. Wagner
                                          S. W. Bennett

Thomas Napier   }
     vs   } Judgment & Stay of Execution
Absolum Jordon }

Came into office the defendant, Who Wishing the Stay of Execution in terms of the Law, paid all Cost and Entered a Stay of Execution for Sixty days, and, at the Same time, Came Duke W. Braswell, his Security, and they, the Said Absolum Jordon & Duke W. Braswell, Acknowledge Themselves jointly & Severally bound to the plaintiff for the payment of Said judgment & all further Cost at the Expiration of Sixty days in terms of the Law. In Witness Whereof, they have hereunto Set their hands & Seals this 25 day of October 1830.

Test. M. Simmons, Clk   Absalom Jordan
                                          Duke W. Braswell

October Term 1830

Joel Bond   } Case and Verdict for the
     vs   } plaintiff for one hundred
Mortimer R. Wallis   } Dollars & Cost

The defendant, being disatisfied With the Verdict of the Jury rendered in the above Cause and having paid all Cost and demanded an Appeal, Brings John L. Mustian and tenders him as his Security, and they, the Said Mortimer R. Wallis and John L. Mustian, acknowledge themselves jointly and Severally bound to Joel Bond, the plaintiff, for the true payment of the Eventual Condemnation Money in Said Cause. In testamony Whereof, they have hereunto Set their hands & Seals this 25th day of October 1830.

Test. M. Simmons, Clk   M. R. Wallis
                                               John L. Mustian

John Philpot } Case & Verdict for the
     vs   } plaintiff for fifty
Owen Brown } dollars & Cost

The defendant, by his attorney in fact Reubin Turner, being disatisfied With the Verdict of The jury rendered in the above Cause and having paid all Cost and demanded an appeal, Brings Henry H. Cone and Tenders him as his Security, and they, the Said Owen Brown, by his Said attorney, & Henry H. Cone, Acknowledge themselves jointly & Severally Bound to John Philpot, the plaintiff, for the true payment of the Eventual Condemnation Money in Said Cause. In testamony Whereof, they have hereunto Set their hands & Seals this 25th day of October 1830.

Test. M. Simmons, Clk   R. Turner, att° in fact
                                               H. H. Cone

October Term 1830

Kimberly & Chisholm }
        vs   } Judgment & Stay of Execution
Thomas McMurrain }

Came into office Thomas McMurrain, Who Wishing the Stay of Execution in terms of the Law, paid all Cost and Entered a Stay of Execution for Sixty days, and, at the Same time, Came Joseph Henderson, his Security, and they, the Said Thomas McMurrain & Joseph Henderson, acknowledge Themselves jointly & Severally bound to the plaintiff for the payment of Said Judgment and all further Cost at the Expiration of Sixty days in Terms of the Law. In Witness Whereof, they have Set their hands & Seals this 25th day of October 1830.

Test. Martin Simmons, Clk   Thomas McMurrain
                                                   Joseph Henderson

David A. Edger } Assumpsit & Verdict for the
     vs   } plaintiff for Thirty two Dollars
Hockey L. Towns} and Eighty Cents & Cost

The defendant, being disatisfied With the Verdict of the Jury rendered in the above Cause and having paid all Cost and demanded an appeal, and brings Alex Richards and tenders him as his Security, and they, the Said Hockey L. Towns and Alex Richards, acknowledge themselves jointly and Severally bound to David A. Edger, the plaintiff, for the payment of the Eventual Condemnation Money in Said Cause. In testimony Whereof, they have hereunto Set their hands & Seals this 25th day of October 1830.

Test. M. Simmons, Clk   H. L. Towns
                                        Alexander Richards

October Term 1830

Thomas Stubbs, Executor &c }
      vs   } Judgment & Stay of Execution
Hockey L. Towns   }

Came into office the defendant, Hockey L. Towns, Who Wishing the Stay of Execution in Terms of the law, paid all Cost and Entered a Stay of Execution for Sixty days, and, at the Same time, Came Alex^r Richards, his Security, and they, the Said Hockey L. Towns & Alex Richards, acknowledge themselves jointly & Severally Bound to the plaintiff for the payment of Said Judgment and all further Cost at Expiration of Sixty days in terms of the Law. In Witness, they have hereunto Set their hands & Seals this 26th day of October 1830.

Test. M. Simmons, Clk   H. L. Towns
                                        Alexander Richards

Abraham C. Byrd}
     vs   } Trover & Verdict for the
George A. Smith } Defendant for Cost

the Plaintiff, by his attorney at Law, Isaac G. Seymour, being Disatisfied With the Verdict of the jury rendered in the above Cause and having paid all Cost, demanded an appeal, Brings [blank] and tenders him as his

Security, and they, the Said Abraham C. Byrd, by his Said attorney, and [blank], acknowledge themselves jointly and Severally bound to the defendant for the payment of the eventual Condemnation Money in Said Cause. In testimony Whereof, they have hereunto Set their hands & Seals this 25th day of October 1830.

Test. Martin Simmons, Clk   Isaac G. Seymour
                                         R. B. Washington

October Term 1830

Ezekiel Smith }
for the use &c } assumpsit & verdict for
vs } the Defendant for Cost
Alexander McGregor }

the Plaintiff, ant by his attorney At Law, Isaac G. Seymour, being disatisfied With the Verdict of the jury rendered in the above Cause and having paid all Cost and demanded an appeal, Brings [blank] and tenders him as his Security, and they, the Said plaintiff, by his Said attorney, and [blank], acknowledge themselves jointly and Severally bound to the Alexander McGregor, the Defendant for the payment of the eventual Condemnation Money in Said Cause. In testimony Whereof, they have hereunto Set their hands & Seals this 26th day of October 1830.

                                         Isaac G. Seymour
                                         R. B. Washington

Thomas Napier } ~~assumpsit~~
vs } Judgment & Stay of Execution
Elijah Cotton }

Came into office the defendant, Elijah Cotton, Who Wishing the Stay of Execution in terms of the law, paid all Cost and Entered a Stay of Execution for Sixty days, and, at the Same time, Came James Thompson, his Security, and they, The Said Elijah Cotton and James Thompson, acknowledge themselves jointly & Severally bound to the plaintiff for the payment of Said judgment & all further Cost at the Expiration of

Sixty days in terms of the Law. In testamony Whereof, they have hereunto Set their hands & Seals this 26th day of October 1830.

Test. M. Simmons, Clk   E. Cotton
                             James Thompson

October Term 1830

Napier & Rylander }
     vs   } Judgment & Stay of Execution
Elijah Cotton }

Came into office the defendant, Elijah Cotton, Who Wishing the Stay of Execution in terms of the Law, paid all Cost and Entered a Stay of Execution for Sixty Days, and, at the Same time, Came James Thompson, his Security, and they, The Said Elijah Cotton and James Thompson, acknowledge themselves jointly & Severally Bound to the plaintiff for the payment of Said judgment & all further Cost at the Expiration of Sixty days in terms of the Law. In testamony Whereof, They have hereunto Set their hands & Seals this 26th Day of October 1830.

Test. M. Simmons, Clk   E. Cotton
                             James Thompson

Campbell & Seymour } Assumpsit & Verdict for the
     vs   } the plaintiff for five hundred
Alex McGregor } Dollars & Cost

the Defendant, being disatisfied With the Verdict of the Jury rendered in the above Cause and having paid all Cost and demanded an appeal, and brings David F. Wilson and tenders him as his Security, and they, The Said Alexander McGregor and [blank], acknowledge themselves jointly and Severally bound To Campbell & Seymour, the plaintiff, for the payment of the Eventual Condemnation Money in Said Cause. In testamony Whereof, they have hereunto Set their hands & Seals this 26h day of October 1830.

Test. M. Simmons, Clk   Alex^r McGregor
                             David F. Wilson

May Term 1831

Georgia } May 2nd 1831
Bibb County }

The honorable the Inferior Court in and for the County of Bibb Meet this day agreeable to adjournment. present, their honors

        Charles Williamson } J. I. C.
        Samuel B. Hunter }

The Court then adjourned till the third Monday inst.

Test. Martin Simmons, C. I. C.

May adjourned Term 1831

Georgia } May 16th 1831
Bibb County }

The Honorable the Inferior Court in and for said County Meet this day agreeable to adjournment. present, their honors

        Charles Williamson }
        Samuel B. Hunter } J. C. C.
        Wm B. Cone, Shff }

The Court then adjourned till the first Monday In June Next.

Test. Martin Simmons, C. I. C.

Georgia } June 6th 1831
Bibb County }

The honorable the Inferior Court in and for the County of Bibb Meet this Day agreeable to adjournment.

Present, their Honors   Samuel B. Hunter} J. I. C.
             Anderson Rice }

The Court then adjourned till the 9th inst.

Test. M. Simmons, Clk

May Term 1831

Georgia } June 9th 1831
Bibb County }

The honorable the Inferior Court in and for the County of Bibb Meet this day agreeable To adjournment. present

                                       Samuel B. Hunter} J. I. C.
                                       Anderson Rice }
                                       Wm B. Cone, Shff}

The Court then adjourned Till the Second Monday in July Next.

Test. Martin Simmons, C. I. C.

Georgia } July 11th 1831
Bibb County }

The honorable the Inferior Court in and for the County of Bibb Meet this day agreeable to adjournment, present, their honors

                                       Timothy Mathews }
                                       Samuel B. Hunter } J. I. C.
                                       Anderson Rice }

The following is the jury Sworn to Serve at This term.

Jury N° 1

1. Charles McCardell
2. Benjamin Terry
3. Whery Buck
4. Lewis J. Groce
5. Isaac Scott
6. Thomas Blanett
7. Williamson Glover
8. Richard A. Cone
9. John McCarthy
10. John Bridges
11. William B. Jordon
12. John Smith

Daniel B. Bruin }
      vs   } assumpsit
J. D. & A. Chapman }

We Confess judgment to the plaintiff in the Sum of four Hundred and Seventy Nine Dollars and fifty four Cents, With interest & Cost of protest.

        C. B. Cole, Def^{ts} att^y

May Term 1831

The Inspectors of }
the Penitentiary }
  vs   } Debt
Zackariah Sims }

I Confess Judgment to the plaintiff for Sixty four Dollars and two Cents, With interest & Cost of Suit.

        C. B. Cole, def^t att^y

Wiley & Baxter }
  vs   } Debt
James Thompson }

I Confess judgment to plaintiff in the Sum of forty one Dollars & Sixty Six Cents principal, with interest & Cost.

July 11th 1831   James Thompson

Kimberly & Chisholm }
  vs   } assumpsit
David McMurrain }

We, the Jury, find for The plaintiffs the Sum of Seventy five Dollars and forty four Cents, With Cost of Suit.

        Isaac Scott, forman

John Mitchell }
  vs   } assumpsit
David F. Wilson }

We, the jury, find for the plaintiff the Sum of fifty Dollars and Ninety three & three fourth Cents, With Interest & Cost of Suit.

         Isaac Scott, forman

Anson Kimberly }
adm^r of N. Cornwell }
  vs   } Assumpsit
C. B. Strong & }
Robert Birdsong }

We, the jury, find for the plaintiff thirty two Dollars, with interest & Cost.

         Isaac Scott, forman

Adjourned May Term 1831

Colin W. Alexander }
  vs   } assumpsit
Nicholas Childers }

We, the jury, find for the plaintiff Seventy three Dollars and twenty three Cents, With interest & Cost.

         Isaac Scott, forman

James Woodard }
  vs   } Assumpsit
William Cumming }

We, the jury, find for the plaintiff the Sum of Eighty one Dollars and Ninety Cents, With interest & Cost.

         Isaac Scott, forman

Hungerford & Stoddard }
  vs   } Assumpsit
William B. Cone }

I Confess Judgment to the plaintiff In the Sum of one hundred Dollars, With interest & Cost of Suit.

Wm B. Cone

John T. Rowland }
    vs   } Casas from justice Court
Wade Hampton }

the Bail Came and delivered the defendant in open Court, it is therefore ordered that Defendant be taken by the Sheriff and Keep in his Custody and the bail be exonerated from his Said bail.

Jury N° 2 Sworn to Serve at this term

1. Caleb Condon
2. Ephram Jones
3. Peter P. Rockwell
4. James Thompson
5. Joseph Henderson
6. Abalum Jordon
7. Wade Hampton
8. E. C. Bulkly
9. Burtran Tesserian
10. Samuel Stanford
11. Calvin L. Howland
12. Rubin C. Baily

Adjourned May Term 1831

M. R. Wallis }
    vs   } Assumpsit
Robert Birdsong }

I Confess judgment to the plaintiff for One hundred Dollars, with interest & Cost. 11th July 1831

R. Birdsong

John Mitchell }
    vs   } Assumpsit
William Cumming }

Jury N° 2

We, the jury, find for the plaintiff the Sum of Ninety Seven Dollars and Sixty Six Cents, with interest & Costs of Suit.

Samuel Stanford, forman

Elias B. Crane }
    vs   } Assumpsit
M. D. J. Slade }

We Confess judgment to the plaintiff in The Sum of Ninety five Dollars And Sixty two Cents, With interest & Cost of Suit.

                      Campbell & Seymour, Defent Att^{ys}

Mitchell & White for the }
use of Peley & Mitchell }
      vs   } Case
Marmaduke J. Slade }

We Confess Judgment to the plaintiff in the Sum of Forty nine Dollars & forty five Cents, with interest & Cost of Suit.

                      Campbell & Seymour, Def^{ts} att^{ys}

Ordered that William J. Price, Alfred M. Hobby, Robert H. Taylor, and Calton B. Cole be Appointed Notory Public for the County of Bibb By them taking the oath required by Law.

Adjourned May Term 1831

John M. McKiney   }
      vs   } Debt
Cornelius Townsend }

I Confess judgment To the plaintiff for the Sum of one hundred and fourteen Dollars, With interest & Cost.

                      C. Townsend

William Fraley and }
Henry Rogers, adm^{rs} }
of John Binion   }
      vs   } Assumpsit
Nicholas Childers   }

We, the Jury, find for plaintiff one hundred and Eighteen Dollars principal, With Interest & Cost.

Samuel Stanford, forman

Ambrose Baber }
    vs   } Debt
Edwin E. Slade }

We, the jury, find for the plaintiff one hundred and forty Six Dollars fifty four Cents, with interest & Cost.

Isaac Scott, forman

Charles Williamson } Casa defendant arrested
    vs   } & bond given by Virtue of
Benjamin Allen   } the Honest Debtors Act

It appearing to the Court that the Said defendant Has been arrested by Virtue of Said Casa and has Given bond Conditioned to his appearing at the present term of this Court to take the Benefit of the Honest Debtors Act and the Said defendant as well as John Curton & Jonathan Mathews, Securities, having been Called and Not appearing. It is therefore ordered that Said Charles Williamson Enter up judgment against the Said Allen and his Securities instanter for the principal, interest, & Cost of Said Casa.

Adjourned May Term 1831

William Quinerly }
    vs   } Casas from Justice Court
David F. Wilson }
Thomas G. Bates }

And Now, at this term of our Court, the defendant and his Securities being regularly Called and they having Made default, it is ordered that the plaintiff do recover against the Defendant & his Sureties the Sum of Twenty Eight Dollars and Sixty Cents, and the Sum of Nine Dollars and fifty Cents for his interest, and also the further Sum of Seven Dollars and Ninety three Cents Cost. 11th July 1831

Prince & Poe, plff[s] att[y]

The Court then adjourned till Morning the 12th at 9 O'clock.

Charles Williamson, J. I. C.
Saml B. Hunter, J. I. C.
Timothy Mathews, J. I. C.
A. Rice, J. I. C.

Georgia }
Bibb County } July 12th 1831

The honorable the Inferior Court in and for the County of Bibb Meet This day agreeable to adjournment. present, their honors

Timothy Mathews }
Samuel B. Hunter } J. I. C.
Charles Williamson }
Anderson Rice }

Ordered that John McCarthur, Thomas Bateman, and John Bailey be appointed Commissioners of Roads in and for Capt Rutland's Dist.

ordered that Mrs Condon be paid fifteen Dollars out of the poor fund.

Ordered that Henry G. Ross be paid twenty five Dollars for his acct.

Adjourned May Term 1831

Kimberly & Chisholm }
       vs   } Assumpsit
Thomas Knight }

I Confess judgment To the plaintiff for Sixty three Dollars & forty Cents, with interest and Cost.

Thomas Knight

Susan Wells, Executrix }
       vs   } Trover
Eliza A. Bullock }

We, the jury, find for the plaintiff Eight Thousand Nine hundred and Sixty five Dollars, Which May be discharged by the Delivery of the property Within Sixty days, With Cost of Suit.

Lewis J. Groce, forman

Abner Cherry & Thomas L. Ross were Sworn Jury N° 1 in place of Isaac Scott & Wm B. Jordon.

The Court adjourned till the Morning at 9 O'clock.

Timothy Mathews, J. I. C.
A. Rice, J. I. C.
Saml B. Hunter, J. I. C.
Charles Williamson, J. I. C.

Georgia }
Bibb County } July 13th 1831

The honorable Inferior Court in & for the County of Bibb Meet this day agreeable to adjournment. Present, their honors

Timothy Mathews }
Samuel B. Hunter } J. I. C.
Charles Williamson }
Anderson Rice }

Low, Taylor & C° }
      vs   } Judgment obtained at October
Keeland Tyner } Term 1830 Principal

on Motion of plaintiff's Counsel, leave is given by the Court to Withdraw the original Note upon which judgment was obtained upon filing a Copy Note in the original declaration.

Adjourned May Term 1831

John T. Rowland } Casa & Bond to take
      vs   } the Benefit of the Honest Debtors Act
Wade Hampton } May Term 1831

The Said Wade Hampton having given bond for his appearance at This term of the Court to take the benefit of the act for for the relief of Honest debtors and the Said Wade Hampton having failed to Make it appear to the Court That he had given the Necessary Notice to the arresting creditor or that he had failed to file his Schedule in Terms of the Law. It is therefore ordered and adjudged by the Court that the defendant, Wade Hampton, be Imprisoned untill he Shall have given the Necessary Notice & filed his Schedule as required by law, to be adjudged of by the Court.

Ordered that the Sum of Twenty Dollars be paid to Sarah Davis, a pauper, for the present year Commencing from the first day of this ins^t and that the Same be paid her out of any Monies in the hands of the treasurer Not otherwise appropriated. July 13th 1831

Seaborn Jones }
Eliza A. Bullock }
adm^r & adm^x &c }
    vs } Trover & Conversion
Irwin Bullock }

We Confess judgment to the Defendant, With Cost of Suit, reserving the right of appeal.

                        Campbell & Seymour, Plff^s att^y

[blank] Peacock }
    vs } assumpsit
Henry Carter }

We, the jury, find for the plaintiff forty Eight Dollars, With Cost of Suit.

                        Isaac Scott, forman

Adjourned May Term 1831

John A. Jones }
    vs } Garnishment
Philip A. Clayton, Def^t }
Isaac B. Rowland }

It appearing to the Court that Isaac B. Rowland, The Garnishee in the above Case, having been Served and having Made default. It is ordered that Said Rowland Shew Cause at the Next term of this Court Why an attachment Should Not issue against Him in terms of the law. july 8th 13th 1831

Rice Durrett }
    vs   } Casa from Justis Court
John Chapman }

The defendant, John Chapman, having complied With the Law. It is ordered that he be admitted to the benefit of The Act & be Discharged.

Nicholas Childers }
    vs   } 2 Casas from Justice Court
John Brady }

The principal in the above Case and his Sureties having been duly Called and having Made default. It is adjudged By the Court that the plaintiff do recover from the Defendant, John Brady, principal, and George Northern & James D. Frierson, Sureties, the Sum of Seven Dollars & fifty Cents for his principal Debt and the Sum of Seventy five Cents for his interest & the further Sum of [blank] for Cost.

Ordered, that Silas Vickers, a pauper, be paid thirty Dollars out of the poor fund of this County.

Adjourned May Term 1831

Calhoun & Fort & others }
    vs   } Attachment
James Taber }

Georgia   } Inferior Court
Bibb County }

It appearing to the Court that a Certain Number of attachments having Been issued against James Taber, late of Said County, But Who has now absconded beyond the reach of Legal process. Which Said attachment Was duly Served upon The Effects of Said Taber returnable to the last term of this Court and Which Said Effects are of a perishable Nature. It is hereby ordered that Said property in all, Save the Land, be Sold agreeable to the terms of the law in Such Case Made and provided.

Mathew Robertson }
  vs   } Assumpsit for rent
Thomas P. Bond }

I Confess judgment to plaintiff for Ninety Dollars, with interest and Cost.

            C. B. Cole, plff[s] att[y]

Cotton & Harrison }
  vs   } Declaration in Attachment
James Taber }

We, the Jury, find for plaintiff One hundred and thirty eight Dollars Eight Cents, besides interest & Cost.

            Isaac Scott, forman

Bigelow & Birch & C[o] }
  vs   } Assumpsit
Mark D. Slade }

We Confess Judgment to the plaintiff for one hundred & twenty Nine Dollars and Eighty Cents principal, With interest & Cost.

            Prince & Poe, Def[ts] att[ys]

Adjourned <u>May Term 1831</u>

R. B. Washington }
  vs   } Case
Young Johnston }

We, the Jury, find for plaintiff one hundred and forty Eight Dollars Eighty one Cents, besides interest & Cost.

            Isaac Scott, forman

Mathew F. Freeman }
Survivor &c   }
  vs   } Debt
W[m] P. Harris }

We, the jury, find for plaintiff fifty Dollars thirty Nine Cents, besides interest & Costs.

Isaac Scott, forman

Wiley & Baxter }
    vs   } Debt
William Bivins }

We, the jury, find for plaintiff two hundred and Eighty one Dollars ten Cents principal, with interest & Cost.

Samuel Stanford, forman

Isaac Harvey }
    vs   } Declaration in Attachment
James Taber }

We, the jury, find for plaintiff Two hundred and fifteen Dollars and Nineteen Cents principal, With interest & Cost.

Samuel Stanford, forman

Wiley, Baxter & Carter }
    vs   } Attachment
James Taber   }

We, the jury, find for the plaintiff Eighty Seven Dollars and fifty Cents, besides interest & Cost.

Isaac Scott, forman

Calhoun & Fort }
    vs   } Declaration in Attachment
James Taber }

We, the Jury, find for plaintiff four thousand five hundred and Sixty one Dollars and Seventy four Cents.

Samuel Stanford, forman

Ordered that B. Rew be paid the Dollars for three days Service as Bailiff at this term.

Adjourned May Term 1831

Georgia } Rushin & Rodgers }
Bibb County } for the use of } Casa from the 564th District
William Porter } principal $8.10 With interest
vs } bond taken under the
Henry B. Horton } insolvent Debtors Act

It appearing to the Court that Said defendant has given bond with Security To Appear at the present Session of this Court and that Said defendant as well as his Securities, William Ward and Leonard Adams, having been Called and failing To Appear Conformable With the Conditions of Said bond. It is therefore Ordered that Said plaintiff Enter up judgment instanter for the principal, interest, & Cost upon Said Ca Sa against Said Defauler & his Securities.

Seaborn Jones & }
Eliza A. Bullock }
adm^r & adm^x &c } Trover & Conversion and
vs } Verdict for the Defendant for Cost
Irwin Bullock }

the defendant being Disatisfied With the Verdict of the Jury rendered in the above Cause and having paid all Cost and Demanded an Appeal, by their attorneys at Law, Campbell & Seymour, ~~and tender Archibald Darragh as their Security~~ and they, the Said Seaborn Jones, adm^r, & Eliza A. Bullock, adm^x, by their attorney as aforesaid, acknowledge themselves jointly & Severally bound To the defendant the Sum of [blank] Dollars, the Eventual Cost of Said Suit. In testimony Whereof, We have This day Set our hands & Seals by our attorney in Law This 13th day of July 1831.

          Eliza A. Bullock }
          administratrix }
          Seaborn Jones administrator }
          By their Atties at Law }
          Campbell & Seymour }

Adjourned <u>May Term 1831</u>

~~Georgia~~ }
~~Bibb County~~ }

~~Susan Wells, Executrix~~ }
~~of Nicholas W. Wells~~ }
~~Surviving Copartner~~ }
~~of Bullock & Wells~~ }
      ~~vs~~ } ~~Trover in Bibb Inferior~~
~~Eliza A. Bullock~~ }

Ordered that William B. Cone be paid Three hundred and Seven Dollars & fifty Eight Cents in full of his bill for jail fees.

The following jury were Drawn to Serve at November Term 183.

1. Joel Harrall
2. Daniel Tucker
3. Hardy Newsome
4. George M. Fingers
5. A. E. Chickering
6. David F. Wilson
7. John McDonald
8. Josiah Johnston
9. Alexander E. Patton
10. Caleb McKinney
11. Thomas English
12. A. R. Freeman
13. Whitman Hardy
14. Joseph Duks
15. Richard Jones
16. Cornelius Henderson
17. John Ellis
18. Benjamin McKinney
19. Charles Crawford
20. Thomas Davy
21. Z. T. Connor
22. William Clements
23. Joseph Wiggins
24. David Dalmeyda
25. Joseph Gainer
26. John Elsworth
27. Jacob J. Todd
28. Samuel Berry
29. Cornelius Townsend
30. Allen James
31. Thomas Sacrey
32. Benjamin Lacy
33. Jessee J. Walls
34. Samuel Bickly
35. Tilman Baker
36. Jessee Hancock

The Court adjourned till Court in Course.

                                            A. Rice, J. I. C.
                                            Sam[l] B. Hunter, J. I. C.
                                            Charles Williamson, J. I. C.

Adjourned May Term 1831

Test. Martin Simmons, Clk   J. I. C.
                                                        J. I. C.

Susan Wells, Executrix	Copy of bond filed in office
of Nicholas W. Wells	Trover in Bibb Inferior Court
Surviving Copartner	Verdict for plaintiff for Eight
of Bullock & Wells	thousand Nine hundred and Sixty
vs	five Dollars & Cost
Eliza A. Bullock	

The Said Eliza A. Bullock, being disatisfied With The Verdict of the jury rendered in the above Cause, and Having paid all Costs and demanded an appeal, Brings Seaborn Jones and Edward Cary and tenders them as her Security. And they, the Said Eliza A. Bullock, Seaborn Jones, & Edward Cary, and Eliza A. Bullock acknowledge themselves jointly & Severally bound to the Said Susan Wells, plaintiff aforesaid, the Sum of Seventeen thousand Nine hundred and thirty Dollars for the payment of the Eventual Condemnation Money in Said Cause.

In Testimony Whereof, they have hereunto Set their hands abd Seals this the 15th of July 1831.

Signed & Sealed in		Eliza A. Bullock
presence of		By her attorney at Law
G. G. Holcomb	Signed	Thomas Campbell
Notory Public		Seaborn Jones
Martin Simmons, C. I. C.		By his attorney in fact
		Thomas Campbell
		Edwd Cary

November Term 1831

Georgia } November 7th 1831
Bibb County }

The Honorable the Inferior Court In and for the County of Bibb Meet This Day agreeable to adjournment. present, their honors

        Charles Williamson }
        Anderson Rice   } J. I. C.
        Seneca Bennett & }
        Cornelius Townsend }

The Court then adjourned till the 21st inst.

        A. Rice, J. I. C.
        C. Williamson, J. I. C.
        S. Bennet, J. I. C.
           J. I. C.

Georgia } November 21st 1831
Bibb County }

The honorable the Inferior Court in and for Said County of Bibb Meet This day agreeable to adjournment. present, their honors

        Charles Williamson }
        Seneca Bennett   } J. I. C.
        Anderson Rice   }

The following Jury Were Sworn to Serve at this term.

Jury N° 1

Thomas Sacre	Thomas Reddick
Joseph Dukes	Daniel Tucker
Albert E. Chickering	Jesse Hancock, Josiah Johnson
Alen James	Joseph Wiggins
Thomas English	Jacob J. Todd
Whitmill Hardy	Isaac Mathews, Samuel Bickley

Jacob Warring }
  vs   } Debt
Ralston & Jones }

We Confess judgment to the plaintiff for five hundred and five Dollars and Ninety one Cents principal, With interest & Cost.

C. B. Cole, Def^{ts} att^y

November Term 1831

Wright, Van Antwerp &c }
    vs } Assumpsit
John B. Wick }

I hereby Confess judgment to plaintiff in the Sum of five hundred & Seventy three Dollars & Cost of protest, With Interest & Cost, reserving the right of appeal.

John B. Wick

John A. Jones }
    vs } Case & Bail
P. A. Clayton }

We Confess judgment to the plaintiff for the Sum of one hundred & Seventy five Dollars, With interest & Cost of Suit, Saving right of appeal.

Campbell & Seymour, Def^{ts} att^y

A. & E. Woods }
    vs } Assumpsit
John B. Wick }

I hereby Confess judgment to plaintiff in the Sum of five hundred & fifty Seven Dollars & one Cent & Three Dollars for Cost of protest, With interest & Cost, reserving The right of appeal.

John B. Wick

The Marine & Fire }
Insurance Bank }
    vs } Assumpsit
Luke Ross }

We hereby Confess judgment to plaintiff in the Sum of five thousand Dollars & three Dollars Cost of protest, With interest & Cost.

C. B. Cole, Def^{ts} att^y

Thomas Napier }
    vs } Case
Solomon Groce }

We Confess judgment to plaintiff in the Sum of one hundred & twenty five Dollars, with interest & Cost, Saving the right of appeal.

Prince & Poe, Def^{ts} att^{ys}

November Term 1831

Thomas Napier }
    vs } Assumpsit
John McMurrian }

We, the jury, find for The plaintiff the Sum of one hundred and thirty three dollars and fifty Eight Cents, With interest from the 10th February 1829 & Cost of Suit.

John McMurrian

Cook & Cowles }
    vs } Assumpsit
Mark D. Clark & }
George A. Smith }

We Confess judgment to plaintiff in the Sum of one hundred Dollars, With interest & Cost.

Prince & Poe, Def^{ts} att^{ys}

Mortimer R. Wallis }
    vs } Assumpsit for rent
Parmelee & Church }

We Confess judgment To the plaintiff in the Sum of two hundred and twenty five Dollars, With interest & Cost.

Tracy & Butler, Def^{ts} att^{ys}

Elias Bliss }
    vs } Assumpsit
Alexander McGregor }

I hereby Confess judgment To plaintiff in the Sum of Six hundred & twenty five Dollars & fifty five Cents & three dollars Cost of protest, With interest & Cost.

C. B. Cole, Def^{ts} att^y

Jones & Sherry }
    vs } assumpsit
John B. Wick }

I Confess judgment to the plaintiff for Six hundred and Seventy Six Dollars & ninety four Cents principal, With interest & Cost, reserving the right of appeal.

John B. Wick

G. Champlain & C° }
    vs } Assumpsit
John Loving }

I Confess judgment to The plaintiff in the Sum of Three hundred and Seventy two Dollars and Ninety Three Cents, with interest & Cost, In^t from 15th july 1829.

John Loving

November Term 1831

Thomas Butler & C° }
    vs } Assumpsit
M. D. J. Slade }

I hereby Confess judgment to plaintiffs in the Sum of Two hundred & forty Seven Dollars & two Cents, with interest & Cost.

Campbell & Seymour, Att^{ys} pro Def^t

Shipman, Robinson & Co }
     vs   } assumpsit
Ralston & Jones   }

We hereby Confess Judgment to plaintiff in the Sum of Six hundred & Seventy Dollars & forty Cents, With & interest & Cost.

C. B. Cole, Def^{ts} att^y

Halsey & Ulter   }
     vs   } assumpsit
Ralston & Jones }

We hereby Confess judgment To plaintiff in the Sum of five hundred & Seventy five Dollars & Sixty three Cents & Cost of protest, With interest & Cost.

C. B. Cole, att^y for Def^{ts}

William Bivins }
     vs   } Sci fa
William Ward }

We Confess judgment to the plaintiff for Eighty one Dollars principal & twenty three Dollars & fifty Cents interest up to the 18th October 1830, With Interest ~~& Cost~~ till paid, With Cost of Suit.

Campbell & Seymour, att^{ys} pro Def^t

Kimberly & Chisholm }
     vs   } assumpsit
Job Magie   }

We Confess judgment To the plaintiff for one hundred & forty three Dollars & forty Seven Cents, With interest & Cost.

Tracy & Butler, def^s att^{ys}

Kimberly & Chisholm }
  vs   } assumpsit
Job Magie, endorser }

We Confess judgment To the plaintiff for fifty Seven Dollars & Seventy one & half Cents, With interest & Cost of Suit.

          Tracy & Butler, Def^{ts} att^{ys}

November Term 1831

Hungerford & Stoddard }
  vs   } Case
Knox & Casterns }

We Confess judgment To the plaintiff for Seventy two Dollars & Sixty Six Cents, With Interest & Cost of Suit, reserving the right of appeal.

         Tracy & Butler, Att^{ys} for Def^{ts}

Hungerford & Stoddard }
  vs   } Assumpsit
George A. Smith }

We Confess judgment To the plaintiff for one hundred Dollars & three Dollars Cost of protest fees, With interest & Cost.

         Prince & Poe, att^{ys} for Def^{t}

The Court then adjourned till to Morrow Morning at 10 O'clock.

         A. Rice, J. I. C.
         C. Williamson, J. I. C.
         S. Bennet, J. I. C.

$2000   Macon Decr 27th 1830

Ninety Days from Date of this My only bill of this Tenor & date, please pay to the Order of Luke Ross Two Thousand Dollars for Value received & charge the Same as ordered to the account of [blank]

		Your Ob^t Servant
To A. R. Ralston, Esqr }		Ralston & Jones
Augusta }		
Ge^o }	Indorsed	Luke Ross
		Henry Solomon

[Vertically across the above note, the clerk wrote the following.]

Notice for Non
payment
1 April 1831
Protested 2 April
1832 W. B. T.
N. P. fees 5.00

Bibb Inferior Court } Judgment having at this term Been Signed November term 1831 } against Ralston & Jones acceptors and Luke Ross, indorser on the above bill, at The Suit of the Marine and Fire Insurance Bank of the State of Georgia and it having been Stated to the Court by plaintiff's Council that Suit has been instituted and is Now pending in the Inferior Court of Twiggs County Against Henry Solomon, the Second indorser on Said bill, Leave is hereby given to Withdraw Said bill from the records of this Court upon filing in the declaration in this Court a Copy of Said bill.

November Term 1831

57.71 on or before the first day of October Next, I promise To pay Job Magie, or bearer, fifty Seven $^{71}/_{100}$ Dollars for Value received this 21st January 1830.   Britain Athens

Indorsed Job Magie

$143^{47}/_{100}$ by the twenty fifth day of December Next, We promise to pay Job Magie, or bearer, one hundred & forty Three Dollars $^{47}/_{100}$ for Value received. Macon May 14th 1830

High & Wiggins
per Rob Ruffin

52.25 Sixty days after date, We, or Either of us, promise To pay Kimberly & Chisholm, or bearer, fifty two Dollars & twenty five Cents, Value received January 20th 1830.

Thomas Knight
Henry Spears

Bibb Inferior Court November Term 1831

Judgment having been Obtained at this term of This Court against one of Each of the parties on the Above Notes & the attorney of the plaintiff having Stated In his place that Suit has been Commenced against The other parties in other Counties. It is ordered by The Court that the attorney of the plaintiff have leave To Withdraw the original Notes on filing a Copy of Each Note in the office of the Clk of this Court.

Ordered that M^r McNeal be paid thirty Dollars out of the poor fund of this County.

Kimberly & Chisholm }
       vs   } Assumpsit
Thomas Knight   }
Henry Spears   }

I Confess judgment To the plaintiff for Thomas Knight for fifty two Dollars & twenty five Cents, With interest & Cost of Suit, reserving right of appeal.

Campbell & Seymour
Att^{ys} for Knight

November Term 1831

Sarah Denton }
  vs } Assumpsit
M. D. J. Slade }

We Confess judgment to The plaintiff for Sixty two Dollars & fifty Cents, With interest & Cost of Suit.

         Campbell & Seymour, att^{ys} for Plff

Sarah Denton }
  vs } Assumpsit
Ralston & Jones }

We Confess judgment To the plaintiff for Sixty two Dollars & fifty Cents, With interest & Cost of Suit.

         Campbell & Seymour, Def^{ts} att^{ys}

Job Magie }
  vs } Assumpsit
Alexander McGregor }

We Confess judgment To the plaintiff the Sum of one Hundred & twenty Six Dollars and Twenty Eight Cents, With interest on Seventy four Dollars & ten Cents from 23rd Feby 1831 & Cost of Suit.

         C. B. Cole, Def^{ts} att^y

McCall & Patton }
  vs } Case
P. & G. Powledge }

We Confess judgment to the Plaintiff for forty four Dollars & fifty four Cents, with interest & Cost.

         Campbell & Seymour, att^{ys} for Def^t

Ordered that the Sum of thirty Dollars be paid to John Wilson, a pauper, out of the poor fund of this County and That he be Discharged from the payment of the County Tax.

Ordered that S. Rose & Co be paid fifty three Dollars and thirty Seven ½ Cents in full of his Acc^t rendered for Stationary up to date.

John B. Ross }
    vs   } Assumpsit
Martin Simmons }

I Confess judgment to the plaintiff for Sixty four Dollars & Eighty Cents, With interest & Cost of Suit.

                                    M. Simmons

November Term 1831

John Scully }
    vs   } Ca Sa from Justice Court & Bond
John T. Blake & } To take the benefit of the
William Ward & } honest Debtors Act
A. W. Randolph }
Sureties }

John T. Blake having been arrested on a Casa & having given his bond for his appearance at this term of this Court to take the benefit of the Act for the relief of Honest Debtors and having failed to file his Schedule & Notify his Creditors in terms of the act & having been Called & having failed to appear & his Securities having been Called & having failed to appear & Surrender Their principal in discharge of their bond. It is therefore ordered & adjudged & Decreed by this Court that the plaintiff, John Scully, do recover of the defendant, John T. Blake, William Ward, & Augustus W. Randolph the Sum of twenty five Dollars & Sixty Eight & three Quarter Cents principal, and three Dollars & Seven Cents interest up to this date, & the further Sum of [blank] for his Cost in this Behalf Laid out & Expended, & he the Defendant in Mercy &c.

                                  C. B. Cole, plff att^y

Ordered that the fifa issued against Thomas Gardner, former Tax Collector, Robert Birdsong, & William Scott, Securities in favour of Bibb County for principal, with twenty five per Cent interest & Cost be Collected With the principal, & Eight per Cent interest & Cost, in Leu of the Said twenty five per Cent interest.

Sarah Denton }
   vs   } assumpsit
Simri Rose }

We Confess judgment To the plaintiff for Sixty two Dollars & fifty Cents, With interest & Cost.

                        Campbell & Seymour, att[ys] for Def[t]

November Term 1831

John Loving }
   vs   } assumpsit
Henry Carter }

Judgment Confessed To defendant for Cost of Suit, With the right of appeal.

                        John Loving

Robert Washington }
   vs   } assumpsit
Alexander McGregor }

I Confess Judgment To the plaintiff for one hundred and fifty Eight Dollars and Twenty five Cents principal, With interest & Cost.

                        Tracy & Butler, Att[ys] for Def[t]

McCall & Patton }
   vs   } Case
E. Alexander }

judgment Confessed to The plaintiff for four hundred and Six Dollars & Eighty five Cents, With interest & Cost.

                        Tracy & Butler, Att[ys] pro Def[t]

T. P. Bond }
   vs   } assumpsit
P. Cunningham }

We Confessed judgment To the plaintiff for three hundred & Seventy three Dollars & thirty Seven Cents, With interest & Cost.

Tracy & Butler, Def^t att^y

George Newhall & Co }
      vs   } assumpsit
Ralston & Jones   }

We hereby Confess judgment to plaintiff in the Sum of Eight hundred Dollars & three Dollars Cost of protest, With interest & Cost.

C. B. Cole, Def^t att^y

George Micklejohn }
      vs   } Assumpsit
John Loving   }

We, the jury, find for the plaintiff in the Sum of Eighty Dollars & twenty two Cents, With interest & Cost.

Jacob J. Todd, forman

November Term 1831

Hyde & Cleland   }
      vs   } Assumpsit
Christopher B. Strong }

I Confess Judgment to the plaintiffs for two hundred and four Dollars and fifty Seven Cents principal, with interest & Cost.

C. Thompson, Deft att^y

T. P. Bond   }
      vs   } Assumpsit
J. D. & A. Chapman }

We Confess judgment to the plaintiff for five hundred & thirty four Dollars & fifty Six Cents, With interest & Cost of Suit.

Tracy & Butler, att^{ys} for Def^{ts}

Jacob Warring }
    vs   } Debt
Ralston & Jones }

We Confess judgment To the plaintiff for five hundred and five Dollars and Ninety one Cents principal, With interest & Cost.

                                  C. B. Cole, Def[t] att[y]

The Marine & Fire }
Insurance Bank   }
    vs   } Assumpsit
Ralston & Jones   }

We hereby Confess Judgment to plaintiff in the Sum of Two Thousand Dollars & three Dollars Cost of protest, With interest & Cost.

                                  C. B. Cole, Def[t] att[y]

Charles Whitehurst   }
    vs   } Assumpsit
The administrators of }
Charles B. Bullock & }
The Executrix of of   }
Nicholas W. Wells   }

We, the jury, find for plaintiff the Sum of two hundred & forty Nine Dollars, With Interest & Cost.

                                  Jacob J. Todd, forman

November Term 1831

The Court then adjourned till tomorrow Morning at ten O'clock.

                                  Sam[l] B. Hunter, J. I. C.
                                  S. Bennet, J. I. C.
                                  Cha[s] Williamson, J. I. C.
                                  A. Rice, J. I. C.

Georgia }
Bibb County } November 23rd 1831

The honorable the Inferior Court in and for Said County Meet this day agreeable To adjournment, present their honors

                               Seneca Bennett }
                               Samuel B. Hunter }
                               Anderson Rice } J. I. C.
                               Charles Williamson }
                               Cornelius Townsend }

Edward D. Tracy, for }
the use of A. Burnett }
      vs   } Assumpsit
E. Bullock & S. Jones }
& Spencer Riley   }

I hereby Confess Judgment to plaintiff in the Sum of Seventy Dollars in eight Cents, With interest & Cost, reserving the right of appeal.

                             Campbell & Seymour, def[t] att[y]

John B. Wick   }
      vs   } assumpsit
Joseph Wainwright }

We, the jury, find for plaintiff the Sum of Sixty one Dollars & fifty Eight Cents, with interest & Cost.

                             Jacob J. Todd, forman

Joseph J. Hamilton   }
      vs   } Debt
Alexander McGregor }
Littleton Atkison and }
Robert Collins   }

We, the jury, find for plaintiff the Sum of one hundred & forty five Dollars, With Interest & Cost.

                             Jacob J. Todd, forman

November Term 1831

John Scully }
    vs   } Assumpsit
James H. Killin }
& John Philpot }

We, the jury, find for the plaintiff fifty two Dollars thirty one cents, With interest & Cost.

                        Jacob J. Todd, forman

Thomas M. Ellis, Guardian }
    vs   } Debt
David Dalmeyda   }
& Martin Simmons   }

We Confess judgment To the plaintiff the Sum of Thirty five Dollars, five Dollars, With interest & Cost.

                        Tracy & Butler, att^y
                        for David Dalmeyda
                        Martin Simmons, Self

Nicholas Childers}
    vs   } assumpsit
David Burks   }

I Confess judgment To plaintiff in the Sum of forty Two Dollars, With interest & Cost.

                        C. B. Cole, Def^t att^y

Talman & Farlin, for the }
use of John H. Farlin   }
    vs   } Assumpsit
Charles S. Lewis   }
the Executrix of   }
Nicholas W. Wells, also }
the administrators of   }
Charles Bullock   }

We Confess judgment To the plaintiff the Sum of five hundred Dollars and three Dollars Cost of protest, With interest & Cost.

        Campbell & Seymour, att^y for Def^t

Faris Carter }
  vs   } Case for rent
John T. Rowland }
L. Atkison   }

We Confess judgment to the plaintiff for five hundred Dollars, With interest & Cost.

        McDonald & Franklin, Def^{ts} att^{ys}

November Term 1831

Elias Bliss   }
  vs   } assumpsit
Marmaduke J. Slade }

We, the jury, find for plaintiff in the Sum of Six hundred & twenty five dollars & fifty five cents & three Dollars Cost of protest, With interest & Cost.

        Jacob J. Todd, forman

A. Baber }
  vs   } Assumpsit
M. R. Wallis }

We, the jury, find for The plaintiff one hundred Dollars, With Cost of Suit.

        Jacob J. Todd, forman

Thos Napier }
  vs   } Inferior Court Nov Term 1831 fifa
Eaton Hollomon }

Same   }
  vs   } D^o d^o April " " "
James E. Jordon }

Same }
    vs }   D° d° d° " " "
M. D. J. Slade }

It appearing to the Court that upon the above fifas the Sheriff Has Made his return of No property and that the Said Sheriff has in his hands Monies belonging to Said plaintiff in the above fifas raised upon other Execution, it is hereby ordered that the Sheriff Pay over to the Clerk of this Court the Cost that May Have Accrued to Said Clerk upon the above fifas.

Nicholas Wagner }
    vs   } Scifa
Samuel Stanford }

We, the jury, find for plaintiff the Sum of forty Six Dollars and Sixty two & a half Cents, with Cost of Suit.

Jacob J. Todd, forman

November Term 1831

Ordered by the Court that, so Soon as Jerry Cowles Shall have finished the Jail in terms of his bond, any three of the Court May receive it & on receiving It the Court, or a Majority of them, Shall Make to The Said Cowles a good and Valid tittle to the Lots from which the jail was removed & on which it Formerly Stood, to wit, N° 5 & 6 in Square 19.

Ordered that William B. Cone, Sheriff, be paid forty Nine $^{23}/_{100}$ Dollars in full of his acc^t rendered up to date.

Ordered that Ellis, Shotwell & C° be paid Eighty Eight $^{35}/_{100}$ Dollars in full of his acc^t up to date for Stationary &c.

John Krier }
    vs   } assumpsit
Joseph Philips }

We, the jury, find for the plaintiff three Dollars & Seventy Seven Cents, With Cost of Suit.

Jacob J. Todd, forman

Randolph L. Mott }
      vs   } Casa
Patrick Cunningham }

It appearing to the Court That the defendant, Patrick Cunningham, has been arrested by Virtue of the above Capius ad Satisfaciendum issued from a Justice Court, That he has entered into a bond With Clark C. Wych and Henry A. Candler as his Securities to appear at The last term of this Court to take the benefit of the act for relief of Honest Debtors, and that Said Patrick Cunningham having failed to appear & to file his Schedule. It is therefore ordered & adjudged by the Court That the Said Randolph L. Mott do recover of the Said Patrick Cunningham, Clark C. Wych, and Henry A. Candler The Sum of Nine Dollars and twenty five Cents principal,

---

November Term 1831

With interest from the twenty Seventh Day of April Eighteen hundred & twenty Nine untill paid and the Sum of Two dollars & Eighty one and a Quarter Cents Cost in said justice Court upon Said Capias Satisfaciendum, Together with the fees, the Sum of four Dollars and fifty Cents Cost in this behalf laid out and Expended, and the defendant in Mercy &c.

                                Campbell & Seymour, plff att[ys]

Prince & Poe }
plaintiffs in Execution }
      vs   } Matger fifa Claim
Josiah Boswell, Def.t in Ex }
and Lewis H. Gregory, Claimant }

We Confess judgment To the Claimant, reserving The right of appeal.

                                Prince & Poe

Scott Cray }
      vs   } assumpsit
Gabriel Capers }

I Confess judgment to plaintiff in the Sum of Sixty Six Dollars, with interest & Cost, reserving The right of appeal.

Campbell & Seymour, Def^t att^{ys}

Howard & Calhoun }
     vs   } Casa
Job S. Cherry   }

It appearing to the Court that The Defendant, Job S. Cherry, has been arrested by Virtue of the above Capias ad Satisfaciendum issued from a Justices Court & that he Has entered into a bond with Leonard Adams & William Riley as his Securities to appear at the Last April term of The Court to take the benefit of the act for the relief of Honest Debtors, & that the Said Job S. Cherry having failed To appear at Said Term to take the benefit of Said act & Still failing to appear. It is therefore ordered, Considered, and adjudged by the Court that the Said Howard and Calhoun to recover of the Said Job S. Cherry & Leonard Adams & William Riley the Sum of Eight dollars fifty

---

November Term 1831

Six Cents principal, With interest there on from the thirteenth Day of August Eighteen hundred and thirty untill paid, & the Sum of one Dollar Eighty Seven and a half Cents Costs in the Justice Court upon Said Capias, & the further Sum of four Dollars and fifty Cents for his Costs in This behalf laid out and Expended, & the defendant in Mercy.

Cooke & Cowles }
     vs   } assumpsit & verdict for the plaintiffs for
M. D. Clark and } the Sum of one hundred Dollars
George A. Smith } and Cost & interest

the Defendant, Mark D. Clark, being Disatisfied With the Verdict of the jury rendered in the above Cause and having paid all Cost and demanded an Appeal, brings Luke Ross and tenders him as his Security, and they, the Said Mark D. Clark and Luke Ross, acknowledge themselves jointly and Severally bound to Cooke & Cowles, The plaintiffs, for the payment of the Eventual Condemnation Money in Said Cause. in testimony

Whereof, they have hereunto Set their hands and Seals this 23rd day of November 1831.

Test. Martin Simmons, Clk Mark D. Clarke
  Lu Ross

Nicholas Childers	}
vs	} fifa from 514 Dist bond taken for
Cynthia Crawford, Deft &	} appearance according The the act of 1823
William Ward, Security	} for the relief of honest Debtors

Cynthia Crawford, the defendant, having been Called and failing To appear and No Cause having been Shewn to the Court. It is therefore ordered and adjudged that judgment be Signed on Said Bond against the Said Cynthia Crawford

---

November Term 1831

And William Ward, Security, according to the provisions of the Statute in Such Case provided.

County of Bibb	} fifa from Road Commissioners of the
vs	} 514 Dist bond taken for appearance
James Wilson, Deft &	} according to The act of 1823 for the
Samuel Stanford, Surety	} relief of Honest Debtors

James Wilson, the defendant, having been Called and failing to appear and No Cause having been Shewn to the Contrary. It is hereby Ordered and adjudged That judgement be Signed on Said bond against the Said James Wilson and Samuel Stanford, Security, according to the provisions of the Statute in Such Case Made & provided.

E. Graves & Son	}
vs	} Casa & Bond to take the Benefit of
Alexander McGregor, principal	} the Honest Debtors act
Spencer Riley and	}
David F. Wilson, Securities	}

Whereas, Alexander McGregor gave bond With Spencer Riley & David F. Wilson as his Securitys for his appearance at this term of this Court, to take the benefit of the act for the relief of Honest Debtors and the Said

McGregor having failed to appear & file his Schedule & Notify the arresting creditors in terms of the Law & having been Called & having failed to answer & his Securities having been Called to Surrender their principal. It is therefore ordered and adjudged by the Court that the plaintiff do recover of the defendant, A. McGregor, & Spencer Riley & David F. Wilson the Sum of thirty Dollars for their principal debt, and The Sum of [blank] for their interest, & the further Sum of [blank] Dollars and [blank] Cost in this behalf laid & Expended, & the defendant in Mercy &c.

C. B. Cole, plff at^y

November Term 1831

Justices of the Inferior Court of Bibb County }
      vs   } fifa
Thomas Gardner, tax Collector and   }
William Scott & Robert Birdsong, Securities }

A petition having been preferred to this Court praying that the penalty of 25 per Cent May be deducted from the amount of principal due from Thomas Gardner, as a defaulting tax Collector. the on Considering The Same do hereby remit the Said twenty five per cent and order that the Said Execution and the Controll and property Therein be and it is hereby transferred to Said William Scott and Robert Birdsong, Securities, upon their payment of The principal & Legal interest in Such proportion as May Be paid by them respectively. It is further ordered that the Sheriff of Bibb County refund to Robert Birdsong any Excess beyond one half of the principal and Legal interest Due on Said Execution, Which Said Birdsong May have paid Said Sheriff and the Said Sheriff is ordered to proceed to the Collection of the Remaining half of principal and interest due on Said Execution from William Scott.

November Term 1831

The following Jury Were Drawn to Serve at May Term 1832.

  1. Daniel Smith   19. Micajah Williams
  2. Balstian Hammock   20. Henry B. Hill

3. Redding Rutland
4. John McRea
5. Ellis French
6. John Linger
7. Oliver Sage
8. Wm Smith
9. Job Allen
10. Henry Candler
11. Angus McCallum
12. Elijah Padgett
13. Wm Dunn
14. Lewis Collins
15. James C. Manguir
16. Hezekiah McKinney
17. Richard W. Lee
18. John Moreland

21. David F. Riley
22. Ge^o W. Ellis
23. Jessee Mauran
24. Leonard Adams
25. A. C. Parmalee
26. Joseph Blake
27. Thos Bancett
28. David McMurrian
29. William Blancett
30. Nathan Jones
31. Rial Griffin
32. Nathan Jessup
33. Berry Rogers
34. John Curbo
35. A. Cox
36. Wm Farrington

The Court then adjourned till Court in Course.

Test. M. Simmons, C. I. C.

	S. Bennet, J. I. C.
I object to the order as regards the }	J. I. C.
transfer of the Jail lots for the }	J. I. C.
Same Reason as published in the }	J. I. C.
Number [illegible] of the 22nd Oct 1831 }	J. I. C.

———

[blank page]

———

Index

———
 Cynthia, 114
 Hardy, 37
 Lewis, 39
 Luke, 171, 172
 Tom, 63
Abell
 Jewett, 95
Abney
 Absolum, 179
 Asalom, 201
Abott
 Henry, 112, 115
Adams, 105
 Alexander, 130
 David, 21, 23
 Leonard, 97, 198, 201, 228, 230, 231, 232, 234, 235, 236, 256, 277, 280
 William, 158
Akridge
 William B., 58
Alexander, 116
 Colin W., 246
 E., 269
 Elam, 25, 117, 151, 197, 213
Allen, 249
 Benj., 23, 106
 Benjamin, 6, 7, 20, 23, 43, 44, 47, 50, 58, 59, 60, 106, 115, 249
 Job, 280
 John, 112
Alston
 James, 117, 146, 148, 215, 227

 James W., 90, 149, 150, 212, 215
 John D., 50
Anderson
 Moses, 112
Arnett, 224, 225
 Felix, 232
Asburry
 James, 21
Ashley
 James, 21
Athens
 Britain, 265
Atkinson
 L., 98
 Stephen, 21
Atkison
 L., 98, 274
 Littleton, 123, 199, 272
 Stephen, 172, 176
Austin
 Samuel, 71
Auston
 Samuel, 67
Baber, 138
 A., 147, 274
 Ambrose, 71, 75, 89, 99, 101, 126, 127, 136, 137, 139, 140, 157, 169, 170, 171, 175, 249
Bacon
 Eliza R., 9
 Francis, 30, 72
 John, 9
Bady
 Alfred, 236
Bailey

John, 177, 250
Baily
  Rubin C., 247
Baird
  Benjamin, 117
Bairfield
  Sampson, 8
Baker
  Tilman, 257
Baldwin
  David T., 46
Ballard
  John P., 21
Balton
  John, 182
Bancett
  Thos., 280
Banks
  Thomas, 7
Barefield
  Sampson, 7
Barker
  Nathaniel, 55, 74, 223
Barringer
  Daniel, 213
Barrough
  Reuben, 66
Barry
  Samuel, 7
Bartlett
  M., 114
Bass
  Edward, 6
  James, 129
  Thomas, 6
  William, 97
Bateman
  Jesse, 237
  Thomas, 250
Bates, 98

Thomas G., 21, 22, 23, 27, 77, 249
Battle
  Thomas, 94
Baxter, 196, 210, 211, 215, 216, 220, 221, 245, 255
Bazmore
  Blunt, 40
Beall
  R. D., 111
  Reason D., 156, 169
Bealle
  Reason D., 11, 21, 22, 184
  Reazon D., 179
  Ren D., 169
  Rezen D., 11, 21
Beard
  Edmund C., 37, 52, 53, 141, 148
Belknap
  William, 144, 172, 173
Bell
  James, 33, 42
  Jesse, 93
Bennet
  S., 259, 264, 271, 280
Bennett
  A., 77
  J., 77
  James R., 17
  Joseph, 9
  S. W., 238
  Seneca, 259, 272
  Smith, 238
Benton
  Robert H., 141, 213, 237, 238
Berry
  Mathew, 86
  Saml., 133

Samuel, 130, 257
Bickley
  Samuel, 259
Bickly
  Samuel, 257
Biddle
  Charles, 67
  Thomas J., 129
Bie
  Andrew, 77
Bigelow, 224, 254
Billups
  Thomas A., 103
  Thos. A., 87, 205
Binion
  John, 248
Birch, 224, 254
Bird
  Ransom L., 180
  Thompson, 31
Birdsong, 101, 111, 279
  R., 6, 30, 54, 75, 247
  Robert, 4, 8, 13, 16, 17, 23, 30, 35, 39, 48, 50, 53, 54, 63, 71, 75, 81, 85, 185, 211, 230, 246, 247, 268, 279
  Robt., 7, 13, 21, 34, 38, 41, 63, 67, 81, 84
Bivins
  William, 29, 98, 123, 202, 255, 263
Black
  John, 182
Blake
  John T., 268
  Joseph, 280
Blancet
  Thomas, 5, 12, 160
  William, 201

Blancett
  William, 198, 280
Blanchard
  Joseph, 8
Blanett
  Thomas, 244
Blanton
  J. A., 229
  James A., 207, 212, 217, 229
  James L., 213
Bledsor
  Rob, 211
  Robert, 212
Bliss
  Elias, 154, 262, 274
Bond, 49, 81
  Joel, 230, 238
  Solomond, 137
  T. P., 269, 270
  Thomas P., 113, 186, 254
Booth
  David S., 13, 47, 54, 59, 65
  Jno. P., 14
  John P., 9, 13, 14, 24, 25
Boren
  Joseph, 129, 133
Boswell
  Josiah, 276
Bosworth
  Richmond, 116, 148
Bowden
  William, 172, 176, 237
Bowers
  E. T., 137
  Enoch T., 101, 103
Bowman
  Leonard, 75
Boyd, 114
  John K., 125
Bozman

John, 49, 83
Brady
　Alfred, 179
　John, 129, 253
　Nathan, Jr., 122
Branscombe
　J. H., 44
Braswell
　Britain, 77
　Davis B., 48, 79, 172
　Duke W., 238
Brewen, 29
　Timothy, 28
Brewin
　Timothy, 98
Briant
　Council, 85
Bridges
　John, 86, 237, 244
　John, Sr., 4, 21, 23
Briggs
　John, 143
Brigham
　James, 112
Brigman
　Thomas, 112, 115, 201
Brinkley
　William, 172
Brooks
　William P. L., 21
Brown, 72, 141, 192
　A. D., 78, 136, 154, 155, 192
　Absolom, 108, 198
　Alexa. D., 133, 144
　Alexander D., 26, 78, 129, 145, 192
　Martin H., 50, 80
　Owen, 101, 103, 206, 212, 239
　William F., 15, 56, 80

William R., 237
Wm. F., 112
Wm. W., 35
Brownell
　John, 57
Bruce
　John, 54
Bruin
　Daniel B., 244
Bryan
　Benjamin, 126, 157, 170, 175
　George H., 160
　James, 145
　Jno., 147
　John, 143, 144, 152, 153, 160, 161, 162, 178
Bryon
　Council, 21
Buck
　Whery, 244
Bugg
　Anselm, 87
Bulkly
　E. C., 247
Bullock, 16, 26, 34, 38, 101, 156, 171, 174, 257, 258
　Charles, 34, 36, 37, 56, 68, 93, 120, 121, 273
　Charles B., 271
　Chas., 68, 121
　E., 272
　Eliza A., 250, 252, 256, 257, 258
　Irwin, 252, 256
　Richard, 8
Burks, 147, 191
　David, 112, 147, 156, 157, 158, 191, 273
Burnett

A., 272
Alexander, 21, 23, 24, 25, 26, 27, 28, 29, 31, 32, 33, 34
Burroughs
  Reuben, 32
Burton, 136
  Robert, 58, 78, 136, 142
Busbee
  Allen, 115
Busby
  James, 4, 172
Bush
  Thos., 97
Butler, 50, 65, 91, 106, 107, 109, 110, 141, 145, 146, 153, 163, 164, 194, 196, 204, 210, 216, 217, 223, 224, 262, 263, 264, 270, 273
  D. B., 167, 168
  David B., 167
  James, 61, 185
  Thomas, 186, 262
  William C., 208
Buzby
  Allen, 112
Byne
  Enoch, 156, 174
Byrd
  Abraham C., 221, 240, 241
Caldwell, 20, 99
  John C., 26, 162
Calhoun, 253, 255, 277
Campbell, 5, 9, 15, 18, 30, 32, 42, 45, 54, 87, 89, 93, 123, 135, 137, 151, 152, 160, 186, 196, 199, 202, 206, 210, 213, 217, 218, 219, 223, 224, 242, 248, 252, 256, 260, 263, 266, 267, 269, 272, 274, 276, 277

J. W., 178
John W., 124
Ramsone B., 55
Thomas, 63, 70, 83, 108, 206, 258
Thos., 71
Walter L., 149
Candler
  Henry, 280
  Henry A., 191, 197, 276
Capers
  Gabriel, 276
Carington
  John, 36, 37
Carter, 255
  Charles C., 40
  David, 40
  Faris, 274
  Henry, 40, 42, 183, 196, 252, 269
  J. A., 20
  Jacob A., 20
  Josiah, 7, 8
  Josiah H., 144
  Mathew, 130
  Nathan, 6, 12, 20, 60, 140
  Silas, 86
  Thomas, 133
Carver
  Stephen, 43
Cary
  Edward, 258
  Edwd., 258
Casterns, 264
Castlebery
  William, 40
Cay
  Wilson H., 191, 197
Chain
  John, 34

Chamberless
  Samuel, 129
Chambless
  Saml., 133, 140
  Samuel, 143
Champion
  Guy, 121
Champlain
  G., 262
Chapman, 224, 225
  A., 26, 34, 62, 88, 210, 212, 214, 218, 219, 222, 244, 270
  Abner, 10, 18, 19, 34, 44, 47, 68, 69, 92, 231
  Ambrose, 47, 68, 69
  George A., 88
  Isaiah, 219
  J. D., 26, 34, 62, 69, 88, 113, 139, 210, 212, 214, 218, 219, 222, 244, 270
  John, 86, 253
  John D., 10, 18, 19, 34, 44, 47, 68, 69, 92, 113, 139, 160, 210, 231
  S. D., 5, 6, 22, 34, 69, 71, 168
  Solomon D., 4, 22, 34, 68, 69, 70, 110, 111, 168, 172, 179, 214, 230, 232
Cherry
  Abner, 37, 251
  Job S., 277
Chickering
  A. E., 257
  Albert E., 259
Childers, 50, 76, 94, 150
  J. S., 68, 227
  John S., 5, 29, 44, 68, 69, 91, 92, 115, 153, 154, 155, 157, 168, 229

N., 142, 143
Nicholas, 142, 143, 145, 223, 246, 248, 253, 273, 278
Chisholm, 45, 88, 134, 161, 164, 202, 206, 212, 222, 225, 239, 245, 250, 263, 264, 266
  M., 65
  Murdock, 65
Church, 261
Clark, 82, 89, 105, 109
  George, 184
  Isabella, 144, 172, 173
  M. D., 277
  Mark D., 261
  Mark Donl., 136
  Noel, 206
Clarke
  Mark D., 278
Clayton
  P. A., 260
  Philip A., 252
Cleland, 59, 60, 64, 270
Clem, 38
  Henry, 37
Clements
  Clemant, 78
  Clement, 24
  P. R., 154, 155
  William, 257
Clemmons
  Clement, 73
Clopton
  A. G., 99, 127, 147, 169, 170, 171
  Albert G., 11, 12, 35, 71, 74, 75, 76, 99, 101, 118, 119, 121, 126, 139, 157, 158, 170, 175
  Allford, 137
Clower

Peter, 44, 69
Coffin, 82, 89, 105, 109
  Ezekiel, 184
Coit
  Gordon C., 135, 178, 210
Cole, 43, 56, 57, 58, 78, 101, 109, 117, 120, 171, 176
  C. B., 134, 137, 142, 180, 213, 214, 218, 219, 222, 225, 230, 231, 245, 254, 260, 261, 262, 263, 267, 268, 270, 271, 273, 279
  Calton B., 217, 234, 248
  Carlton B., 122, 234
Coleman, 32
  Robert, 10, 35, 219
Collins, 80, 171
  Andrew, 112
  Charles, 10, 18, 19, 194, 200
  George, 43, 112
  Joseph, 88, 112
  Lewis, 67, 73, 80, 129, 143, 202, 280
  Robert, 10, 18, 19, 41, 80, 91, 92, 96, 103, 125, 126, 170, 175, 177, 191, 224, 225, 272
  Robt., 41, 103, 170, 175
Colquhaun
  Archibald, 62
Colt
  Willis F., 118
Condon, 250
  Caleb, 201, 247
Cone
  H. H., 103, 239
  Henry B., 32, 84
  Henry H., 103, 183, 184, 196, 239
  Richard A., 237, 244

  William B., 67, 71, 129, 141, 142, 146, 176, 183, 189, 190, 197, 246, 257, 275
  Wm. B., 133, 134, 136, 139, 141, 143, 145, 146, 147, 149, 150, 151, 155, 156, 158, 159, 160, 163, 190, 243, 244, 247
Conner
  Henry W., 180, 199
  T. C., 146
  Torrance C., 143
Connor
  Z. T., 257
Cook, 177, 261
  Philip, 152, 161, 221
  Samuel, 47, 68
Cooke, 277
Cooledge, 82
Coolidge, 61
Coopie
  William, 198
Corbett
  John, 125, 135, 136, 137, 139, 151
Corning, 134
Cornwell
  N., 246
Cosey
  Allen, 8
Cosnard
  Henry, 50, 67
Cotton, 55, 254
  Charles, 55
  Cyrus, 5, 7
  Daniel, 7
  E., 70, 106, 139, 168, 169, 204, 242

Elijah, 47, 69, 91, 101, 106, 139, 168, 169, 204, 222, 241, 242
Coutch
  Watson, 112
Cowart
  Zacha., 133
  Zachariah, 140, 143
  Zackariah, 21, 130
Cowles, 261, 275, 277
  Jerry, 275
  Thomas F., 46
Cowly
  James, 76
Cox
  A., 280
  John T., 129
Coxwell
  Michiel, 179, 182
  Mitchell, 49, 198
Crain
  John, 74
Crane, 26, 27, 40
  Elias B., 248
Crawford
  Charles, 112, 115, 257
  Cynthia, 278
  Thos., 86
  William C., 33
Cray
  Benjamin G., 17
  Scott, 170, 173, 175, 276
Crew
  Elbert, 85
  Henry, 110, 151
Crocket
  David, 153
Crockett
  David, 138
Crowell
  John, 176
Cumming, 38
  Andrew, 155
  John B., 78, 100, 121, 125
  William, 34, 38, 49, 72, 117, 128, 129, 140, 150, 166, 171, 181, 188, 196, 218, 219, 227, 233, 246, 247
  Wm., 81, 140
Cummings
  William, 6
Cunningham
  P., 269
  Patrick, 124, 130, 276
Curbo
  John, 280
Curley
  James, 7
Curry, 159
  Peter M., 159
Curton
  John, 249
Cutler
  H. S., 167
  Henry P., 99, 113
  Henry S., 77, 163, 177, 195
Dalamaten
  B. W., 118
Dalemyda
  David, 224
Dalmeyda
  David, 146, 257, 273
Danelly
  James M., 215
  Louisa B., 216
  Maria P., 216
  W. J., 168
  William J., 13, 82, 91, 106, 114, 123, 165, 215, 216, 226

Wm. J., 13, 21, 138, 139, 216, 220, 221
Danely
  William J., 7, 8
Danforth, 88
  Jacob, 124
Darnell
  John, 201
Darragh
  A., 175
  Archibald, 11, 174, 236
Daughtry
  William C., 61
Davidson, 116
Davis
  A. D., 33
  Ashburn D., 23
  Eleanor, 40, 59, 83
  Elenor, 26, 49
  Marther, 83
  Mather, 49
  Sarah, 252
Davy
  Thomas, 257
Dawson
  Matha, 37
  Matha B., 36
  William W., 36
  Wm. W., 37
Dean, 63
  David, 237
Dennis, 182
Denton
  Sarah, 267, 269
Dickson
  Thos., 86
Dingley
  Joseph, 14
Dismuke
  Betheny, 182

Dixson, 38
  Josiah, 38
  Thomas, 86
Dole, 16
Dorman
  Wiley, 40, 43, 112, 149
Douglass
  Hezekiah, 118
  James, 67, 73, 129, 133, 158
  John, 21, 23, 129
Ducks
  Joseph, 8
Dudly
  Kinchen C., 67, 71
Dukes
  Joseph, 259
Duks
  Joseph, 257
Dun
  Wm., 228
Dunn
  William, 198, 201
  Wm., 280
Durdon
  Washington, 40
Durrett
  R., 154
  Rice, 39, 154, 253
Dwight
  Sereno H., 11
Earby
  James J., 164
Earl
  James, 176, 177
Earnest
  Asa E., 172, 176
Eaton
  James L., 172
Echols
  Abraham, 136

Absalom, 133
Clement, 158
Eckley
  Levi, 237
Eckly
  Levi, 226, 236
Edgar
  David A., 189, 200, 235
Edger
  David A., 199, 240
Edwards
  William L., 86
  Young, 21
Egan, 4
Elliott
  Alfred M., 20
Ellis, 83, 108, 117, 275
  Addison, 86
  Geo. W., 280
  John, 56, 257
  Richard W., 114, 123, 188, 197, 198
  Thomas, 89
  Thomas M., 183, 184, 196, 273
Ellsworth
  John, 198
Elsworth
  John, 112, 115, 201, 203, 204, 205, 206, 211, 212, 213, 218, 219, 220, 221, 222, 223, 224, 225, 229, 230, 232, 257
English
  Thomas, 257, 259
Enis
  Nathaniel, 86
Erby
  James J., 132
Ernest
  A. E., 176, 177, 178, 179, 181, 183, 185, 186, 187, 188
Etherage
  Elijah B., 67
Etheredge
  Elijah, 112
Evans, 50, 67
  John, 67
  R. K., 68
  Rufus K., 12, 13, 19, 55, 67, 71, 119, 125, 160, 172, 176, 187, 188, 189
Everett
  James A., 89
Ezekiel
  Emanuel, 198
Fairchild, 107, 129
Farington
  William, 198, 201
Farlin, 273
  John H., 273
Farrington
  Wm., 280
Felton
  Shadrick R., 79
Fergerson
  James, 40, 43, 97
Fessendon, 105
Field
  Thompson, 67
Fields
  Thompson, 73
Finch
  William, 169, 187
Fingers
  George M., 257
Fitch
  Lewis, 108, 150
Fitzgarrald

James, 116
Fitzjarrel
  James, 39
Fitzjerold
  James, 38
Fitzpartrick
  R., 102
  Rene, 102, 177, 178
Fitzpatrick
  Rene, 86, 96, 99, 134
Flewellen, 38
  James, 38, 135, 145, 173
Flowers
  John, 143
Fluker
  Baldwin, 152
  Sarah Q., 234
Folds
  William, 85, 86
Folker
  Joseph, 111, 125, 126
Fort, 196, 210, 211, 253, 255
Foster
  Arther, 146
  Arthur, 138
Foy
  Henry R., 5
  Lewis, 67, 73, 141, 145, 153, 172, 176, 187, 228
Fraley
  William, 248
Franklin, 221, 274
Frederick
  Mary, 205, 206
Freeman
  A. R., 182, 257
  J., 11, 21, 139
  James, 145
  Josiah, 25, 59
  M. F., 218

  Mathew F., 218, 223, 254
French
  Ellis, 280
  John, 9, 22
  William, 228
Frierson
  James, 51
  James D., 253
  James S., 33, 44
Fryeron
  Js. S., 11
Fryerson
  Js. S., 12
Fuller
  John M., 56
Gadist
  John, 67
Gainer
  Joseph, 257
Gainey
  Edmund, 7
Gallagah
  Hugh, 20
Gamble
  James, 97, 122, 127, 143, 164
  John, 237
  William, 179
Ganey
  Edmund, 8
Gardner
  Thomas, 185, 268, 279
Garrett
  Elijah, 40
Garry
  Benjamin E., 53, 56
Gaudry
  John B., 10, 74, 77, 116, 118, 119
George

Jephtha V., 46
Gibb, 19
Gibbs
  Phillip H., 19
Gillespie, 101, 111
  James, 125
  S., 70, 107
  Saml., 105, 140
  Samuel, 16, 17, 30, 48, 50, 69, 72, 85, 100, 101, 105, 107, 123, 128, 140, 152
Gillis
  A., 178, 180, 181, 199
  Angus, 181
Ginn
  Arthur, 144, 155
Glover
  George, 21
  Williamson, 244
Goddard, 93, 160
  Bailey, 109, 111, 134, 159
  James, 134
Godfrey
  F. H., 119, 130, 131
  Francis H., 131
Good
  Precilla, 233
  Priscella, 233
Gordon
  George W., 228
  John W., 43
Goulding
  A. D., 198
Granberry, 89
Graves
  E., 278
Gray
  Seaborn, 10, 12, 27
Green
  Charles, 237
  Enoch, 40, 42, 237
  James, 78
Greene
  Enoch, 172
Gregory
  David, 181
  Elliott W., 25
  Lewis, 129
  Lewis H., 9, 276
Griffin, 217, 229
  B. S., 211, 229
  Bennett S., 191, 229
  John W., 5
  Rial, 280
Grimes
  Thomas, 67, 71
Groce
  Lewis J., 105, 141, 143, 173, 237, 244, 251
  S., 85, 105, 173
  Solomon, 36, 37, 85, 90, 105, 108, 124, 160, 162, 173, 205, 261
Grubb
  Benjamin, 15
Grubbs
  Benjamin, 23, 172
  George H., 237
Gunn
  Daniel, 44
Habersham
  J., 10
  R., 10
Hagen
  E. P., 109, 111
  W. H., 109, 111
Hall
  James, 231
  John, 4, 43
Halsey, 263

Hamilton
  Joseph J., 272
Hammock
  Balstian, 279
  Harrison, 40, 43
  James, 237
  Johnson, 67, 71, 101, 176
  Lewis, 4, 85
Hammond, 59, 62
  Abner, 43, 60, 62, 112
  Lewis, 43
Hampton
  Wade, 247, 251, 252
Hancock
  Jesse, 259
  Jessee, 257
Hansell, 29
  Wm. G., 29
Hardeman
  Thomas, 133, 136
Hardeway
  J. H., 181
Hardin
  John, 71
Harding
  Martin L., 112, 115
  William, 21
Hardy
  Whitman, 257
  Whitmill, 85, 86, 259
Harper
  H. W., 185
Harrall
  Joel, 257
Harrilson
  William, 172
Harris, 14, 52
  A. W., 82
  Alvanus W., 56, 73, 75, 81
  Benjamin F., 160

  D. L., 237
  Ehud, 30, 72
  Elias, 97
  Hannah, 47
  W. P., 30, 173, 174
  Wade, 11, 172
  William, 46, 86, 174, 237
  William P., 86, 135, 173, 196
  Wm. P., 254
Harrison, 55, 129, 154, 157, 185, 186, 254
  Bartholomew, 141
  David, 182
  John, 55
  R. B., 196
  William, 107, 129, 137, 155, 204
  Wm., 157
Harvey
  Isaac, 255
Hatch, 135, 189, 190, 193
Hatcher
  William, 85, 97
Heard, 177
Hegen
  E. P., 117
  W. H., 117
Helpburn
  Barton, 13
Henderson
  Cornelius, 257
  Daniel, 172, 179
  Joseph, 239, 247
Hendrickson, 136
Henshaw
  David, 177
  John, 177
Hepburn
  Burton, 87
Herring

James, 73, 87
Hickenburg
  Francis H., 110
Higgins
  C. A., 167, 168
  Charles A., 167
High, 266
Hill, 20, 99
  H. B., 132
  Henry B., 40, 42, 55, 99, 114, 127, 159, 171, 180, 279
Hoag
  M., 137
Hobby
  Alfred M., 248
Hodges
  John L., 117, 130
Hogan
  William, 134, 174
Hoge
  William, 218
Holcomb
  G. G., 258
Holderness
  James, 36, 37
Holensworth
  James, 86
Holeyworth
  James, 86
Holezworth
  John, 112
Hollaway, 88
Hollingsworth
  John, 122, 140, 159
Hollingworth
  John, 162
Hollomon
  Eaton, 228, 274
Holmes
  Findley, 57, 64

James, 10, 16
Holt, 29
  D. J., 202
  David, 28, 29
  T., 51, 52
  Tarpley, 4, 6, 7, 8, 23, 30, 34, 35, 38, 39, 41, 42, 51, 63, 67, 71, 75, 76, 85
Holzendorf
  John, 5, 6, 137
Horton
  Henry B., 256
Howard, 277
  Harmon H., 80, 233
  Hermon H., 36
  James W., 6
  Ralph O., 171
  Thomas, 40, 129, 133, 148, 150, 151, 155, 156, 168
  Thos., 40, 168
Howland
  Calvin L., 247
Hoy
  Quinton, 38, 39, 179
Hudron
  Jonathan A., 29
Hudson
  Jonathan A., 116
Huff
  Needham, 129
Hughes
  James, 198
  Mathew, 133
Hughs
  James, 83, 201
  John, 129
  Mathew, 129
Humphries
  Solomon, 66
Hungerford, 161, 246, 264

Hunt
  Robert C., 67
Hunter
  Sam B., 120
  Saml. B., 115, 123, 128, 130, 133, 140, 147, 162, 166, 172, 180, 199, 209, 226, 232, 250, 251, 257, 271
  Samuel B., 113, 115, 120, 148, 162, 171, 176, 181, 201, 209, 226, 232, 243, 244, 250, 251, 272
Hutcherson
  J. W., 202, 203, 205, 206, 209, 211, 212, 213, 215, 216, 217, 220, 221, 222, 223, 225, 226, 227
  Jehu, 198, 201
  Jehu W., 43, 233
Hyde, 270
Imlay, 100, 119
Ingersol, 12, 61, 82
  S. M., 9, 33
  Stephen M., 51, 189
Ingham
  Charles, 198
Inglish
  James, 7
Ingram, 39, 182
  Charles, 14, 24, 39, 182
  Charles, Jr., 66
Isaacs
  Robert, 61
Isler
  Frederick B., 237
Ives, 32, 66
Ivey
  Jerdon, 112
  Jordon, 15
Ivy

Jordon, 122
Jackson
  Absolom, 198
  George W., 72, 202
  John W., 237
James
  Alen, 259
  Allen, 257
  John, 71, 112, 114
Janes
  Austin, 92
Jarrett
  James, 228
Jessup
  Nathan, 280
Jeter
  A., 230
Jhonson
  Jacob, 8
Johnson
  Aferd, 7
  Arnold, 233
  Jacob, 8, 10, 11, 12, 13, 14, 15, 16, 17, 18
  Jeremiah, 198
  Joshua, 172, 237
  Josiah, 259
  Otis, 135
  William, 172, 176, 198, 201, 233
  Young, 17, 18, 94
Johnston, 49
  Arnold, 24
  Henry, 129
  John, 86
  Josiah, 257
  Y., 204
  Young, 48, 79, 81, 82, 83, 132, 142, 150, 168, 186, 210, 220, 254

Jones, 117, 130, 135, 152, 189, 190, 193, 259, 262, 263, 265, 267, 271
  Edmond, 129
  Edmund, 133
  Ephram, 86, 237, 247
  James, 40, 43, 86
  Jno. L., 130
  John, 67, 129
  John A., 178, 252, 260
  John L., 21, 130
  John R., 122
  John W., 56
  Jonathan, 67
  Mathew, 42, 237
  Moses, 40
  Nathan, 40, 67, 280
  Richard, 172, 257
  S., 272
  Seaborn, 27, 31, 41, 144, 252, 256, 258
Jordan
  A., 55, 56, 57, 62
  Absalom, 238
  Absolam, 47, 48, 49, 50, 51, 52, 60, 61, 62
  Joshua, 144, 150, 161
Jordon
  A., 56
  Abalum, 247
  Absalom, 74
  Abslom, 40
  Absolam, 45, 46, 48, 52, 53, 54, 55, 73
  Absolom, 73
  Absolum, 42, 203, 238
  James E., 197, 214, 274
  John, 40
  Joshua, 37, 115, 190, 192
  William B., 244
  Wm. B., 237, 251
  Zachariah, 74
  Zackariah, 21, 66
Judson
  Philander, 110, 111, 198, 237
Kaigler
  J. J., 31
  John J., 48, 49, 57, 67, 84, 114, 234
Keeney
  E., 33
  Ebenezar, 19
  Ebenezer, 17, 18, 40, 42
Keith
  Iseral, 67
  Israel, 95, 106
  Whiten, 42
  Whiton, 40
Kelsey
  C., 24
  Charles, 15
Kendrick
  Harvey, 107
  Harvy, 129
  Isaac, 137
Kenon
  Thomas, 58
Kid
  David, 129
Kidd
  David, 143
Killan
  James H., 166
Killen
  James H., 166
Killin
  James, 181
  James H., 273
Killingworth
  Ambrose, 40, 42

John, 129
Kimberly, 45, 88, 134, 161, 164, 202, 206, 212, 222, 225, 239, 245, 250, 263, 264, 266
   Anson, 45, 47, 48, 49, 51, 69, 90, 110, 149, 150, 215, 217, 227, 246
Kimbro
   John H., 21, 115, 198, 201
Kinchen
   Uriah, 28
King
   G. C., 237
   Ralph, 46, 54
   Thomas, 147, 156, 158, 191
   Winefred, 153
Kirkpartrick
   John, 90
Knight, 266
   Thomas, 7, 95, 96, 130, 250, 266
Knowland
   Thomas, 237
Knox, 205, 221, 264
   David, 11
   Hugh, 221, 228, 236, 237
Krier
   John, 275
Lacklain
   George, 91
Lacy
   Benjamin, 86, 257
Lamar, 36, 38, 72
   Benjamin B., 136, 142
   Henry G., 133, 157, 175, 201
   J. T., 167
   John T., 38, 163, 164, 167, 168, 195, 206
   L. Q. C., 72, 85, 162, 173
   Lucius Q. C., 138, 173

   Zackariah, 227
Lamb
   Henry, 21
Lanford
   William, 148
Langdon, 93, 160
   Amon W., 178, 179, 182, 183, 186
Langford
   Carter B., 129
   James, 100, 119, 152
   Lewis B., 129, 133
Larchan
   John, 186
Lauchea
   Lewis, 38
Lawson
   Devenport, 90
   Roger, 147, 169, 170
   Rogers, 127
Lay, 136
Leavenworth
   Melins C., 24
Ledbetter
   Washington, 35, 65
Lee
   Joseph H., 7, 172, 176
   Richard, 143
   Richard W., 280
Legueux, 26, 27, 40
   Martha, 119
Leguiexx
   Peter, 25
Leonard
   William W., 13
Leseur
   Drury M., 93, 94
Lesuar
   M., 89, 104
Levi

Josephus, 133, 136
Lewis, 39, 45
  Charles S., 67, 71, 73, 76, 77, 79, 83, 107, 108, 178, 179, 182, 183, 186, 220, 273
Linger
  John, 280
Long
  Nimrod W., 154, 155
Loving
  Hugh, 107
  John, 27, 31, 46, 88, 100, 101, 105, 120, 123, 142, 188, 211, 262, 269, 270
Low, 128, 194, 207, 208, 251
  Andrew, 61, 82
Lowery
  Abram, 7
  Alexander, 5
Lundy
  Thomas, 36, 153
Lunsford
  Enoch, 188
Lynch, 143, 235
  Christopher, 143, 234, 235
Lyon, 107, 129
Macarthy
  Roger, 93, 154
Mackey
  William, 96, 103
Mackie
  William, 53
Magee, 176, 177
  Job, 179
Magie
  Haines H., 90
  Job, 183, 263, 264, 265, 266, 267
Malden
  Caleb, Jr., 177

  Caleb, Sr., 177
Malloy
  John, 237
Malsby
  John, 201
Man
  Hiram, 4, 176
Manard
  Francis A., 220
  Stephen, 149, 220
Mandell, 5, 9, 15, 18, 30, 32, 42, 45, 54
  A., 111
  Addison, 19, 82, 87, 93, 123
Manereth
  William, 40
Manguir
  James C., 280
Mann
  Hiram, 164, 165
Marshall
  J. W., 151
  James, 139
Martin
  James, 156, 169
Matherson
  M. L., 11
Mathew
  Timothy, 96
Mathews
  Elijah, 4, 86
  Isaac, 259
  Jonathan, 249
  Timothy, 4, 6, 23, 30, 34, 35, 38, 39, 41, 42, 51, 52, 53, 54, 63, 67, 71, 75, 76, 81, 85, 86, 96, 113, 115, 120, 123, 128, 130, 131, 132, 133, 140, 147, 148, 162, 166, 171, 172, 176, 180,

181, 187, 199, 201, 209,
226, 232, 244, 250, 251
Maulsby
  John, 179
Mauran
  Jessee, 280
McAlister
  Charles, 21
  John, 88
McAllister
  John, 104
McBryde
  A., 15
  Andrew, 4
McCall, 267, 269
  Eleazer, 96
  Elezar, 11, 22, 23
  Elezer, 96
  Rodger, 95
  Roger, 96, 100, 121, 122, 125
McCallum, 194
  Angus, 67, 182, 193, 280
McCardell
  Charles, 233, 244
McCarder
  Thomas, 237
McCardle
  Charles, 198, 201
McCarthey
  Roger, 43
McCarthur
  John, 250
McCarthy
  John, 237, 244
  Peter, 172
  Roger, 102, 157
McClendon
  Burrell, 4
McCluskey
  Thomas J., 124
McCluskie
  Thomas J., 118
  Thos. J., 114
McCree
  William L., 67
McDonald, 221, 274
  Alexander, 155
  C. J., 148
  Charles J., 21, 33, 66, 135, 146, 149, 150, 155, 162, 170, 183, 191, 192, 197, 236, 237
  Chs. J., 20
  John, 257
McGregor, 143, 165, 279
  A., 143, 279
  Alex, 145, 226, 236, 242
  Alexa., 143
  Alexander, 80, 88, 93, 95, 143, 160, 165, 203, 206, 207, 212, 216, 223, 241, 242, 262, 267, 269, 272, 278
  Alexr., 203, 207, 208, 235, 242
  Charles, 185, 200
McIntire
  Charles, 30
McIntyer
  Charles, 15
McIntyre
  Charles, 65
McKay
  Hugh, 11, 22
McKennie
  Hezekiah, 23
McKiney
  Benjamin, 85, 86
  Hezekiah, 21, 198

John M., 248
McKinney
  Benjamin, 257
  Caleb, 257
  Hezekiah, 201, 280
McKinnie
  Hezekiah, 233
McLaughlain
  Alexr., 237
McLaughlan
  Jared, 198
  John, 197
  Rhoda, 198
  Sally, 198
  William, 198
McLaughlin, 4
McLean
  Angus, 5
McMarrian
  John, 40, 42, 104
  Thomas, 104
McMurrain
  David, 245
  Thomas, 239
McMurrian
  David, 280
  John, 4, 88, 261
  Thomas, 225
McNeal, 266
  Hugh, 19
McNeil
  Hugh, 18
McRea
  John, 280
McRee
  William L., 71
McSumner
  Benjamin, 237
Meeker, 176, 177
  Jonathan T., 107, 109

Melborn
  Henry, 197
Melbourn
  Henry, 183
Menard
  Stephen, 86
Merewether
  Alexr., 110
Merrell
  Lemuel, 53, 70
Merrewether
  Alexander, 148, 176
Merriman
  Charles P., 25
Metcalf
  Isaac, 21, 23
Micklejohn
  George, 126, 270
Milburn, 146
  Henry, 146, 211
Miles
  Thomas, 8
Miller, 122
  Thomas, 122
Milles
  Thomas, 8
Mills
  John, 131, 132
Milner
  James M., 118
Mims
  Henry, 54
  Williamson, 116, 148
Miner
  Mary, 34
Minor
  Mary, 5, 12, 160
Minzins
  Robert, 53
Mitchel

Henry, 163
Mitchell, 248
  Henry, 167
  John, 245, 247
Mixson
  Micheal, 67
Molesby
  John, 179, 235
Molsby
  John, 97, 198, 233
Montgomery
  Edward, 198
Moor
  Thos., 97
  William, 16
Moore, 49, 50, 67, 132
  Thomas, 70, 131, 132
  William, 52, 57, 70, 71, 81, 84, 142, 234
Moreland, 76, 107, 108, 119, 129, 154, 157, 185, 186
  John, 280
  Tuttle, 107
  Tuttle H., 106, 107, 129, 155
Morgan
  John, 40
  Joseph, 71, 75, 76, 99, 101, 126, 127, 147, 157, 169, 170, 171, 175
  Luke J., 50
Morrison
  Hugh, 67, 71
Mosely
  Joseph, 8
Moses
  Neal, 172
Mott
  Randolph L., 276
Munroe, 86, 94, 146
  Nathan C., 41, 148, 149

Murphey
  John, 9, 15, 22, 52, 77
Murray
  Alexander, 13, 18, 19
Mussellwhite
  Thomas, 143
Mustian
  John L., 238, 239
Napier, 86, 94, 146, 222, 242
  Thomas, 26, 27, 31, 34, 40, 41, 91, 92, 135, 151, 156, 173, 174, 197, 202, 203, 204, 205, 209, 212, 214, 228, 238, 241, 261
  Thos., 71, 274
Neal, 38
  Eliah, 21
  Jonathan, 37
  McComick, 17
Nesbit
  John, 55
Newcomb
  L., 143
  Lem, 200
  Lemuel, 199
Newhall
  George, 213, 214, 270
Newsom
  Henry, 135
Newsome
  Hardy, 257
  Henry, 173
Newton
  Josiah, 45
Nichols
  C., 108
  J., 108
Nims
  Theodore, 79
Nobles

Edmund, 112
Norman
  William S., 19
Northern
  George, 253
Norton
  Isaac, 208, 223
Nothern
  George, 172
Nunn
  Mary, 93
Oakley
  Daniel, 109
Oler
  John, 225
Oliver
  John, 24, 180
Orick
  Henry G., 78
Owen
  Hardeman, 152
Owens
  J. L., 167
  Jesse L., 163
  Jessee L., 167
Pace
  Samuel, 8
Padgett
  Elijah, 280
Palmer
  Jesse, 67
Parish, 134
Parker
  Joseph, 198
  Nathan, 172
  Thomas, 141
Parmalee
  A. C., 280
Parmelee, 261
Parriot
  Tyra, 85
Parrish
  D., 207
  Q., 221
  T., 207, 221
Parrot
  Tird, 7
Partrick
  A. P., 115, 117, 118
  Abraham P., 112, 115
Patrick
  A. P., 120, 123, 124, 125
Patterson, 181
  Jeremiah, 112, 122
  John, 40
  Thomas, 40
Patton, 214, 267, 269
  Alexander E., 257
  David, 7, 8
  Robert S., 17, 79, 80, 118, 226
Peacock, 252
  Jonathan, 5
Pearson, 95
  Charles, 126
  James, 89, 137
Peley, 248
Pendergrast
  M., 181
Perkins
  John, 67, 71
  Uriah, 94
Perry, 32
  Jno., 35
  John, 74
  Michael W., 148
  William, 14
Pettis
  Moses, Jr., 4
Philips

Benjamin, 40, 43
Joseph, 275
Philpot, 166
   John, 16, 45, 54, 62, 65, 70, 77, 166, 181, 206, 239, 273
Pickard
   Samuel, 40
   Thomas, 18
   William, 7, 8
Pickart
   Benjamin, 146
Pitman
   Sir James, 222
Pitt
   Willis, 21
Pittman
   Sir James, 159
Pitts
   Willis, 198, 201
Plummer
   Samuel A., 28, 50, 56, 57, 61, 62
Poe, 43, 57, 61, 62, 82, 131, 135, 136, 137, 148, 151, 152, 156, 185, 249, 254, 261, 264, 276
   Washington, 140, 179
Polhill, 43, 56, 57, 58, 78, 101, 109, 117, 120, 171, 176
   John G., 53, 96, 103, 122, 124, 134
Porter, 135, 140, 189, 190, 193
   Vincent R., 133
   William, 256
Potts
   John, 40
Powell
   David, 21
   George, 143
   Samuel, 32
   Thompson, 21, 97
   Thompson, Sr., 21
   William C., 228
Powledge
   G., 267
   Gideon, 152
   John H., 198
   P., 89, 105, 267
   Philip, 79, 89, 104, 152
   Phillip, 237
Pratt, 92
   Daniel, 92
Preston
   David, 198
Price
   William J., 248
Prince, 43, 57, 61, 62, 65, 82, 131, 135, 136, 137, 148, 151, 152, 156, 185, 249, 254, 261, 264, 276
   Oliver H., 19
Pullain
   Thomas N., 116
Puryear, 21
   Wm. M., 21
Puryer
   William M., 20
Quinerly
   William, 249
Quinn
   Edward, 9
Rabon
   Burrell, 66
Radford
   Shadrick, 201
   Shedrick, 198
Raiford
   Alexander G., 176
Raines

Cadwell W., 78
Nathaniel, 58
Rains
  Cadwell W., 27
Ralston, 117, 130, 135, 152, 189, 190, 193, 259, 263, 265, 267, 271
  A. R., 265
  D., 63, 115
  David, 23, 30, 31, 51, 52, 53, 54, 71, 76, 80, 84, 85, 86, 95, 96, 97, 98, 112, 130, 131, 132, 165, 183, 195
Ranalds
  Thomas A., 82
Randolph
  A. W., 268
  Augustus W., 268
Ranolds
  Thomas A., 109
Ransone
  James B., 8, 29
Ray
  Murdock, 86
Rea
  James, 8
Reddick
  John, 33, 42
  Noah, 33, 42
  Thomas, 259
Redding
  John, 161
Reed
  Luke, 211
Reid
  John H., 73
Relph
  George, 30, 31, 65, 73
Reneid
  John, 172

Timothy, 172
Rew
  B., 255
  Beverly, 57, 61, 110, 177, 191, 195, 233, 237
Rhodes, 181
Rice
  A., 250, 251, 257, 259, 264, 271
  Anderson, 243, 244, 250, 251, 259, 272
Richards
  Alex, 240
  Alexander, 27, 46, 47, 58, 59, 97, 233, 240
  Alexr., 240
Rilander, 222
Riley, 190, 192, 193, 205
  Charles, 30
  David F., 280
  Martin, 72
  Spencer, 6, 20, 39, 93, 95, 98, 102, 111, 112, 114, 132, 163, 171, 174, 189, 190, 192, 193, 194, 195, 200, 217, 220, 272, 278, 279
  William, 8, 227, 277
Robenett
  Jesse, 163
Roberts
  John, 172
  John W., 15, 54, 65
Robertson, 89
  Aaron, 73
  Alexander Y., 74
  John, 74
  M., 6, 13, 21, 51, 75, 81, 84, 211, 229

Mathew, 4, 7, 8, 13, 35, 42, 51, 71, 75, 81, 85, 94, 104, 229, 254
Robinett
  J., 167
  Jessee, 167
Robinson, 263
Rockwell
  C. W., 117
  Charles W., 15, 30, 31, 54, 65
  Peter P., 55, 56, 79, 237, 247
  Samuel, 26
Rod
  Thomas, 182
Rodgers, 13, 14, 18, 39, 57, 59, 62, 138, 256
  Benjamin W., 161
  Berry, 58
  George, 78
  George A., 27, 33, 51, 85, 86, 87, 88, 89, 90, 91, 92, 93, 94, 95, 97, 100, 103, 104, 108, 109, 110, 111
  J. C., 111, 119
  James, 176
  James H., 41, 91, 97, 101, 103, 122, 125, 127, 147, 163, 164, 174, 181, 187, 191, 195, 197, 201, 209, 226
  Jas. H., 41, 104, 174, 180, 187, 199, 209, 226, 232
  John C., 44, 63, 91, 130
  Temperane, 44
Roe
  Charles, 77
Roffe, 136
  Robert, 15, 23, 78, 130
Rogers

Berry, 280
Henry, 248
James H., 232
Roland
  Thomas, 138
Rolph
  George, 15
Rose, 236
  H., 110
  S., 267
  Simri, 210, 222, 229, 269
  W., 110
Ross, 12, 32
  H. G., 24
  Henry G., 24, 32, 42, 84, 140, 234, 250
  John B., 268
  Lu, 112, 120, 123, 128, 131, 278
  Luke, 33, 42, 86, 96, 99, 113, 115, 120, 123, 128, 131, 132, 164, 165, 172, 176, 180, 181, 187, 195, 199, 230, 233, 234, 260, 265, 277
  Thomas L., 251
  William, 86
Rouell
  James, Sr., 8
Rowell
  James, Sr., 7
  Voluntine, 7, 8
Rowlan
  John, 129
  Thomas, 130
Rowland, 253
  I. B., 165
  Isaac B., 252
  John T., 54, 113, 194, 195, 247, 251, 274

Thomas, 138
Ruffin
  Rob, 266
Rushin, 13, 14, 18, 39, 57, 59, 62, 119, 130, 256
  J., 22, 41
  Joel, 5, 12, 22, 26, 27, 28, 31, 33, 41, 51, 160
  John, 91, 95, 96
Rushing, 111
  John, 120
Russell
  B., 196
  Benjamin, 32, 45, 67, 68, 81, 144, 159, 189
  William, 8
Rutland, 12, 32, 250
  Redden, 154
  Reddin, 17, 21, 86, 87, 89
  Redding, 23, 280
Rylander, 242
Sacrae
  Thomas, 143
Sacre
  Thomas, 259
Sacrey
  Thomas, 130, 257
Saffold, 140
Sage
  Oliver, 17, 106, 112, 151, 196, 280
Sander
  John M., 226
Sanders
  John M., 17, 48, 218, 221, 225, 227
  William, 36, 81
  William L., 178
  Wm., 82
Sayer

William H., 17
Scott
  Isaac, 237, 244, 245, 246, 249, 251, 252, 254, 255
  John, 146
  W. F., 111
  William, 4, 40, 146, 268, 279
  William F., 145
Scully
  John, 16, 23, 38, 53, 55, 56, 68, 70, 75, 76, 81, 84, 86, 120, 121, 182, 233, 268, 273
Scurly
  Thomas, 21
Seacry
  Thomas, 233
Seymour, 87, 89, 93, 123, 135, 137, 151, 152, 160, 186, 196, 199, 202, 206, 210, 213, 217, 218, 219, 223, 224, 242, 248, 252, 256, 260, 263, 266, 267, 269, 272, 274, 276, 277
  I. G., 199
  Isaac, 83
  Isaac G., 107, 113, 200, 240, 241
Sharp, 37
  John A., 10
Shaw
  Joseph, 21
Shelman
  Jno. M., 85, 142
  John M., 43, 57, 60, 63, 64, 65, 85, 90, 109, 142, 151, 218
  R. B., 8, 64, 65
  Robert B., 58, 64, 109
Sherrard
  Joel, 44

Sherrod
 Arthur, 164
Sherry, 262
Shipman, 263
Shotwell, 83, 108, 117, 158, 275
 Jacob, 158, 200
Sibley
 Amory, 177
Simmons
 M., 103, 104, 131, 132, 167, 168, 169, 170, 173, 174, 196, 199, 229, 237, 238, 239, 240, 242, 243, 268, 280
 Martin, 7, 8, 19, 20, 22, 23, 24, 30, 34, 39, 40, 41, 42, 63, 70, 84, 85, 86, 96, 121, 132, 138, 154, 168, 169, 175, 176, 184, 186, 189, 193, 200, 239, 241, 243, 244, 258, 268, 273, 278
Sims
 A., 187
 Amanda, 188
 Benjamin A., 198, 201
 Z., 46, 106
 Zackariah, 45, 50, 187, 188, 225, 227, 245
Singer
 John, 198, 201
Skaggs
 Samuel B., 79
Slade, 236
 E. E., 157
 Edwin E., 172, 206, 249
 M. D. J., 130, 151, 248, 262, 267, 275
 Mark D., 254
 Marmaduk J., 130
 Marmaduke J., 203, 248, 274
Slate
 Samuel, 81, 112, 115
Slatten
 Shadrach F., 29
 Solomon L., 29
Slatter
 Shadrick F., 204
Smiley
 William R., 194
 Wm. R., 182
Smith, 50, 63, 76, 94, 116, 150, 159, 194, 209
 Benjamin, 7, 43, 52, 172, 176
 Caleb, 15, 85
 Calub, 86
 D., 202
 Daniel, 73, 130, 142, 279
 Eason, 169
 Ezekiel, 233, 236, 241
 Geo. A., 113, 133, 200
 George A., 90, 97, 99, 100, 113, 133, 185, 200, 221, 240, 261, 264, 277
 George W., 208
 H., 188
 Harrison, 33, 51, 66, 141, 169, 170, 188
 Henry, 12, 21, 23, 32, 49, 57
 James, 40, 42, 198
 Jered, 198
 Jeremiah, 58, 91, 92, 114, 224, 225
 Jno. P., 184
 John, 143, 176, 234, 235, 244
 John P., 184
 Josiah P., 97
 Robert, 112
 Turner, 21

Williamson, 91, 125, 198, 201
Wm., 280
Smithheart
  David, 233
Snow
  John W., 237
Solomon
  Henry, 265
Spear, 214
Spears
  Henry, 266
Springer
  William G., 90, 105
Stanford, 95
  Samuel, 89, 247, 249, 255, 275, 278
  William W., 7
Starr, 59, 60, 64
Stewart
  Henry, 237
  Randal, 40
Stockton
  E. S., 8
Stoddard, 161, 246, 264
Stokes
  John, 146
Stone
  H. S., 193
Stoors
  Oliver A., 172
Stovall
  George, 6, 116
Strawbridge
  John, 196
Stringfield
  E., 196
Strong, 36, 72
  C. B., 133, 219, 246
  Christopher B., 270
Strougher
  William, 172
Stubbs
  Thomas, 230, 231, 240
  Thomas B., 217, 219, 222, 230, 231, 233
Sumerlin
  Elerson, 198
Summerlin
  Ellerson, 172
  James, 67, 201
Swearingin, 36, 59, 62
  E., 60, 62
  Josiah, 85
  Van, 114, 172
Sweet
  Rachael R., 55
Taber, 253
  James, 253, 254, 255
Talman, 273
Tapley
  William, 138, 153, 164
  Winefred, 153
Tarpley
  William, 132
Tarver
  Elisha, 9
Tate
  Isaac M., 73, 87
  Zenire, 87
Taylor, 128, 194, 207, 208, 251
  Robert H., 248
  Thos., 86
  William, 40
Terrell
  Henry, 14
Terry
  Benjamin, 237, 244
Tesserian
  Burtran, 247

Tessrau
  Bertrand, 77
Tharp, 196
Thomkins
  Samuel, 44
Thompkins
  Samuel, 36
Thompson
  C., 134, 174, 270
  Charlton, 134, 174
  Drury, 130
  Isaiah E., 160
  J. E., 134, 153
  James, 4, 29, 38, 39, 43, 52, 70, 73, 74, 75, 93, 102, 138, 157, 174, 179, 180, 182, 183, 187, 189, 241, 242, 245, 247
  James, Sr., 67
  Jas., 139
  Jeffrey E., 116, 117, 134, 153
  John F., 4, 72
  Tabitha, 116
  William H., 25
Thweatt
  Thomas, 43, 63
Tice
  Abraham, 42
Tinsley
  Thomas, 187
Tobin
  James, 16, 38, 67, 73, 76, 82, 83, 84, 85, 165, 226
Todd
  Jacob J., 257, 259, 270, 271, 272, 273, 274, 275
Tompkins
  John, 112
  Samuel, 69, 156, 203
  William P., 212

Town
  Hockey, 22
  Hockey L., 199
Towns, 205
  H. L., 200, 240
  Hockey L., 11, 21, 189, 199, 200, 205, 213, 224, 231, 235, 240
  Joseph H., 180, 199
Townsend, 76, 107, 108, 119
  C., 248
  Cornelius, 93, 106, 119, 248, 257, 259, 272
Tracy, 50, 65, 91, 106, 107, 109, 110, 141, 145, 146, 153, 163, 164, 194, 196, 204, 210, 216, 217, 223, 224, 262, 263, 264, 270, 273
  E. D., 33, 74, 124
  Edward D., 19, 65, 79, 229, 272
  Edwd. D., 229
Trice
  Abraham, 33
Tripp
  Henry W., 79
Troup
  George M., 32, 33, 35, 51
Tucker
  Daniel, 257, 259
  John, 112
Turner
  James R., 159
  R., 99, 105, 112, 115, 120, 123, 128, 130, 132, 140, 147, 162, 166, 239
  Reuben, 9, 15, 22, 52, 77, 80, 96, 99, 104, 113, 133, 140

Reubin, 86, 115, 120, 122,
  123, 128, 131, 148, 162,
  168, 171, 239
William, 73
Turpin
  William H., 9
  Wm. H., 12, 24
Tyner
  K., 207, 209, 224
  Keeland, 139, 165, 194, 202,
    204, 207, 208, 209, 210,
    214, 219, 224, 232, 251
Ulter, 263
Van Antwerp, 260
Vance, 205, 221
  John P., 198
Varner
  Edward, 79, 178
Veasey
  Zebulon, 133, 136
Venters
  James, 55
Vickers
  Silas, 253
Victery
  John, 137
  Thomas, 87, 103, 205
Vigal
  George, 36, 164, 205
Vincent
  Payton, 198
Vines
  Hiram, 114
Visage
  James, 36
Voluntine
  Andrew, 40
Wade
  Samuel, 67
Wadsworth, 37

Daniel, 104
Wafford, 99
  James T., 59
Wagner
  N., 142, 238
  Nicholas, 126, 130, 133, 142,
    143, 213, 237, 238, 275
Wainwright
  Joseph, 73, 272
Wakeman
  Mark H., 215
Walker
  B. G., 201
  Benjamin G., 202
  George, 83
  Hiram, 129
  John D., 87, 108, 201, 202
Wallace
  John S., 35, 65
  Norman, 128
Wallis, 49, 81
  M. R., 19, 45, 121, 183, 239,
    247, 274
  Mortimer R., 19, 78, 100,
    103, 114, 121, 124, 125,
    148, 165, 230, 238, 261
Walls
  Jessee J., 257
Walton
  R., 14
Ward
  James P., 144
  Richard W., 144
  William, 21, 83, 227, 256,
    263, 268, 278
Wardlaw
  Geo. B., 32
  George B., 14, 25, 32, 84,
    124, 217
Wardsworth

Daniel, 51
Wardworth
  Daniel, 88
Ware
  B., 12, 20
  M., 12, 20
  Robert D., 46
Warren
  John, 142
  Joshua, 42
  Robert, 161
Warring
  Jacob, 259, 271
Washburn
  J., 188
  Joseph, 165, 187, 188
Washburne
  Joseph, 63
Washington
  R. B., 241, 254
  Robert, 269
Watkins
  Cornelius, 91
  James C., 143
Wats
  Hampton B., 102
Watson
  Douglass C., 179, 235
  John, 172
  Leroy, 112
  Thomas, 67
Wattons
  Hezekiah, 172
Watts
  H. B., 102
  Hampton B., 172, 179
Wayman
  W. J., 206
Weathers
  J. D., 44, 54

Weed
  H., 74, 210, 215
  N. B., 74, 210, 215
Week
  James S., 46
Weeks
  James S., 112, 122
Welch, 217, 229
Wells, 26, 34, 101, 156, 171, 174, 257, 258
  Elijah, 46
  N. W., 220, 227
  Nicholas, 34
  Nicholas W., 46, 156, 174, 175, 257, 258, 271, 273
  Susan, 186, 206, 207, 220, 227, 250, 257, 258
Whalley
  Maven, 7
Whatley
  Green, 172
Wheless
  Edmund, 21
White, 32, 66, 248
Whitehead
  George, 172, 201, 233
  George, Jr., 198
  Masten, 88
  Maston, 86
Whitehurst
  Charles, 271
Whithead
  Mastern, 86, 104
Wick
  John B., 260, 262, 272
Wiggins, 266
  Joseph, 7, 8, 40, 42, 86, 257, 259
Wilabee
  John, 5

Wilder, 45
  Green, 112, 115
  Jonathan, 8, 233
Wiley, 196, 210, 211, 215, 216, 220, 221, 245, 255
Willee
  John, 5
Willey, 165
  Francis, 165, 179, 226, 235
Williams
  Henry, 17, 18
  Hubbard, 144
  James, 67, 73
  Micajah, 227, 279
  Peter J., 27, 28
  Reuben, 7, 8
  Reubin, 112, 115, 237
  Stephen, 67, 71, 112, 115
  Thomas, 112
  W., 101, 106, 107, 108, 111
  Whitmill, 85, 97, 98, 102
  William, 7, 179, 184
Williamson
  C., 259, 264
  Charles, 243, 249, 250, 251, 257, 259, 272
  Chas., 271
  Littleton, 67
  Reuben, 4, 21
  W. W., 127, 147, 169, 170
  Zackariah, 112
  Zackariah, Jr., 67
Willson
  James, 151
Wilson, 80, 95, 235
  David F., 32, 45, 48, 56, 57, 80, 84, 95, 97, 98, 189, 224, 234, 235, 242, 245, 249, 257, 278, 279
  James, 278
  John, 172, 267
Wily
  Francis, 182
Wimberly
  E., 147, 169, 170
  Ezekiel, 126, 127, 157, 170, 175
  James, 126, 157, 170, 175
Winship
  Isaac, 183, 184, 196
Wise
  Barnett, 7
Wofford
  James T., 29
Woodard
  James, 246
Woodruff
  Charles, 150, 190, 192
Woods
  A., 260
  E., 260
  Edmund, 40
Woodson
  A. R., 157, 202
  Archibald, 83, 121
Woodward
  Isham, 121
Wooten
  Howell, 43, 62
  John R., 61
Wooton
  John R., 185
Wordsworth
  Daniel, 79
  William, 173
Worrin
  Joshua, 40
Worsham
  D. B., 113
  D. G., 82

Daniel B., 88, 112, 113, 141, 205, 211
David G., 81
Wright, 159, 194, 209, 260
  E. W., 106
  Edward W., 31, 41, 91, 92, 113, 125, 152, 219
  Edwd. W., 113
  George, 7

Gillis, 112
Glover, 21
Wych
  C. C., 179, 182, 191
  Clark, 197
  Clark C., 276
Young
  Henry F., 140
Youngblood, 83

www.ingramcontent.com/pod-product-compliance
Lightning Source LLC
Chambersburg PA
CBHW020056020526
44112CB00031B/198